Sandwell
Metropolitan Borough Council

Please return this item to any Sandwell Library on or before
the return date.

You may renew the item unless it has been reserved
another borrower.

You can renew your library
hotline numb
or FREE online at

THANK YOU FOR U

THE REAL PRIME SUSPECT

**FROM THE BEAT TO THE SCREEN.
MY LIFE AS A FEMALE DETECTIVE**

JACKIE MALTON

WITH HÉLÈNE MULHOLLAND

ENDEAVOUR

First published in Great Britain in 2022 by Endeavour, an imprint of
Octopus Publishing Group Ltd
Carmelite House
50 Victoria Embankment
London EC4Y 0DZ
www.octopusbooks.co.uk

An Hachette UK Company
www.hachette.co.uk

First published in paperback in 2023

Distributed in the US by
Hachette Book Group
1290 Avenue of the Americas
4th and 5th Floors
New York, NY 10104

Distributed in Canada by
Canadian Manda Group
664 Annette St.
Toronto, Ontario, Canada M6S 2C8

ISBN 978-1-80419-015-9

A CIP catalogue record for this book is available from the British Library.

Printed and bound in the UK

10 9 8 7 6 5 4 3 2 1

Typeset in 12.5/18pt Garamond Premier Pro by Jouve (UK), Milton Keynes

This FSC® label means that materials used for
the product have been responsibly sourced

To my sister Sue, who has always watched out for me, and Peter.

You can't connect the dots looking forward; you can only connect them looking backwards. So you have to trust that the dots will somehow connect in your future. You have to trust in something – your gut, destiny, life, karma, whatever.

–Steve Jobs, Stanford University commencement address,
12 June 2005

AUTHOR'S NOTE

I have recounted my memories to the best of my abilities, given the passage of time. Anything I have misremembered is purely accidental. Some names and identifying details have been changed to protect the privacy of individuals.

CONTENTS

CONTENTS

CHAPTER 1
WATCHING THE DETECTIVE

A street. London. It is night-time. A car pulls up and two men emerge. Police radios hum in the background as more cars arrive on the scene. The destination is a first-floor bedsit. A woman has been found murdered.

From out of a car steps a heavyset man with a nonchalant air; he's wearing a dark coat, a cigar in mouth. He walks across the road with a swagger. Flashing his warrant card to the uniform police officer at the entrance, he says: 'DCI Shefford. I'm in charge.'

Not for long: the next day he drops dead at work from a heart attack. It is left to Detective Superintendent Michael Kernan to break the news to the all-male murder squad that a woman is going to take charge of the investigation: Detective Chief Inspector Jane Tennison.

'I know how you must all feel, but give her the best you've got,' Kernan tells the team.

'I'll give that tart the best I've got, all right,' fires back a detective sergeant sarcastically. Tittering all round.

This should have been Tennison's case from the off. She was on call the night that the victim – identified as Della Mornay – was found. But Shefford was sent instead. On learning of Shefford's untimely death,

Tennison wasted no time arguing her corner to take over the investigation. And her boss reluctantly agreed.

*

I watch the scenes play out from the darkness of an auditorium, my heart in my mouth. It is 1991, and I am at the preview of the first episode of *Prime Suspect* before it airs on ITV on Sunday 7 April. Women barely featured in the cop shows I watched avidly as a child, so watching a female lead character in a cutting-edge television police drama is a seminal moment in my life. In more ways than one – because the character depicted on the screen is inspired by me, one of only three female DCIs in the entirety of the Metropolitan Police at the time.

In the room are journalists, cast and crew and a few friends of mine from the Met, including my good pal Bob, who is sitting by my side. Bob squeezes my hand reassuringly. He knows how nervous I am, and he knows why: there, on the big screen – finally – is the lot of a senior-ranking female officer operating in an overwhelmingly male institution.

This is all thanks to Lynda La Plante, the formidable author and screenwriter who listened to and absorbed my stories and experiences over many months of conversation to create a compelling character and storyline from my point of view: a woman in a man's world. La Plante establishes Tennison's role as an outsider early on. We see witnesses talking to junior male colleagues, unable to believe that a woman is in charge; detectives frowning defensively as she lays out her investigative approach to find the culprit responsible for rape and murder. La Plante cooks it perfectly.

I watch Lynda's script unfold on the big screen. I chuckle as Tennison channels my quips courtesy of the redoubtable Helen Mirren.

'Listen, I like to be called "guvnor" or "the boss"; I don't like "ma'am".

I'm not the bloody Queen, so take your pick,' Tennison tells a detective constable.

'Yes, ma'am,' comes the defiant reply. She has her work cut out on asserting her authority over the troops.

My delight at La Plante's brilliance is tempered by nerves: how will this show be received? It was only a few months ago that an actor cast in the show had announced to the producer Don Leaver that 'it's a load of bollocks'. This was the verdict of police friends that the (now-dead) actor had shown the script to. It played on concerns that they may have a turkey on their hands. Cue a subdued conversation between me and Leaver, a kindly, respectful and thoughtful man. 'Should we be worried?' he asked me gently.

An avalanche of negativity descended upon me as the self-doubts I was often plagued with crowded in. I questioned whether my views were of value and whether I really knew what I was talking about. Maybe my experiences were wrong? Perhaps the sense of being an outsider was all in my head? It was a wobble of seismic proportions, of feeling an impostor, but then my mind cleared.

The fact that a bunch of men were trying to discount my experiences spoke volumes. This was déjà vu. I was a DCI with 20 years of policing experience under my belt already – 11 of which were spent in the Met. I had no idea who these fellow officers were, but how on earth would they know what it was like to be a female officer? The attempt to drown out my voice reflected my daily reality. There was no room for a woman's perspective in the Met.

'You can show this script to 25 officers, and 25 will give you a different point of view,' I told Leaver evenly. 'What I have given Lynda is my account of policing life. My experience. Imagine my surprise that male officers don't agree. It's kind of my point. They haven't got a clue what it's like to be a woman on the job.' I returned Leaver's gaze for what felt like the longest time. Finally: 'OK, Jackie. I trust your experience. We will go with that.'

As I sit in the auditorium watching the finished work, the qualms ebb away. La Plante's well-crafted plot is gripping stuff. As the screen fades to black, the brief seconds of silence drag. Then enthusiastic applause breaks out. It seems that dust may have gotten into my eye.

Lynda La Plante turns to me from her seat. 'What do you think of it, Jackie?'

The damp eyes are probably a clue. 'I think it's brilliant,' I reply. 'Thank you very much.'

What I don't realize that night is that this drama Lynda has created will prove a massive hit. For me, nothing will ever be the same again. But, of course, DCI Tennison is not me, and I am not Tennison. There are many similarities, but there are differences too. This is my story.

CHAPTER 2

THE APPRENTICE

Langland Bay, Wales, 1969. I was living with my parents and had dropped out of college halfway through my A levels following disappointing mock-exam results.

My plan had been to become a probation officer, which required a degree. I'd set my heart on this career path because I'd thought it would satisfy my innate nosiness about people and why they did what they did. I also had a fascination with crime and punishment, sparked by studying prison reform at secondary school and reading Dickens's *Little Dorrit*. Dropping out of college meant a rethink.

I'd ruled out being a prison officer because I was worried that the job would just involve herding prisoners about with a large set of keys rather than engaging with them in any meaningful way. With my father working in the newspaper industry, the notion of becoming a crime reporter was another short-lived idea. One occupation I'd often wondered about was policing, an interest largely attributable to my love of watching police dramas.

I grew up watching the BBC's *Dixon of Dock Green*, where Britain's most friendly bobby, George Dixon, played by Jack Warner, pounded the beat. The show was a regular fixture in our house as my parents, my older brother and sister and I settled down for our Saturday-evening viewing while tucking into sweets as a special weekend treat.

The show was tame fare and a far cry from the gruesome yet compelling blood and gore that would crescendo in cop dramas across the ensuing decades. PC Dixon was depicted as a safe pair of hands who offered a reassuring presence. At the end of each episode he would sign off with a 'Goodnight, all.'

It was the same with another of my favourites, *No Hiding Place*, centred around Scotland Yard detectives. The police officers were characterized as straightforward, trustworthy and by the book – not like the maverick characters so often depicted in the genre later down the years. The detective team was led by Detective Superintendent Lockhart, played by Raymond Francis. The sleuths would piece together the evidence and outsmart the criminal by the time the credits rolled. Sally Jordan, played by Rowena Gregory, was the 'woman detective'. Suffice to say her sex meant she had few lines to learn.

The virtual invisibility of women police officers did little to deter my 18-year-old self as I wondered what to do with my life. I chose to overlook the fact that all the exciting action I had seen on the telly involved male characters; instead, I focused on the vision of policing that these shows portrayed.

I didn't think my parents would approve of a career in policing, but they were very supportive. My father decided to contact Police Superintendent Syd Page, a former neighbour of ours back in Leicester, for some advice. Mr Page no doubt smiled when Dad called him. Some years previously, when we were still neighbours, he had invited my parents to his home and shown off the new décor. 'Ooh,' said my mum, 'did you use Durex? Jeff always uses Durex. It gives such a lovely finish.' Laughter all round. Now, hearing of my interest in policing, Mr Page advised that I join the cadets – he said this would allow me to see if I was suited to it.

In many ways, the fact that I chose uniform service wasn't very surprising. Service was embedded in my family. My parents, Jeff and Olive, were both born in 1919 and met in Lincolnshire while working for the Royal Air Force during World War II: Dad as a pilot and Mum as a civilian telephonist at the aerodrome. My paternal grandfather had enlisted in the Royal Navy during World War I despite initial difficulties getting in because of his name. To us kids he would later be known as Pop, but to his huge regret he'd been christened Karl Marx Malton. This was thanks to my great-grandfather, who had either a sense of humour or strong political allegiances – I never did find out which. Mum's father, meanwhile, had worked as a policeman in the Metropolitan Police during the Great War.

After the war, Dad wanted to stay in the RAF, but my mother yearned for the normality of civilian life, so he carved out a successful career in newspapers instead and Mum gave up paid work to raise a family. I came along as a surprise pregnancy that left my mother reeling. By then, my brother, Trevor, was eight and my sister, Susan, was four. Mum, who had grown up with five brothers, cheered herself up with the thought of a second son, whom she would call Nicholas. Boy came there none. I arrived on 7 July.

Though I was born in the cathedral city of Lincoln in 1951, we relocated to Leicester before my first birthday, after Dad traded in his job at the accounts department of the *Lincolnshire Echo* for a step up to manager of the *Leicester Evening Mail*. We moved into a three-bedroomed semi-detached house, with bay windows and a garden front and back, in Broadway Road, situated in a residential area called the Way Roads in the south of the city.

We were well-fed, lived comfortable lives and were instilled with solid values by our parents: honesty, a strong work ethic, and the importance of helping others. Dad would walk home for his lunch during the week, which meant that I got to see him regularly. Sundays, without fail, was a day trip somewhere. My parents always had a car and the first one I remember was a black Morris Eight. Off we would go to visit stately homes or to picnic somewhere scenic. The fact that Dad was a bit of a petrol-head meant that, as the years passed, the family car was always replaced by a flashier model. The deal was that Mum would get to pick the colour and Dad would choose the make: first the Cortina, later a Triumph 2000 and then the much-hailed SD1 Rover. We were incredibly lucky that our parents could afford a holiday every year, Salcombe in Devon being our favourite resort.

Alliances had been established within the family by the time I came along: Trevor was close to Mum, Sue to Dad. My best pal and confidant at home was the family dog – a Wire Fox Terrier called Penny. Growing up, given the age gap, my relationships with Trevor and Sue were not close. I'm sure I was the pain in the proverbial. I shared a bedroom with Sue, who understandably resented her younger roommate. She was brightest of the three of us. By her teens, she was kicking fairly hard against boundaries: coming home later than agreed; trying to subvert the strict uniform standards set by her grammar school; and not necessarily putting her all into her schoolwork, despite her natural abilities. Trevor was tall, dark, handsome, and taciturn by nature, keeping to himself and with a small circle of trusted friends. By contrast, I fulfilled the role of the compliant child in a bid to court approval.

Dad was a lovely, gentle man. Tall, slim, smartly dressed and always sporting a moustache. The more stable and patient of our two parents, he was the one to attend to us if we hurt ourselves because Mum couldn't cope if we were in pain. Dad was a protective and supportive figure to all of us, including our mother, and made us feel safe. Sadly, my mother was a more complicated, troubled soul.

With her brown eyes and hair so dark it was almost black, Mum was an attractive woman who dressed her slender figure tastefully and was blessed with charisma. She had a knack for storytelling and making people laugh, helped by her natural acting ability, which she put to good use as a member of the local amateur dramatic society. But regrettably she was also cursed by anxiety, which overshadowed her life and made her rather temperamental. Living with Mum often felt like walking on eggshells, never knowing what mood she would be in when I got home.

Back then it wasn't the done thing to share one's mental anguish, and I can only guess what the source of Mum's emotional struggles may have been. All I knew was that she had been born into a family of sons following the death of another daughter; she had suffered with alopecia during her adolescence, and one of her brothers had killed himself.

Mum wanted us to match the ideals of the time and worried far too much about what the neighbours thought, even what perfect strangers thought. Her preoccupation with 'standards' and how other people saw us was a key driving force. On the plus side, Mum's attention to appearance drilled home the benefits of being neatly turned out, of having the right shoes for the right outfit – something I have applied all my life. 'Better to have one good outfit that you can wear seven days a week than seven cheap ones,' she would say.

The pressure she put on herself to be the ideal wife and mother, combined with her fretful state, made for an unhappy combination. Like many women of her generation, my mother had acquired a lifelong dependency on tranquilizers prescribed by her doctor. Criticisms dropped from her lips on what seemed to be a daily basis: for not pronouncing words properly; for not having perfect table manners; for failing to measure up to an ideal. These criticisms were usually conveyed by comparing us to other children. Her thinking could be summed up thus: 'You'll never amount to much unless you do *this*, and you do *that*.' Later in life, we would joke with her that she was a real-life Hyacinth Bucket, the pretentious character famously played by Patricia Routledge in the BBC sitcom *Keeping Up Appearances*. Mum saw the funny side, but it certainly wasn't funny when I was growing up. Perhaps she believed that the tactic of making unfavourable comparisons would spur us to raise our game, but all it did was chip away at my confidence. The frequent ridiculing of my thoughts and opinions left me feeling crushed and simply not good enough. This would cast a long shadow over my life. Sadly – for us *and* for Mum – the hugs, kisses or even words of affection that could have helped offset the harsher aspect of her parenting style were not part of her maternal repertoire.

My refuge from home life was playing outdoors with my best pals, Trevor Nunn and Gareth Miller, who lived in the same street as me and remain two very important friends to this day. My friendship with Trevor began as tots in nursery school. We first met Gareth aged seven, when he moved into our road. Together we played football and cricket day and night. Mostly football. We set up our own team, called the Broadway Rangers. I was the only girl. I was passionate about football, but the limits placed on females in so many walks of life were rudely impressed on me at Linden Junior School. Thanks to an enlightened teacher, I made the school football team – but this inclusion was short-lived as our opposing teams one by one objected.

When Trevor, Gareth and I weren't running about, we were inventing all manner of ways to pass the time, from making homemade telephones using tin cans and string, to building go-karts without the luxury of brakes. Uniform clubs were the only social occasions where the three of us were segregated. Off I would go to Brownies and they to Cubs. We mixed it up a bit wherever we could. When the Cubs and Brownies held a fancy-dress party one Christmas, Gareth turned up as a Brownie and I came as a Cub. We won first prize.

I loved my time at Linden. I had marvellous teachers, mostly, and plenty of football at lunchtime. But one day the headmaster invited my parents in for a chat. He was worried that I spent so much of my time playing with the boys: when we all hit puberty, he said, I would be abandoned by them and have no friends. I'm glad to say that this touching concern was wide of the mark. In my teens I found it as easy to make friends with girls as I did with boys.

When my primary-school years were almost up, the question on my family's lips was, 'Where next for Jackie?' My siblings attended grammar school but my eleven-plus result confirmed that I would not be following in their footsteps. My first epic fail. What made it worse was accidentally overhearing my parents holding a post-mortem in the front room. I was sitting at the top of the stairs when I heard their disappointment first-hand.

'What are we going to do with her?' said Mum. My face flushed with shame.

'We can afford to send her to Evington Hall Convent,' said my dad, always ready with a solution.

'She won't like that. It's an all-girls school, and it's run by nuns,' said my mum. 'And we're not even Catholic.'

'The school takes children who are Church of England.'

Given that the other option was Spencefield, a secondary modern that my mother was heavily against, Mum took me to Evington to sit the entrance exam. As we walked along the long lane to the school, which looked like a huge mansion house, I was feeling pretty nervous.

'How are nuns going to play football in their long frocks?' I asked my mother.

A pause. 'Oh, you know . . . they manage,' she replied.

The exam took place in an attic room, where a one-bar electric heater failed spectacularly to bring warmth to the vast space. My mind made up, I turned over the paper and ticked the 'don't know' box with abandon. Spencefield, here I come . . .

I soon settled in at the large secondary modern. Being sporty certainly helped me to fit in. I worked hard in English and in history; but as for the rest, I clowned around far too much because I sensed we were somehow being written off by the system. Lessons about how to bring up babies, for example, seemed like a pretty clear message about the low expectations set for secondary-modern pupils.

Purgatory for me was needlework on a Monday afternoon. An entire academic year passed before I finished making a dress – I wasn't helped by the fact that the punitive teacher insisted on teaching me to use my right hand, when I was left-handed. Most of my domestic-science efforts ended up being fed to the appreciative family dog.

In my early teens I began going to fencing classes at a local club – inspired by Gareth, who had started lessons and made it sound a lot of fun. I loved the intensity of fencing and the agility of mind and body that it requires: nimble foot and wrist action, fast movement – forwards, backwards, forwards, backwards – and above all, quick thinking. Here, my left-handedness played to my advantage and foiled my opponents. This was a sport I would pursue for years.

I was about 14 when I started thinking about what I would do when I left school. As a regular churchgoer at St Philip's (C of E), I briefly considered becoming a nun. The church felt like a safe place: I enjoyed the rituals, the smell of the building, the silence, and the belief there was something else bigger than man; not necessarily God but definitely some kind of spiritual power. It made sense to wonder whether this was where I belonged. The fact that I had deliberately flunked my entrance exam to a convent school three years previously was probably a clue that my interest in this potential vocational path would be short-lived, as indeed it was.

I moved on to the idea of working with criminals, a thought sparked by gazing out at the local probation service from the top deck of a bus one day. I thought I'd be good at helping the underdog rehabilitate.

It was also when I was 14 that my father announced we were leaving Leicester, because he had been appointed general manager at the *Grimsby Evening Telegraph*. My youthful voice of protest held no sway. I decamped with my parents to a detached house in Daggett Road, Cleethorpes, leaving behind my friends, my lovely school and the only life I had known to date.

It's amazing how quickly a heart can mend. I soon settled in at my new school and over the summer got a job selling candyfloss and ice creams on the seafront at Cleethorpes, chatting all the while to customers.

Two years later, I passed my CSEs. I was just about to start my O levels (the old version of GCSEs) when my dad was appointed manager of the *South Wales Evening Post*. This meant moving to Wales, but it was agreed that I would live with my grandfather Pop and his wife while I went to college. Pop was the person that I felt the happiest and safest with. An engineer after World War I, he was a gentle, kind and popular man. He'd been widowed before I was born, and had remarried – to a woman we knew as Auntie Vi. Unlike home, with Pop and Auntie Vi there was no telling off, no comparing me with others, no wishing that I was someone else. I loved their company.

I was a late developer by anyone's book and didn't start dating until I was 17. Glyn was fun and always lovely to everyone; I was very fond of him. The fact that he owned a car made me feel very grown-up. With him,

I started smoking and drinking socially, but I was too 'straight' to ever try drugs. Through his wide circle of friends, I met a girl called Jo, with whom I became close. Sometimes, as I lay in my bedroom with my Dusty Springfield posters on the wall, I would guiltily acknowledge that I was spending more time daydreaming about Jo than Glyn. The absence of gay role models in those days meant I was left confused by some of the feelings I was experiencing (not for the first time) but couldn't name. The relationship with Glyn petered out, eventually.

In 1968 I passed two O levels, in English and English grammar. My history and religious studies grade 1 CSEs were equivalent to O levels, giving me a total of four. Maths proved to be my Achilles heel. Without A levels, I didn't have the qualifications to apply for a degree, so my hopes of becoming a probation officer were laid to rest. Once I had decided on the cadets, though, I opted to apply back in Leicester. Syd Page gave me a reference and I was accepted on the scheme.

Being a cadet was essentially a policing apprenticeship for 16- to 19-year-olds. The role was an opportunity to observe up close what a police officer's life was like. Would policing be for me, I wondered. I was about to find out.

*

In the early autumn of 1969, I set off with my parents for Leicester with a sense of excitement at the thought of my first real taste of independence and the beginnings of a career. At last, I had a sense of purpose and direction in my life. I dumped my bags at the house where I would be lodging and spent the weekend with Mum and Dad.

On the Monday morning, I was raring to get started. As I turned up at the Blackbird Road cadet centre, based in the grounds of a police station, the smell of biscuits wafted in my nose from the nearby Frears & Blacks biscuit factory.

Roughly a quarter of my cohort were female, aged between 16 and 18. On our first morning, we were issued with kit: a pillbox hat, a skirt, a blue shirt, a jacket and white gloves. All I had to provide was the black stockings and sensible shoes. We were categorized according to age, as yellow, green or blue cadets. As an older entrant, I was a blue cadet. The cadetship promised to be a great introduction to becoming a public servant and to build skills that would serve me well if I went on to proper police training. The programme was designed to help us to learn to work as part of a team, to follow discipline, to foster good relations with the community and to familiarize ourselves with aspects of the law.

The training schedule involved a mixture of activities. A lot of our time was spent competing in sport, be it running, swimming or gymnastics, or doing organized events such as the Duke of Edinburgh awards to build up the team spirit. Given my sporty nature, this suited me down to the ground. We were expected to work in a community setting of some kind and also to serve as gofers in the various police departments at force headquarters. The course tutor, John Peacock, would take us through different elements of policing – learning what constituted criminal offences such as theft, robbery and burglary and the like. He was supportive and encouraging, and provided me with a great start to my fledgling career.

I wasn't expecting to go out and nick collars, investigate crime or do traffic stops as a cadet, though. We had no powers of any sort, so we were not allowed to walk the streets with a police constable since we would probably have got in the way of business. Clerical work was also part of the remit for all recruits. Males and females were treated the same, with no noticeable discrimination other than the fact that I don't recall the boys being asked to make the tea.

What I quickly learned was the importance of rank, rather like the military. The chief constable in post at the time came across as an approachable leader: he took his black Labrador to work with him most days and had a reputation for knowing the names of everyone at HQ.

My first posting was a stint at Staunton Harold Cheshire Home, a residential home for adults with physical disabilities situated north of Leicester and near to the Derbyshire border. We cadets would help out and spend time with residents alongside other volunteers. One of the carers presented himself as an aristocrat, but intuitively it seemed to me that something about him didn't fit: he seemed too obsequious with residents and staff, a little too keen to befriend. What was he really doing there? He was a popular man and everyone else seemed to take what he said at face value, but my suspicions grew when he invited me to his room, where I clocked several shopping bags from expensive shops in Ashby-de-la-Zouch. Something about him wasn't adding up. I had no evidence but reported my hunch to a sergeant at the cadet school, who acted on my concerns. A bit of digging soon revealed him to be a conman who was busy obtaining money by deception. I had detected my first crime! I had spotted that something was off and raised my concerns despite the risk of looking like an idiot to experienced police officers if I was wrong – and this boosted my confidence considerably. A couple of days later, I crossed the path of a female superintendent called Hilda Parkin, who gave me a 'Well done, Miss Malton.' My cheeks reddened with pride.

After two wonderful summer months spent at the home, it was back to the administration department at force headquarters. My cup of enthusiasm ran dry when it came to making the tea. I failed to see how it taught me anything about the actual job of policing and resented the fact that only female cadets were expected to stick the kettle on. This thought brewed in my mind until one fateful day when I was asked to make a round of drinks for senior officers in a meeting being led by the slightly intimidating Deputy Chief Constable Eric Lacey. He stirred the sugar in his tea as he talked to colleagues, took a sip, then promptly spat it out. 'You've given us salt instead of sugar,' he said, his face as red as a traffic light. Clearly I had absentmindedly dipped the sugar bowl into the wrong brown bag.

My reaction was to laugh and put my hand on his shoulder. 'I'm so sorry, sir,' I said. 'It wasn't intentional – but if my mum knew that being a cadet was just about making the tea, she wouldn't be very happy.' Thankfully my cheeky quip made him smile. Lacey remembered me after that.

The rest of my cadetship went off without a hitch. Sergeant Peacock told me that I'd been recommended as a suitable candidate for the police. I applied to Leicester and Rutland Police, where I was given an interview and a medical. The medical involved me stripping down to my bra and knickers, touching my toes and being weighed and measured. I have no idea whether male recruits had to undergo the same exam in only their pants, but as an 18-year-old I assumed it was normal procedure for everyone. (This practice would eventually be phased out in favour of a fitness test, where recruits could wear tracksuit bottoms and T-shirts, and the presentation of a GP's letter.) Fitness standards were quite strict: flat feet, varicose veins, hammer toes and lung, ear or eyesight defects were enough to rule out a prospective candidate. At 5ft 5in, I was an inch above the minimum requirement for women at the time.

As soon as I arrived back at the cadet school, Sergeant Peacock called me in to his office. 'You've been accepted,' he said. I could have hugged him. When I called my parents, they were as overjoyed as I was. It offset the personal turmoil I was going through at the time as I began to realize that I was more attracted to women than men and was probably gay – a fact I couldn't bear to acknowledge because I knew that being a lesbian was seen as shameful. Being a police officer, on the other hand, was viewed as respectable. I wanted the police to be my life. I was determined to give my career everything that I had.

CHAPTER 3
PW8

I swore my police oath on the day I turned 19. On 7 July 1970, I was down at the Magistrates Court in Town Hall Square in Leicester city centre, taking my bible in my right hand:

> I do solemnly and sincerely declare and affirm that I will well and truly serve our Sovereign Lady, The Queen, in the office of Constable, without favour or affection, malice or ill-will, and I will to the best of my power cause the peace to be kept and preserved and prevent all offences against the persons and properties of Her Majesty's subjects, and that while I continue to hold the said office I will, to the best of my skill and knowledge, discharge all the duties thereof faithfully and according to law.

I felt a mixture of nerves and excitement that day, not to mention a huge sense of responsibility for the role I was assuming.

The first two years would be a probationary period. This entailed being frequently observed on the job by a more experienced officer to assess whether we were suitable to be confirmed as police officers in terms of attitude, our knowledge of the law and our confidence to do the job. Our paperwork was also supervised by a sergeant. The blue shirt was switched for a white one. The hat was similar to the pillbox hat that I had worn as a cadet but with a chequered police band and badge. My officer number was PW8. The skirts had no pleats, which restricted movement a bit, but trousers were out of the question for women then. Male probationers were issued with whistles, batons and handcuffs; female recruits were just given a handbag, the whistle and handcuffs. My vision of walking the beat with my baton ended right there. What I didn't realize on my first day was that discrimination went further than a lack of equipment . . .

I attended the training school at Ryton-on-Dunsmore, near Coventry. The new recruits, a mix of ex-cadets and people who had applied directly, hailed from forces from various parts of the country outside London. There were 17 men in my class (460C) and 6 women. The training-school site was a sprawl of Nissen huts, some equipped as classrooms and others as accommodation. We were housed in billets for the duration of the 13-week course, each with a bedroom not much bigger than a prisoner's cell and containing a single bed, a wash basin, a modest wardrobe and a small desk and chair. Despite the restricted space, we were expected to keep our rooms ship-shape to pass muster at routine inspections.

We reported every morning to the parade square, where we had to wait for the arrival of the formidable drill sergeant Jim Suthers, known as the Drill Pig. A former soldier from the Black Watch Regiment, Sergeant Suthers would bellow with a pace stick tucked under his right armpit: 'Eyes front!'

Our uniforms were inspected every day. To meet requirements, the creases on the sleeves of our jackets were ironed in with brown paper so sharp you could cut your finger. I spent an hour each night bulling the toecaps of my shoes: using a lit match to burn in the polish, then spit and finally a good shine with a yellow duster. When Suthers was unsatisfied by my efforts he could be brutal: 'I need to see what you had for your breakfast when I peer into your toecaps, miss.'

Suthers would shout at us and throw in the occasional threat of putting his pace stick up 'every orifice I can find' to knock us into shape. This dramatic flourish was his way of making us focus, and it worked. No one wanted to be singled out for failing to do as he asked. We marched to the music of the Top 20 records, including 'Cottonfields' by the Beach Boys, 'Spirit in the Sky' by Norman Greenbaum and 'In the Summertime' by Mungo Jerry. I was fortunate enough not to be one of those who march in 'tick-tocking' style, with the arm and leg on the same side moving forward together.

The gruff and bullish culture of the time was a bit like the BBC drama *Life on Mars*, but it was soon forgotten on Passing Out day. Witnessed by our parents and siblings, we could march with heads held high as well as any other army squadron to 'Colonel Bogey'. In a short space of time, Sergeant Suthers had instilled in us pride in our appearance, punctuality, discipline and teamwork.

Our class leader, Sergeant Laurie Cyples, from West Mercia, taught every aspect of the law: the legal definition of different offences (theft, robbery, burglary, firearms, traffic offences and so on) and the Judges' Rules, which at the time set out the guidelines about questioning suspects and holding people in custody. We were taught how to direct traffic (to the tune of 'The Blue Danube') and how to give evidence in court, and we role-played arresting suspects. The rest of the training involved basic first aid, life-saving swimming classes and self-defence. Ninety-five per cent of the job, we were told, was talking. 'On the streets, you can talk yourself into or out of trouble. It's your choice,' Sergeant Cyples would say.

If I had time in the evenings after doing my homework, pressing my uniform and cleaning my shoes, I would head to the bar to catch up with the others. I bonded with everyone in my class, but especially Mary and Pauline. Sometimes the three of us would dress up on nights out, get on the stage in the dining hall and mime to Three Degrees songs. Good times.

Everything changed when the course ended and I headed to the women's department in Leicester, based in a building at the rear of Charles Street Police Station. In line with segregation practices in place up and down the country, female officers worked in a self-contained unit based in another building, with its own hierarchy and rank.

Segregation was a bit of a shock. I had not come across the women's department during my time as a cadet, since most of the time I'd been based at force headquarters, where the cadets were of both sexes and treated the same. What I didn't initially realize was that the work the women officers did was very different from what the men at the main station did. A female officer's role was to support the work of the male officers over the road, and to deal with issues relating to women and children in the main – essentially welfare duties: missing children, child neglect and abuse cases, and domestic disputes.

The department also dealt with female offenders of low-level crime, such as shoplifting and theft of monies from home electric meters. We were also expected to search female prisoners. The remit of our work seemed to align with the all-pervasive maternal role attributed to women in those days, but that wasn't how I wanted to be seen. It seemed to me that we were merely complementing the proper policing being done by the men over the road. Yet while I saw the women's department as acting as a secondary service, many of the female officers I worked alongside saw their role as highly valuable.

The pay for women was nine tenths of men's and the shift slightly shorter at 7.5 hours, compared to the 8 hours worked by men. The annual pay for a

19-year-old was £745, which went up to £850 for seniors (age of 22 and over). We also received an allowance for shoes and lodgings.

I made friends in the department easily enough, but it took me a while to settle down. I guess I was a bit of a cheeky recruit. I was harmless with it, but it was not to the liking of Superintendent Hilda Mary Parkin, who held the command over women police officers across Leicester and Rutland Constabulary. Stocky of build, upright of posture, and exacting by nature, the superintendent was quite a character and undeniably scary. She had her eye firmly on me.

Superintendent Parkin wore bright-red lipstick and brushed her thick grey hair up from the nape into what was popularly known as a DA (duck's arse). She had an accent that revealed her Halifax roots and a deep voice she would use to full effect when displeased. She would walk along the corridor, past the small restroom where we made the tea and coffee, and shrill, 'Cream of the milk please, cream of the milk!' – her way of ensuring that her coffee had the top of the milk and was delivered in a china cup with saucer. We duly obliged, hoping that this would set her up in a good mood for the day. Offering her one of our cigarettes was another ruse to keep on her good side. The super only smoked other people's supplies since her sister Ethel, with whom she lived, had no idea that she smoked.

While the superintendent could be direct and sharp, we all knew where we stood with her. She would make routine checks of our police-issue handbags to ensure the contents complied with regulations and she measured the length of our skirts. To her constant irritation, the seams on my stockings were like two slithering snakes, going this way and that. Superintendent Parkin's were, of course, always as straight as a ruler.

Policemen over the road called us Peewees. I would later discover that choice derogatory terms like 'Office Doris' and 'Plonk' (Person with Little or No Knowledge) were used by men in other police forces. It probably wasn't much worse than the casual sexism that women in those days faced in civvy street, but then again it wasn't any better. If a male officer ever referred to me as a 'bird' – common parlance both in and out of the job in the 1970s – I would always fire back that 'women are called birds because of the worms they pick up'.

We spent a lot of time updating files with relevant information on individuals or families received from children's officers or mental-welfare officers – specialist roles that predated the generic social-worker title. The job also involved a lot of work at the juvenile court, where a police officer needed to be present, or at the magistrates', to guard female prisoners in the dock and escort those sentenced to Risley prison – or 'Grisly Risley', as we called it – near Warrington, Lancashire.

Women often ended up in court for offences such as shoplifting, loitering or soliciting 'for the purposes of prostitution', theft and common assault. Usually they would receive a fine – though many failed to pay, resulting in a warrant being issued by the court. In these instances, we would arrest the women and remand them in a police cell overnight ready for their appearance before a magistrate the next morning. Non-payment would invariably see the women sent to Risley for a period of weeks or months. I once paid a fine on behalf of a single mum with a young son to prevent her from ending up in prison.

On the other side of the spectrum, female officers could act as plain-clothed security guards at society balls to keep an eye on the furs and jewellery. I didn't think looking after rich women's fur coats was our job, so was thankful to never be picked for that particular duty.

Taking statements from female victims who reported indecency or assaults – sexual or otherwise – and passing the information on to the male officers across the road was also part and parcel of a policewoman's duties. We handled missing-from-home enquiries too, and domestic incidents.

When a major incident occurred, such as a murder, women officers would often be used to record all the information on an index-card system. Domestic violence was not treated as seriously as it should have been by the police, nor was the long-term impact on the children witnessing violence and abuse registered. There was a general tendency from both men and women to treat it too lightly.

Then there was the extreme end of domestic violence, which shocked me to the core. My training had also left me ill-equipped to deal with it. What was not understood then – and for many years thereafter – was the impact on victims of coercive behaviour. I can still remember the case of an Indian woman who turned up to hospital with a deep slash across her face – acquired, she said, from 'falling down the stairs'. A doctor beckoned us over: 'No way are her injuries due to a fall,' he said. 'I'd say they're more consistent with a machete. This was no accident.' I gently interviewed the woman. She looked absolutely terrified and stuck to her story. I never forgot her.

As a young officer, I was often involved on decoy work to apprehend marauders reported for flashing, groping or, in the worst cases, rape. The job involved changing into civvy clothes and walking along dark alleyways or canal paths, for example, where previous assaults had taken place. Ironically, the job meant that you were actually *hoping* someone would pounce. It was adrenalin-pumping stuff, though you had the safety net of knowing that you were in sight of other officers who were monitoring what was going on. Since I was never attacked I never did get to catch someone in this particular act.

*

Occasionally, women officers were sent out to patrol areas of the city centre, though not every day like their male counterparts. Walking the beat was the only time I really felt like a proper police officer, able to deal with whatever came my way. My favourite patch was in the Highfields, a rough part of the city, and I was sent out on patrol alone, with a pocket police radio to contact base.

The Highfields area, patterned with rows of terraced red-brick houses, was plagued by high levels of unemployment, deprivation and despair. A disused old workhouse operating as a hospital dominated the landscape. As someone who had been lucky enough to grow up in a warm, comfortable home where making ends meet was not a daily worry, I found the Highfields an eye-opener. The poverty and self-neglect were shocking. I'll never forget the overwhelming stench when entering certain homes, only to find that excrement was the source – with soiled nappies (and sometimes worse) scattered about the house. The fetid odour in some people's homes could be so powerful that it made every part of you hanker to get out as soon as possible. I witnessed kids who looked as ill-fed and dishevelled as their parents, mired in a pit of hopelessness; I saw homes with a lack of basic furniture and with musty-smelling threadbare carpets whose replacement was simply an unaffordable luxury.

Unsurprisingly, crimes in these areas were more often directly linked to dire straits: people were so poor that they were bashing the meter boxes to bump out the coins they had previously slotted in to stay warm. Other crimes included thefts of things like prams – expensive items that could easily be sold second-hand. Many women at a loss about making ends meet turned to sex work. Often, they were coerced into it by boyfriends who sat back and counted the money.

A few weeks into the job, I made my first arrest after a group of children playing in a street alerted me to the presence of a man they'd seen hanging around a derelict building. I looked up and spotted him scurrying away, carrying a plastic bag that appeared to contain something heavy.

'Stop!' I shouted, running towards him.

He looked up.

'What have you got in the bag?' I asked when I'd caught up with him.

'The site foreman gave it to me,' he answered, looking very shifty.

As I took hold of his arm to arrest him, the man punched me in the stomach and threw me against the wall. He then dropped the bag and scarpered, shouting as he ran off: 'I'm a gunman, I'll shoot!'

Winded, I called for help on the radio. It seemed only seconds before a male colleague arrived in a police car. I jumped in and only then opened the bag, which was full of heavy lead. The theft of lead from derelict houses was quite common at the time, since it could be sold on. As my colleague drove around the area, we quickly spotted our culprit. I got out of the car to make my first arrest.

The lead thief was an unemployed labourer called Ted Cox. The paperwork involved preparing my statement and checking the offender's details and previous criminal history, which were all sent to the police's prosecution department. Cox had a string of convictions for assault, larceny (theft), drunkenness and burglary. I wasn't needed for court, as Cox pleaded guilty to stealing 15lb of lead and assaulting a police constable in the execution of her duty. He received a three-month prison sentence. The case made the *Leicester Mercury*, though to my disappointment the reporter misspelt my name as 'Moulden'. The headline was 'Man said: "I'm a gunman, I'll shoot", court told'.

There were many 'firsts' on the job. A memorable one happened when I was on the beat in the town centre just a few months into my probation and a harried-looking woman rushed out from a pub and beckoned me inside.

'Quickly! My husband has collapsed.'

The couple lived in accommodation above the pub. The wife raced back upstairs, explaining breathlessly as I followed behind that her husband had dropped like a stone after clutching his chest, unable to breathe. I arrived in their sitting room to find the husband sprawled on the carpet. My pulse quickening, I checked myself to remain calm as I knelt beside him to look for a sign of life and told his wife to call an ambulance.

'Is he dead?'

I looked at the woman while feeling for a pulse.

'It's OK,' I sighed. 'He's still breathing.'

At this the woman's tense features visibly relaxed. The ambulance crew soon arrived. 'I felt his pulse and he's still alive,' I declared, feeling utterly useful.

The two ambulancemen looked at the man on the floor, a knowing look sweeping across their faces. One of them knelt down next to him while the other ushered the wife out of the room.

The ambulanceman turned to me. 'Can you show me how you did that, please?'

'Of course.'

I replayed exactly what I had done, placing my thumb on the inside of the poor man's wrist.

'You felt your own pulse, you silly cow.' I deflated like a balloon. It was my first corpse – clearly I'd forgotten my training on 'how to tell if someone is dead'. I had the unenviable task of breaking the news to the wife, now a widow.

Dealing with death goes with the territory of policing, whether it's at the hands of others, suicides or sudden deaths. A 'sudden death' means a death by natural causes, rather than because of violence of some kind. I would encounter so many in Leicester that I earned the nickname 'Sudden Death Queen'. I didn't choose the jobs that I was called out to, of course. Often, alerts would come through to the police from concerned relatives who hadn't been able to get in touch with their loved one for some time.

Usually, we would go around and find that everything was fine. Occasionally, though, it wasn't.

During my first year, one such call came through. A woman worried about a relative asked if we could pop in to see if she was OK. I went round to the address with my supervising officer and knocked on the door of the terraced house. No answer. I peeked through the letterbox, cold air wafting onto my face, and saw a rough pile of unopened mail on the hallway carpet. According to a neighbour, the occupant – a woman in her fifties – had not been seen for several days. I don't recall how we got in, but as I stepped into the house I called out: 'Hello, anybody home?'

An eerie silence met my call as we walked into the living room. The house was barren: no photographs, no knick-knacks, nothing to give the property a warm, homely feel. A palpable gloom pervaded. A smear of blood on the banister caught our attention and a red trail led upstairs. As I followed it, my heart pounded in anticipation of what we were about to find. In the bedroom we discovered a lifeless woman lying on a double bed. She had killed herself. The cold and depressing feel of the house seemed to mirror how she must have felt. I didn't allow my emotions to surface. My job was to deal with the practicalities, not to fall apart.

I contacted a doctor to come and confirm the death, then called the Co-Op funeral directors to collect the body. There is something particularly sad about a suicide, the way it highlights the utter despair that triggers someone to end their life prematurely. When I got home that night, I imagined how the news of this woman's death at her own hands would affect those who knew her or cared about her. It was easier to think about the impact on invisible strangers than to consider how finding her had left me feeling.

The anxious anticipation I felt when I was expecting to find a dead body was often worse than being confronted by the reality. Dealing with death can be an education: my sergeant, Bettie Buxton, told me about the time she attended a death while still a rookie, and heard a rattle emanating from the body as the funeral directors moved it. She ran out of the house until she could run no more. It took her months to recover from the fear she experienced that day. The 'death rattle' is merely a result of a build-up of mucus and saliva that can cause the throat to make a rattling sound shortly after a person has passed away. But you don't know what you don't know, and Sergeant Buxton learned the hard way. Finding bodies that have lain undiscovered for months is harrowing. Police officers can be met with the sight of a body being eaten by maggots.

Some incidents stick in the mind more than others, and some affect you more than most, but no one at work ever talked about how cases may have affected them; it just wasn't done. You were expected to weather the blows of human misery and continue onto your next task. I used the uniform as a shield to protect myself from my emotions. My strategy was to take a deep breath, pull back my shoulders and get on with it. Occasionally you would get unwelcome reminders of the scene you'd just witnessed: I often found that the smell of death clung to my uniform throughout the remainder of my shift. When I got home, I would soak in a bath to cleanse myself of the smell and hang my uniform outside to air. In the evening, thoughts of a particular case might float up, but as much as possible I kept the lid tightly shut on my feelings.

Troubling sights that connected with my own anxieties sometimes did pierce through. The ones that always got me were the people who died alone, since dying alone without anyone I loved by my side was my biggest fear. I'll never forget the elderly woman I found dead in a chair in front of an electric fire, with patterns on her thin-skinned legs from being so close to the heat.

A few days after finding the elderly woman, I was called to another death. I knew before I arrived that the body that had floated to the surface of a river was probably the Indian woman suffering with dementia who had been reported missing from her home 24 hours earlier. Premature endings of this kind often left me with questions that could never be answered. What led her to the river, and how did she end up in the water? Did she mean to do it, or was she just confused? It was a dark winter's day, and I shuddered at the thought of how cold she must have felt in her final moments of existence. All that she had been wearing was a pale-blue sari.

Dealing with instances like this could get to you if you didn't find ways of distracting yourself. I was young and I focused on the good times. Even at work I would occasionally try to have a bit of a laugh to lighten the day – much to Superintendent Parkin's disapproval. I could always count on her to be in the wings, ready to rebuke me.

I was amusing my colleagues one day by recounting an exchange I'd had that morning with a motorist who had been speeding. 'Having difficulty taking off, sir?' had been my opener to the sheepish driver. As my small but appreciative audience laughed, the superintendent appeared from nowhere to suck the air out of the room. 'We are public servants and being rude to them is not part of the role, PW Malton.'

Christ, I thought to myself, *how on earth did she overhear that all the way from her office?* Lowering my head, I feigned a chastened response while quietly savouring the fact that the girls had heard my witty repartee.

The decision to buy a 99 ice cream on a particularly hot day on patrol was another moment of joy killed dead – because who should just happen to walk past in the opposite direction as I savoured my treat? As the super loomed closer, her anger palpable at 20 paces, I braced myself for what was coming.

'What on earth are you doing, young lady?' she shouted.

'I was hot,' I mumbled, lowering my ice cream from her gaze. Glaring, she pointed to a rubbish bin. 'In there.' My half-eaten cornet was gone.

Despite her strict ways, Superintendent Parkin could be very protective of her crew, especially if any of her girls fell ill or were assaulted; she made sure we didn't return to work until we were ready to do so. Occasionally, she would let her hair down a bit. She loved my impersonation of Frank Spencer, the dim but well-intentioned character depicted in the 1970s TV comedy *Some Mothers Do 'Ave 'Em*. The super was such a fan of my performance that she would later insist I do a rendition at her retirement dinner, held at the Grand Hotel in 1975. But if I were to bump into Superintendent Parkin again today, I think I'd automatically return to that impish child state that she tended to bring out in me.

*

Establishing good relationships on our patch wherever possible was very much part of the job, so I got to know locals of interest on my beat – particularly women who worked as prostitutes (as sex workers were then known). I'd pop round to their homes for a cup of tea and a natter. The chats were always interesting: they would regale me with stories about the strange sexual demands made by customers, prompting my jaw to drop. Aside from the gossip and the humour, as the trust built up the women began giving me helpful bits of information about the local scene and the characters to watch. Sometimes, they would inadvertently say things that were of use. This occasionally paid invaluable dividends and led to some good crime arrests. The relationships forged were mutually beneficial, since the police made sure to take an interest in crimes committed against this social group about which society generally held its nose. I had a good rapport with many of them and if they were arrested would make sure to look after them at the station, getting them a cup of tea and a magazine to read.

The relationships I established paid off in other ways too. One day, a sex worker reported her baby missing: she had left the child with a friend called Julie who promptly vanished. I knew Julie, who was also on the game. For a case deemed of high importance, any intelligence held by women officers would be handed over to male police officers over the road. I went and gave all the details I had about Julie. Ordinarily this would be where my role as a female officer stopped. It was over to the male officers at Charles Street Police Station to quickly set up a search party, but there was no trace of Julie or the baby. Julie had left the seven-month-old with another friend, who on reading the news about a missing baby had realized what Julie had done and returned the child to the mother. Two days later, Julie called me to say that she wanted to turn herself in to me. 'I just wanted a baby,' she told me. Her attempt to find love by stealing another woman's child was a symptom of her poor mental health. Julie was a needy soul due to a troubled background, which she had told me about over several conversations. She pleaded guilty to taking the child by force with the intent of depriving his mother of him, and of burgling a flat. She was put on probation for two years and ordered to go into inpatient psychiatric for six months.

Women officers' skills and abilities were seen by some in the CID as secondary to the main role of the male detectives. Some men stood out for their more collegiate approach, however. Detective Sergeant Maurice Jones, for example, always gave female officers credit where credit was due: whenever I shared information with him or his team, Jones would keep me abreast of developments. If it led to an impending arrest, he would sometimes offer to take me along.

When Jones dealt with a complaint from a man who had been robbed during a visit to a sex worker, I knew the obvious suspect to approach and contacted Jones. I had come to know of a man called Harry Turner, who was very camp and equally charismatic. Harry was tight with a terrifying female pimp called Ellen, as coercive and predatory as any man.

More than once, some of the sex workers I knew had whispered to me that Harry was involved in a sting whereby punters would be divested of their wallets while their jackets were hanging up and their trousers were around their ankles. After I shared the intelligence with Jones he allowed me to be present at the arrest, which saw Harry held in the cells overnight. I was still learning the ropes and making my fair share of blunders. When Harry confided that he was terrified of prison, I – like a fool – reassured him. 'It probably won't come to that,' I said.

He was sent down for two years.

The lesson for me, as I watched Harry's face crumple in court, was that however good your intentions, you should never promise what you can't guarantee.

CHAPTER 4

THE ROAD TO BECOMING A DETECTIVE

Diana Morris was only six years old when she disappeared. She was on her way back from school to her grandparents but never made it home. It was June 1971, and I was still in my first year in the job. A mobile incident room was set up on the Braunstone Estate, a socially deprived area southwest of Leicester city centre, where Diana's grandparents lived in a council house on Corfield Rise. It was all hands to the pump, and I was sent to assist. I vividly remember the anxious atmosphere in the incident room as detectives worked against the clock to try and find Diana before it was too late. My job was as a gofer: to make constant rounds of tea, carry pieces of paper from one end of the incident room to the other, jump when told to, and generally be as useful as I could.

At the helm was Deputy Chief Constable Lacey, the man to whom I had served salty tea a few months before. The search for Diana ended two days later, when her body was found in a tea chest dumped on a refuse tip near a church on the edge of the estate. Diana had been sexually assaulted and suffocated with a pair of child's pants. When the news came in, my instant reaction was shock, despite having anticipated that she would not be found alive. A sombre mood infused the incident room as everyone digested the news. I looked over to the seasoned, no-nonsense

DCC Lacey sitting at his desk, head in hands, looking deeply shaken. Clearly everyone was feeling as ghastly as I did that afternoon. I felt for the police officer given the job of informing the grandparents that Diana was dead. The mission now was to find out who had committed such a heinous crime.

This was an analogue era, where detectives operated in a world with no CCTV footage, no mobile phones and no DNA to help with crime detection. The investigation depended solely on footwork, knocking on doors and talking to people who may have seen something.

The local community rallied to ensure that Diana's killer could be found. A crucial lead came through when someone reported that a local man had been seen walking down the road pushing a wheelbarrow containing a tea chest. Diana had been hidden in plain sight. The culprit who had paraded her through Braunstone was quickly identified as Kenneth William Patrick, who lived on the estate. He was apprehended and charged with murder. At court he was convicted after pleading guilty to manslaughter on the grounds of diminished responsibility and sentenced to life imprisonment with a psychiatric order attached.

The sense of shock that I felt was huge. This wasn't like watching crime on a TV police drama; it was real time and real life. How anyone could do what Patrick did was unfathomable. When I got back to my room the night that Diana's body was found, my thoughts swirled on the emotional toll that her brutal murder must be having on her family. I felt their pain. Their lives would never be the same again. It's fair to say that the roof on my pretty sheltered life began to dismantle rather quickly during my first year as a probationer.

*

Almost as soon as I had started working in the policewomen's department, I had been itching to go over the road to the main police station, where the men were based. *That's where the real action is*, I told myself.

The Diana Morris murder case was the first time I'd had a chance to watch detectives at work and the experience fortified my resolve to join their ranks one day. How satisfying it must be, I thought, to liaise with witnesses and suspects, to engage with the evidence, follow leads and refer to the slew of experts, such as forensic scientists and pathologists, to find out whodunnit – and sometimes why they'd done it too.

When I confided my ambition to my parents on a weekend visit, my mum chirped up that she for one was not surprised. 'You were always curious as a child about people and what made them what they were,' she said to me over lunch. 'Always asking questions, always wanting to know about people. It's you all over.'

It felt good to have my parents so interested in the job I was doing and so encouraging about my ambitions. But would the force see it that way?

Female and male rookies alike were given a one-week stint attached to CID as part of our probationary period. But my desire to join CID permanently was pretty fanciful for two key reasons: the first was that I was only a probationer, months into the job, which virtually ruled me out for a couple of years at least; the second was that the opportunities for women to become detectives were few and far between. There was only one permanent female detective in the CID at Charles Street, in contrast to around 20 posts for men. There was also a woman detective posted in Special Branch.

Seeing how the odds were stacked, I put my head down and got on with the job at hand: admin, beat, traffic stops. By getting good results, I hoped to get noticed for the right reasons – and not because I was the bane of Superintendent Parkin's life. I notched up several arrests during traffic stops on the Highfield patch. I'd like to think that it was due to my diligent questioning of drivers and my insistence that I take a look in their boot. As luck would have it, I found drugs stashed in vehicles on several occasions.

As the months passed, my confidence grew. Nine months into the job, and not even halfway into my probation, I successfully applied for an attachment to the Drug and Vice Squad over the road. Young female officers like me were needed to frequent dancehalls and pubs to identify drug dealers and users.

I was as excited as a Jack Russell. I switched my uniform for a smart skirt suit that would have met with my mother's approval, ditched the police handbag and joined an office of ten male officers in the squad.

The office was shared with detectives from the Force Crime Squad and the Regional Crime Squad. The latter was part of a bigger team consisting of detectives from neighbouring forces, dealing with major and cross-border crime. I was thrilled to be there. Having my own desk was quite the novelty.

Being with the squad was a more relaxed affair than life in uniform. My direct line of command was a cool-looking detective sergeant who sported a beard and had a penchant for wearing open-neck shirts, a brown leather jacket, flares and Cuban heels. Taking me under his wing, he inducted me into the culture and the processes of detective work, which were different from uniform work. Instead of dealing with calls or complaints from the public, the Drug Squad relied on tips, informants and intelligence gathering. My DS underlined the importance of being able to talk to people in order to penetrate and obtain intelligence from any source.

I'd been in my new role for only five minutes when the phone rang on a desk belonging to the Force Crime Squad. As I was the only person in the office, I picked it up.

'Detective Policewoman Malton,' said I proudly.

The voice of a very well-spoken woman asked for the detective chief inspector. 'I'm sorry, madam,' I replied in the most professional voice I could muster, 'but he's not at his desk at the moment.'

The caller sounded irked. 'I need you to give him a message. It's very important. Do you understand?'

'Yes, madam.' I grabbed hold of some paper, my pen poised at the ready as she went on.

'The message is this: the fox has got out of its hole and the *Queen Mary* has sunk.'

Temporary pause my end. 'Could I just repeat that back to you, madam? "The fox has got out of its hole, and the *Queen Mary* has sunk." Is that correct?'

'That's it. And if the detective chief inspector is not there right now, you need to tell Scotland Yard immediately. Ask for the commander. He is also known as the Pied Piper, so you might try that.'

I replaced the receiver with a trembling hand. My heart raced a little. I was now part of a world of undercover operations and secrecy, where codes were part of everyday parlance. With still no sight of my DS – or anyone else from the squad – I picked up the phone and dialled New Scotland Yard. Sure enough, the commander in question was not available.

'He's also known as the Pied Piper,' I said a tad awkwardly, spurred by a sense of urgency.

Still no joy. I relayed the message: 'The fox has got out of its hole, and the *Queen Mary* has sunk.'

'Are you having a laugh?' asked the voice at the other end.

'No, this is the message, sir.' I felt quite indignant at his tone.

As I put the phone down, I started to wonder whether I'd done the right thing.

I think 'idiot' was among the choice words that passed the DS's lips when I told him what had happened. The woman who left the message, it turned out, was a fantasist who made regular calls to the station, prompting much mirth in the office. The boss wasn't laughing much when he was forced to ring up the Crime Reserve Office at New Scotland Yard to smooth things over. This was not the world of John le Carré. The ordinariness of reality came crashing down. But you live, and you learn.

I was ribbed by colleagues over it, as you would expect. Overall, though, no one on the Drug Squad gave me any stick as the rookie in the team. I had proved my worth by the amount of drug arrests I had garnered as a uniform officer. Moreover, they knew they needed a woman in the team to assist with certain operations. Working the vice aspect of the team's remit meant enforcing the Street Offences Act 1959, which covers loitering and solicitation of prostitution. Male detectives would pose as customers then arrest the women – often called 'toms' or 'tarts' by police. The woman would have to have two cautions for loitering, from two separate occasions, before she could be charged with the offence. Where information suggested that a house was being used as a brothel, officers would spend hours on observation.

Having forged connections with many of those at the sharp end of sex work, I didn't really enjoy arresting the women. I knew the dire circumstances – poverty, drugs, coercive boyfriends-come-pimps – that led to women and girls heading down this sordid route. I was also aware of the awful realities that their line of work involved. Nevertheless, our job as police officers was to uphold the law, no matter how it was framed and to whose disadvantage. What didn't make sense to me was why only the woman was penalized. The only hassle the men would get were letters sent to their home address saying their car had frequently been seen in an area where prostitutes were operating.

When I was out on patrol looking for missing young girls, street workers would invariably help me with information as to their whereabouts, saying, 'I don't want these young girls ending up like me.' Sometimes, if they knew that the new girl on the block was missing from home, they would tip me the wink to come back, assuring me that they would get her for me so that she could be returned to her family.

When a sex worker called Rosina Hilliard was found dead after sustaining serious head injuries, local working girls were asked to attend the police station to see if they could shed any light or identify worrying red-flag behaviour by regular clients or newcomers. It appeared that someone had tried to strangle Rosina and that she had been hit by the suspect's car when trying to get away.

I was tasked with driving the women home in the police van after the interviews, dropping them off at corners or at their homes to avoid their pimps knowing that they had talked to the police. The banter en route was unforgettable: they managed to laugh about some pretty harrowing experiences in their grim lives. I admired their resilience and their ability to laugh in the face of what they did to get by. Despite the humour that day, it was clear that the women were scared about there being a murderer on the street, particularly one who had targeted one of their own. They resolved to be more alert and to look out for each other. Young Rosina's killer was never caught.

One of the women in the van that day was a raucous character called Maisy. She was pimped by her trilby-wearing boyfriend Steve, who would often wave to me from his Chevrolet when driving past. To them, an existence in the underbelly of life was normal. Years later, while on a house-to-house enquiry in west London concerning the case of a missing child, I came across Maisy once more. She looked at me with recognition on her face. 'I know you, ya bastard!' she screeched. 'Your name's Jackie and you nicked me in Leicester!' We arranged to meet up in the pub for a proper reunion with Steve. It was quite a night.

*

Cannabis was at the heart of most of our operations in the Drug and Vice Squad, although LSD was growing in popularity. The Misuse of Drugs Act 1971 classifies drugs as A, B or C. Class A included heroin, cocaine, crack, MDMA, LSD and others; Class B included, among others, amphetamines, barbiturates and cannabis; Class C included GHB, diazepam and other tranquilizers. Working in the squad, I soon realized that cannabis was often a gateway to harder drugs. We also dealt with cases of forged prescriptions used to obtain drugs from chemists.

My youth meant I was frequently sent to dancehalls and pubs to detect users and, with a bit of luck, the dealers. The quantities were relatively small beer. Our biggest haul during my stint on the squad was 8lb of cannabis, valued at £2,500. The same amount today would be worth around £35,000. We were tipped off that someone from Birmingham was planning to bring the stash to the city, intending to sell it to local dealers. The out-of-towner set himself up in a motel and arranged to meet his newly found contacts in a hotel, where he handed over 6lb of the cannabis. Four men turned up, took the package and duly scarpered without paying. We weren't far behind, thanks to the intelligence that we had received about the deal. The hapless dealer saw himself as a victim of crime. All five men were apprehended, arrested and charged. They pleaded guilty to various charges and were sent to prison: two for five years, two for four and one for three years. All the cannabis was recovered. A good result.

My time on the squad taught me that cultivating a good informant could reap dividends in terms of tip-offs, and that having a reliable source gave a detective kudos. My main informants, however, continued to be of the informal kind: usually female, usually sex workers. Back at the office, I would tune in to the chat about jobs the Regional Crime Squad were working on with other forces to nail crime gangs operating across large geographical areas. I found the conversations fascinating. It made me all the more determined to carve out a career as a detective.

My one-year posting flew by and was over far too quickly for my liking. A woman's role had a certain shelf-life: Leicester is not a huge city, so after a few police operations working in dancehalls, I'd be easily recognized. I was sent back to the female section to enable another woman to join the team.

*

My departure from the Drug and Vice Squad turned out to be well timed. In its progressive wisdom, my force decided to appoint half a dozen women to be trained alongside men to drive the new brand of patrol cars, the Triumph Dolomite. The aim of patrol-car drivers was to provide a faster response to incidents in the city centre: the drivers would be the first, or among the first, at the scene. Nowadays these response cars would be described as 'police interceptors'. To qualify, you had to pass Advanced Level Driving as part of a three-week course. I'd already passed my driving test at my first attempt, aged 17, and I loved driving. I wasted no time throwing my hat in the ring. One for me, I decided.

Three female officers had already been trained and passed the tough two-hour test. I was accepted on the course as part of the second tranche and was determined to succeed.

Training involved being given a scenario that would require a fast response, and then taking the appointed route. We were taught how to down-shift gears smoothly at speed, using double de-clutch, and to use the whole of the road, driving on the wrong side where necessary to give more visibility of the road ahead. It was a liberating experience, but one that required huge amounts of sustained concentration.

Sergeant Ken MacDonald brooked no small talk as he invited me to sit in the driver seat for the test. When we reached the deep Leicestershire countryside, he instructed me to stop the car on a very narrow road. The task set was to respond to an urgent call from the force control room. I was expected to give a running commentary as I drove. Off I sped, applying all that I had been taught on my intensive course: zipping down the country lanes, keeping an eye out for all the potential obstructions ahead, while articulating in detail my observations, my actions and which manoeuvres I was doing and why. At the end of the test, it seemed like an age until he said those magic words: 'You've passed.'

The rush of driving fast or being a passenger in a police car on the blues and twos – blue lights flashing and siren going – would remain with me throughout my policing career, none more so than when being driven by a squad driver in an unmarked car.

My partner in crime in the Dolomite was Doreen Newton. We were the second double-crewed all-woman traffic patrol. Tall, slim and blonde, Doreen was self-assured, professional and a very capable police officer. She was also extremely funny. She always kept a straight face, so it was difficult sometimes to work out whether she was joking or not. We had a lot of laughs together and made a good team.

One of our first shouts was when colleagues called for assistance at a disturbance at a 21st birthday party on the Braunstone Estate. The fire brigade had responded to a report of a child hanging from the ledge of a house. Arriving quickly on the scene, we knocked on the door to be met by a woman who began to scream hysterically at the sight of police officers and the fire brigade outside her house. She had no idea what was going on. The woman's son – the birthday boy – came out and also began shouting at the police; he was restrained after punching a police constable in the face. Another partygoer then rushed out, holding a lager glass in his hand. He smashed the glass against the front wall of the house and thrust the jagged edge into the side of PC Maurice Williams's head. Maurice – known as 'Mo' – was standing next to me and had blood gushing from his temple alarmingly fast.

Rather than wait for an ambulance, we helped Mo into the patrol car and drove at speed to Leicester Royal Infirmary, where doctors stemmed the bleeding and performed an emergency operation. According to the doctor, Mo's fate could have been quite different had we waited for an ambulance.

The 20-year-old culprit who attacked Mo was sentenced to three years' imprisonment. The birthday boy, who had been released from prison only two days before the fracas, received nine months. The call to the fire brigade turned out to be a hoax. Whenever I bumped into Mo thereafter, he would thank me and Doreen for saving his life.

Being an area-car driver had its lighter moments. Doreen and I would occasionally park the car at Leicester racecourse and wait for my sister, Sue, to drive by before putting on the blues and twos and pulling her over. Doreen would step out of the car with a clipboard and do the full formal, 'Good morning, madam. Can you tell me what speed you think you were doing back there?' I never failed to find it funny; Sue, on the other hand, found it all a bit exasperating.

My social life at this stage centred around the job. Our regular haunt was the police club, situated above a garage at the back of Charles Street Police Station. It was the venue for leaving dos and for regular meet-ups after shift, when everyone could let their hair down. I enjoyed the banter, the camaraderie, the drinking and the smoking. I was known as 'Cocky Chops' and gave as good I got.

My sense of fun didn't distract from the job. I took the earliest opportunity to sit my sergeant's exam once my two-year probationary period had ended. Still only 22 years old, I passed. In fact, my exam results put me in the top 200 passes in the country that year, which automatically allowed me to be considered for the 12-month Special Course for sergeants – effectively a fast-track promotion scheme. If successful, I could expect consistent mentoring and support to rise through the ranks. Off I went to Surbiton in the London borough of Kingston upon Thames to face an interview panel comprising three middle-aged men, humourless one and all. I felt that it was going quite well until midway into the interview they lobbed me a curveball.

'If you went to a public house and saw two women canoodling in the corner, what would you do as a police officer?' My confusion must have been visible to all. As the panel waited for an answer, I sat stumped. I wondered what the point of the question was, since being a lesbian was not a crime, nor had it ever been one. What on earth was the correct answer?

'Sorry, I'm not quite sure what you mean, sir,' I said, playing for time. The question was repeated. 'I wouldn't do anything,' I answered finally, 'since they haven't committed an offence, sir.'

The panel moved on to other questions, and then it was all over. About a week later, I learned that I had failed the interview. The fast-track route was out.

Whether the 'lesbian question' was to blame for my failure to make the grade, and whether this question was asked of every candidate, I will simply never know. This was the first time that the issue of sexuality had arisen on the job. I had been thrown by it that day because I'd only recently admitted to myself that I was gay.

I embarked on my first gay relationship at the age of 21 with a woman called Gill. My attraction to women had lurked for a long time but I had pushed it away for as long as I could. The overt hostility towards homosexuality at the time made the prospect of being gay seem frightening: it was seen as a flaw, an inadequacy, a marker for bullying. Acting on my feelings wasn't something I'd ever envisaged doing.

Gill and I met in a pub with a group of friends. She was older than me and, like me, had never had a relationship with a woman before. With her sparkling blue eyes, short hair and sporty look, I found her very attractive. She drove a fast sports car, had a great sense of humour and made me laugh when she took the mickey out of me. We played a lot of squash at the local sports club. I enjoyed Gill's company greatly.

It was a slow burn before we became sexually involved. It started with a kiss one evening at my house. But with the joy of intimacy came a feeling of shame and a pact of secrecy. We were both scared of anybody finding out, so we told no one; even Gill and I barely discussed it. To this day, I don't think anyone has known about it.

Until my relationship with Gill, the only other person I knew who was gay was my old friend Gareth, who wrote to me from university to say that he had fallen in love with a fantastic man called John. What was confusing for me – and no doubt countless other gay women at the time – was that being sexually attracted to a woman felt normal, yet society as a whole viewed us as an aberration and our sexuality as deviance. *Who wants to belong to that particular club?* I thought. I hated the word lesbian, and still do. I'd rather have been called queer, because that's how it felt.

I saw my sexuality as a natural part of me, but it never defined me or my world. It was not something that I wanted to campaign about; forging a career as a woman in a predominantly male world was hard enough without throwing my private life into the mix. I didn't lie about it, but nor did I bring it to people's attention – certainly not to my parents'. When I finally came clean to them, many years later, the conversation proved as painful and as difficult as I had feared.

It was hard to sustain a relationship in those days, when you were unable to share it with anyone else or to go out in public together for fear of gossip. There were few places you could go where you could be openly gay, but being a police officer prevented me from attending anyway. Living your life in fear of being exposed brings pressure with it. Gill and I eventually parted.

After Gill, I found it easier to suss out other gay women who, like me, kept it under the radar. Some I worked with; others I met from other stations and other forces through the police hockey league. Again, the elephant in the room was not discussed. In public, there was no display of affection, given the climate, so the notion of two women canoodling romantically in a bar was completely out of touch with reality. Perhaps this was the answer that I should have given the panel in my Special Course interview.

I parked the failure of not making the fast-track and seized the first opportunity for promotion. As soon as I spotted an advert for a female sergeant in Leicestershire, I applied.

The three-strong interview panel was chaired by Chief Constable Alan Goodson, with Superintendent Parkin as an observer. Near the end of the interview, Goodson laid bare his doubts about me: 'You're only 22, Policewoman Malton. You need a couple more years of experience before you can be considered seriously for the role of sergeant.'

A succession of emotions coursed through me: deflation, frustration, determination. I went for broke: 'But aren't you the youngest chief constable in the entire country, sir? So, with the greatest respect, I think it's pretty rich for you to be saying this to me, since somebody must have given you a break. I'd just like the same.'

An amused smile crept across Goodson's face. It's amazing the absolute cheek that I got away with. I carried on: 'It's true that I've not been in the job for that long, but I do think I have notched up a fair few skills and experience already, including my time on the Drug and Vice Squad and now on traffic patrol. I took the sergeant's exam at the first opportunity, I passed, and I want to make the police my career.'

Suffice to say, I got the job.

My appointment led to a small piece in the *Leicester Mercury*, under the headline 'Police officer sets record'. I was the youngest policewoman ever to be promoted from the beat to sergeant in Leicester and Rutland Constabulary. The article noted: 'Although promotion for young officers can be accelerated by select courses, Sergeant Malton, the youngest of three children of former Leicester newspaper executive Jeffrey Malton, has won her promotion through the ranks.'

CHAPTER 5

SARGE MALTON

On 17 April 1973, I rocked up in my first sports car – a second-hand navy-blue Spitfire – for my first sergeant's shift at Syston, north Leicester. The station was smaller than Charles Street and everybody was friendly enough. The downside of the new job was that by leaving traffic patrol, I was back in the female department under the watchful gaze of Superintendent Parkin. Now, though, I had a little bit more maturity and experience to curb the prospect of a dressing down. And anyway, the super's visits to Syston station weren't very frequent, which limited the number of potential brushes with her.

Under segregation, I was a sergeant for two police departments in an area of Leicestershire, whereas my male peers covered just one station. My rank required me to draw up duty rotas and fulfil supervisory duties for the first time. I was responsible for making sure that the records of women and children were kept up to date, warrants had been executed and inquiries regarding missing persons were being well conducted. I still went out on the beat, and there was still no truncheon.

I made a point of eschewing the authoritarian approach modelled by Superintendent Parkin in favour of a more relaxed style of management.

As a sergeant with just three years of policing under my belt, I was on a steep learning curve and not too proud to take advice.

You'd imagine that police constables with many years' service might have rolled their eyes when they found out they were to be managed by a young upstart. Perhaps some of the women did, but they never showed it. Notably, I gained support from a very able and experienced constable on my team called Sue Glazebrook, who quietly advised me when I was flailing. At times, I felt I was less of a sergeant to her than she to me. She really had my back and I owe her a debt of gratitude.

Women officers with seniority of rank were not supposed to go on patrol together, but Inspector Pat Perry and I didn't always adhere to this rule. Pat was a supportive colleague with whom I got on famously. When we decided to drive to see Sue Glazebrook at Blackbird Road station in my Spitfire one day, we spotted Superintendent Parkin in the station car park. I stifled a laugh as Pat literally slid down from her seat to hide in the footwell of the car.

We responded to the usual grim roll call of crimes affecting women and children: indecent exposures and assaults; rapes; children missing from home; and violence within the home, including incest and sexual abuse, which seemed to be a too common occurrence. The control room had a telex printing machine on which we received messages from other stations about local crimes, suspects wanted by the police and missing persons. The printing moved at a snail's pace. We would take people's statements and provide victim support while the detectives investigated. Sometimes we'd liaise with the CID on a case. I seized every chance to work with the CID to garner more knowledge and insight into the role that I ultimately wanted to do.

By this time, I was earning enough to buy my first house and my first new car, trading my old Spitfire for a new Volkswagen Beetle. When

I wasn't working, I played football and hockey, socialized and dated. I smoked, and I drank.

After a two-year stint as a uniform sergeant, a detective-sergeant vacancy came up and I decided to apply. I gave it my best shot and to my delight got the job – back at my old hunting ground, Charles Street Police Station.

I had big shoes to fill when I arrived in CID. The woman I was replacing was the popular Wanda Stanley, who had clearly had strong abilities since she had been moved on to the Force Crime Squad – a team made up of the most experienced detectives pursuing major criminals operating force-wide. Women were such a token feature of CID that when Bettie Buxton became a detective policewoman at Leicester City Police in the 1960s, the chief constable's office had to resort to using a typewriter to adjust her warrant card: where it said 'this is his warrant and Authority for executing his office', 'his' was crossed out and 'her' was typed rather awkwardly above it.

Despite having the rank of sergeant, joining CID felt to me like starting at the bottom again. Everything was different, and there was plenty to learn – preparing court files for my own cases was a new responsibility, for example. As a newbie, when I was unsure what to do, I would muster up the courage to ask the more experienced men on the team. Otherwise, I observed, kept my mouth shut and learned as much as possible by diligently doing as I was told. I knew that I'd have to prove myself before I'd be allowed to work on more serious cases. I made sure I was out on the streets as much as possible to garner useful information.

My arrival in the detective squad coincided with the implementation of equal-opportunities legislation that signalled the end of segregation. The Equal Pay Act (1970) and the Sex Discrimination Act 1975, which both came into force in 1975, meant that employment terms and conditions for male and female officers must now be the same. By then my force, which had been renamed Leicestershire Constabulary in 1973, had already made some headway in giving women more opportunities. The advanced driving course I had taken advantage of, for example, and the inclusion of a woman in CID. Women officers became involved in the recruitment and supervision of female cadets too – something traditionally done by male officers. In anticipation of the legal requirements to integrate, Leicestershire Constabulary had conducted a pilot scheme in one division whereby some female officers were freed of their specialist responsibilities and allowed to join their male colleagues on ordinary foot duty. Now it was official in all areas, all over the country: policewomen and policemen were merged as one.

This meant that policewomen would now do the same work as men, on the same shift patterns and the same pay scales. Not all women were delighted by the decision to integrate; many wanted to carry on as before, continuing with the specialist work around women and children that they had found meaningful and rewarding. A reduced women's department was renamed the Special Enquiry Unit and enabled the institutional knowledge and experience to be retained: useful intelligence about local problem families, vulnerable children and people with mental-health problems, for example. This sort of information was useful to the police and may have been lost, had responsibility for it been handed over to the collator's office, where information received from both uniform and CID officers was recorded and disseminated and where police officers turned for case-relevant information. The SEU remained women-only, since not one man asked to work there. By contrast, most women went over the road to join the men.

I was excited by the change but was soon to be disappointed by the practice on the ground. Legislation may have dismantled the walls of segregation and paved the way for equal opportunities but, in truth, meaningful change was slow to come in this institution defined *by* straight men *for* straight men. Institutionally sexist attitudes prevailed.

The CID's welcome to a new woman detective was 'station stamping'. It wasn't pleasant and it wasn't remotely welcoming. My initiation happened as I was booking off duty in the CID admin office at 11 o'clock at night. Two officers grabbed me by my arms while a third put his hands up my skirt, pulled down my pants and stamped my bottom with the CID ink stamp – all as four or five other men from the team looked on. There was little point fighting them off; I knew it was going to happen, however much I resisted. It was utterly humiliating, just as I suspected this ritual – which was meted out only to women – was meant to be. I didn't dwell on my treatment. I focused on the privilege of being a detective.

In November 1975, a few weeks after starting my new post, I was sent off to Bishopgarth Police Training School in Wakefield, West Yorkshire. My rank as a sergeant meant that I was put on the advanced CID course. I set off in my new bright-yellow VW Beetle in fog so thick that I couldn't see anything ahead of me. I was scared stiff at the thought of having an accident and drove extremely slowly, arriving at my destination several hours later than expected.

When I entered the reception, I noticed shields mounted on the wall representing the emblems of police forces who sent their officers there. The centre had a sports field with a running track and (crucially) a bar. I dropped off my gear in the room that would be my private haven for the next ten weeks and went down there to meet some new faces. I couldn't see any women colleagues anywhere.

Confirmation that I was the only woman on my course came the next morning, when the group met formally for the first time in class. My heart sank a bit. I had hoped to have a female classmate as a break from conversations dominated by male banter. So be it, though.

The course covered every aspect of criminal investigation, with a breadth of topics that included dealing with sexual offences, investigative techniques and forensic evidence. One of the first things we were taught was something called Locard's Exchange Principle, which was that everything leaves a trace. Whenever two objects come into contact with each other, there is always a transfer of material – so preserving a crime scene is paramount to any investigation. Crime-scene officers in those days wore ordinary clothing (though I recall gloves and perhaps overshoes being worn), so the fewer the officers at a scene, the better, to avoid hair or fibres cross-contaminating the forensic evidence in any way. The trail to a murder scene would be set out with markers and only the crime-scene officer and the senior investigating officer were allowed near the body. Cups of coffee and cigarettes stubs were absolute no-nos in case the discarded items were mistaken by the forensic team as possible clues about the prime suspect.

A Home Office-approved forensic pathologist came in to talk to us about the process of calling them to see a dead body in situ and the importance of it not being moved beforehand. We learned about rigor mortis, which sets in after death: once the blood stops circulating, it sinks to the lowest areas of the body; if left undiscovered for a period of time, the body starts to putrefy and the body tissues begin to liquefy. An array of crime-scene photographs was used as prompts to explain the forensic evidence to look for in murders committed by stabbing, shotgun or strangulation, and in suicide by hanging. I made myself look at the photographs being passed around the class to try to detach the idea of the dead body having once been a person. What didn't come across in the photographs, of course, was the repellent smell of a corpse.

A fingerprint expert taught us about identification: the print needed to have at least 16 points of comparison to match it to its owner. A ballistics expert explained that by assessing the crime scene he was able to determine where a killer had been standing when he discharged his gun. He was also able to match a bullet to the gun it was fired from, providing both items were recovered.

We learned the importance of gathering evidence after sexual assaults. In rape cases, fibres, hair, semen and other fluids and any other remnants left behind constitute vital evidence and their preservation is essential. Back then, if the victim reported the attack to the police immediately, she would be taken to a station and asked to stand on a large piece of brown paper rolled out on the floor and then one by one hand over each item of her clothing, which would be bagged up separately. The paper was to catch fibres that could help prove whether or not any of them belonged to the accused with the forensics available at the time. The brown paper would be preserved and submitted to the forensic-science lab with all the other bags of forensic exhibits.

Victims and offenders needed to be taken to different police stations to be interviewed to eliminate potential claims of cross-contamination by the defence. The importance of the preservation of forensic evidence and Locard's Exchange Principle were drummed into us at every opportunity.

We were taught techniques for interviewing suspects, too, which we practised using role play. The use of silence, for example: the tutor explained that staying quiet often resulted in the suspect filling the void by talking. (This was an era when the 'no comment' response was unusual.) We also learned the benefit of beginning interviews with a bit of chit-chat, before using open questions to zone in on the particulars surrounding the offence being investigated.

Many of the men in my class were from northern police forces and seemed to bring with them a harsher, far more sexist culture than the one I was used to. The banter from a couple of the officers was memorable: 'If she's ugly I'd still shag her, but I'd have to put a brown paper bag over her face first.' If a woman refused their advances when we went down the pub, you'd overhear quips such as 'She's probably a lesbian.' Maybe she was, or maybe she just didn't like the look of them – but it appeared that, in their own minds at least, these men were irresistible to the opposite sex. Sometimes, one of them would try it on a bit; you almost got the impression that they felt obliged to.

As for the job, I got the distinct impression that my classmates were setting the bar higher for a female detective than for her male colleagues, and that she would have to prove herself as a particularly good thief taker to be accepted.

I took the jibes from the northern chaps on the chin. Their company made me feel grateful to be in the Leicestershire force: whatever the banter and the attitudes of some of my male colleagues, my employer had not blocked me from being a response-car driver or a young sergeant.

It was just as well that I wasn't fazed by being surrounded by men, because one day we were sent to HMP Wakefield. The aim was for us to gain insights from prison officers about managing a group of potentially volatile men on a daily basis. This Category A men's prison housed the most dangerous types of criminals you could meet: lifers, armed robbers and IRA terrorists. I had never set foot inside a prison before, since whenever I'd escorted women to Grisly Risley I'd handed them over to prison officers at the gate. I was curious to see what it was like inside.

As we waited for a series of locked doors to be opened, I remembered with a wry smile my schoolgirl fascination with prison. The claustrophobic environment made me wonder why anyone who had been an inmate once would risk a return visit. Yet by this time, I had come across several repeat offenders in Leicester who clearly thought that committing crime was worth the downside; either that or they held the grandiose belief that they wouldn't get caught on the next job.

Wakefield was built in Victorian times. Each floor had a central hub for staff surrounded by clusters of prison cells on various wings, a design that gave prison officers a 360-degree view of what was happening on the landings. As you would expect, there was not much variety in a prisoner's day. As part of their routine, they would work in the kitchens or clean the wings; studying was also available to those who wanted to improve their education. Officers spoke about how quickly the inmates would become institutionalized. The visit confirmed to me that I would not have enjoyed being a prison officer. I wanted to catch the criminals, not watch over them.

The hard work done on the course in the day was offset by some fiercely entertaining evenings. We found a pub near Halifax run by drag queens who would stand on the bar and tell jokes and mime lyrics to Dusty Springfield and Cilla Black songs. The pub was always packed to the brim and the atmosphere was electric. Those evenings remain fond memories.

*

When my ten weeks were up, I returned to Charles Street keen to apply my new skills. It was good to be back in the old stomping ground, since I had already built alliances with the Highfields community. I worked hard and made sure to remain curious. I knew my biggest skill was my ability to chat to anybody, be they a company chairman or a homeless person, so I played to my strength. I continued where I'd left off, renewing the relationships I'd made previously as a young PC and cultivating new ones. This was essential to gathering intelligence and keeping abreast of new suspicious faces appearing on the block. I talked to market-stall holders, pub licensees, newspaper sellers and greengrocers – all the local tradespeople – listening to any concerns they had and paying attention to nuggets of information that might prove relevant to an investigation at some point. Most of the cases I cut my detective teeth on related to low-level crime such as theft, of which there was a lot thanks to the poverty in the area. It was the kind of crime you'd expect to have assigned to you as a trainee detective, known as a CID aide, rather than what you'd expect to be given as a sergeant. I suspected that a man with the same rank and experience as me would have been put on some juicier cases than this, but there wasn't much I could do about it. The only thing I could do was to crack on, assist where I was asked and earn a reputation as a detective who could get results whatever was thrown her way.

My arrest rates were good, but I harboured the distinct notion that there was resistance to me as a female of more senior rank. The glass ceiling for women was set pretty low, and as a DS I was the highest-ranking female detective in Leicestershire at the time and, despite integration, the only female in CID at Charles Street.

It's not as if my position in the force was actually high. In a provincial force, the running order was: constable; sergeant; inspector; chief inspector; superintendent; and chief superintendent. The ranks were the same for both uniform and detectives. Above that was assistant chief constable; deputy chief constable; and chief constable at the top.

Undeterred, I ploughed on with my aspirations and successfully passed my inspector's exam in 1977. My achievement turned out to be a mixed blessing, however, as in late 1978 I was moved from CID back into uniform to serve as an acting inspector in Hinckley, a market town in southwest Leicestershire.

At inspector rank – albeit in a temporary post – I spent the bulk of my time inside the station fulfilling myriad responsibilities. I had to ensure that proper procedure had been followed for prisoners locked up at the station, for example, and check that inquiries on pressing cases were being carried out correctly. I was also responsible for supervising junior officers and conducting officers' appraisal reports. Whenever possible, I would go on patrol.

I'm afraid that I didn't gel with Hinckley. A posting of higher rank had appealed, but the environment was also important to me, and I found Hinckley parochial, grey and without character. Oh, for the Highfields – grim for sure, but its buildings and the colourful characters who lived there made it a more interesting place to police. I never really settled in at the station either. It felt like walking into a party where everyone knew each other well and didn't feel the need to include the newcomer – but then, I didn't make much effort either. I hated the place. The thought of working there for a few years was too depressing to contemplate, not least in an acting capacity. After a year of proving myself as an able inspector I looked around for opportunities within my force for a permanent inspector post.

What I didn't realize at that point was that my head was pressing against an invisible ceiling. I thought I was stuck in my temporary post because the person I was filling in for was on a secondment and was, for administrative purposes, still part of Hinckley station's headcount. Making my post permanent would mean exceeding allocated numbers. It didn't dawn on me at this stage that this was only part of the story.

Playing hockey paved my way forward in life. It was during a home game against the Metropolitan Police that I met Pauline, who was the team captain and, in her day job, a detective sergeant at Scotland Yard. Pauline was older than me and cut quite a gamine figure with her slender frame and short, dark hair. She was a snazzy dresser, and good fun. We soon became an item. Pauline had a huge personality and was very popular with the rest of the hockey team, so it felt like a bit of a coup when she asked me out. We travelled between Leicester and Pauline's southwest London home for a while to see each other. I got to know her circle of friends and it was they who gave me the spur I needed.

'Come to London!' they chorused at the pub one night. 'You'll get more opportunities in the Met than you will anywhere else in the country. You'll love it in the Met.'

Listening to them, I realized that they were probably right about there being more scope in the Met for advancement of a female police officer. There was clearly a better gay scene in the capital too and I was young and wanted to have fun. I requested a meeting with Chief Superintendent Michael Hirst to discuss my future.

'I've made some new friends in London, sir, and they're encouraging me to apply for transfer to the Metropolitan Police. I'm not sure what to do,' I told him.

Hirst's response was far from encouraging: 'If I were you, Jackie, I would go. They don't know what to do with you.'

'What do you mean?' I asked, crestfallen.

'The men aren't used to reporting to a woman, and it makes them feel uncomfortable. I know it's not fair, but it's the way it is.'

My face was burning as I left the room: a mixture of hurt, disappointment and bewilderment. It was galling to hear that I was seen as a problem because I was doing well and rising up the ranks. I was in limbo. Despite passing my exam, my promotion rested on getting a permanent position as an inspector, which didn't look as if it would happen any time soon. I didn't want to do a run of acting-inspector posts. Realizing that my career had run out of road gave me the kick I needed to apply for a transfer to the Metropolitan Police force. It felt like a huge step. Was I ready for policing the metropolis? I was about to find out.

CHAPTER 6

LONDON: HERE I COME

It was a wrench to leave my lovely new Georgian-style terraced house in Leicester, but it had to be done. A colleague and friend of mine who was divorcing his wife needed a new home and new furniture, so I sold my house and most of its contents to him: a win-win for us both. I packed up all my things, and moved in with Pauline in Kingston, southwest London. By then I had acquired a rescue dog called Herbie. Although Pauline wasn't a dog lover by nature, she welcomed us both into her home regardless. There was no garden, but the flat was located just outside the gates to Richmond Park, so Herbie was happy.

My parents were relieved that I was flat sharing as they knew how daunting and expensive moving to the capital could be. They had been living in northwest London for some years while my dad worked as the group manager of Associated Newspapers, which meant that he oversaw all the company's provincial newspapers. Company policy required him to step down from the role at 60 years of age, but Associated Newspapers suggested that he might want to take up the post of managing the *Western Morning News* and the *Evening Herald* based in Plymouth. Dad took up the offer since he felt too fit and healthy to retire. They had grown to love London and it was a shame for all of us that they were leaving just as I was arriving. They met Pauline several times and liked her. I didn't declare that we were a couple and they never asked.

Moving to the bright lights of London to be with Pauline was full of promise, and I felt privileged to join the country's most famous police force.

When I applied for a transfer to the Met, it was explained to me that I'd have to take the inspector's exam again because the Met didn't recognize the national one taken in the provinces. The Met version of the exam expected you to show an understanding of its own policies and procedures (General Orders). I was taken on as a uniform sergeant and I was quite happy with that. My posting was in the leafy borough of Richmond upon Thames, southwest London, which was part of T Division.

With nine years of experience under my belt, I should have felt fairly confident when I arrived for my first day as a Met officer on 30 April 1979, but in truth I was pretty nervous.

London's police force served a population of close to 7 million residents and was predictably busier than Leicestershire, and more intense. The culture also seemed more rough-and-tumble, more hard-edged. Each rank had greater responsibility than had been the case in Leicester, so a detective sergeant in the Met would deal with armed robberies, whereas in Leicestershire that level of responsibility would have been assigned to a detective chief inspector.

The Met had more senior ranks too, each with their own portfolio. At the helm of policing the metropolis was the commissioner, below which he – and it was always a he – had a deputy commissioner (DC) and a number of assistant commissioners (AC). Under this tier there was a deputy assistant commissioner and below that commanders – equivalent to assistant chief constable (ACC) rank back in Leicester.

The pecking order went by role as well as by rank: area-car drivers had kudos, for example. They were usually very experienced constables, often more so than a sergeant or an inspector, and were seen as the premier among equals; a good response driver was definitely someone that you wanted on your team. All round it was a steep learning curve, and it would take me some time to catch on to the dynamics of how the relief worked. When I didn't know something, I said so; experience had already taught me that colleagues responded better to humility than to 'know-alls' who blagged their way through.

I was more interested in getting the job done right than in making friends, though I made no secret of the fact that I lived with Pauline. How people interpreted that was their business. By this time it didn't particularly bother me if people realized I was gay, but I respected the fact that Pauline was a very private person and didn't want people to know.

As a newcomer, I was braced for a bit of ribbing, and I was not to be disappointed: colleagues seized on my transfer from a provincial police force and jokingly called me a 'carrot cruncher'.

I was grateful that a uniform inspector took me under his wing early on. 'I will teach you everything in the correct and proper way,' he said. 'Once you have the foundations, if you choose to take a shortcut, that's up to you.'

The inspector supervised me while I learned the ropes. My role involved responsibility for the 'comms team' – the area where calls from the public came in; the station office, where members of the public went to report crimes; and the charge room (now called a custody suite).

Being station sergeant – now known as a custody sergeant – had its moments. I was responsible for the care and welfare of persons detained and needed to be satisfied that the arrest was lawful based on the information given. Some were drunk, some up for a fight, and some gave false names and addresses. Anyone arriving at the station with an injury had to be seen by a police surgeon. Big pub fights led to multiple arrests, and a snaking queue of people in the charge room waiting to be processed. Then I would check on those placed in the cells.

I remember a heart-stopping moment when I slid back the metal shutter on a cell door and faced a prisoner staring ahead with a blank look on his face, his head at an uncomfortable angle. *Shit*, I thought in a panic. It looked as though he had hanged himself. My heart racing, I quickly unlocked the door.

As I did so, the prisoner bent over double and laughed his head off as he watched the fear on my face. It took me a while to calm down. I never did have a death in custody under my watch, thankfully.

I was warned about the three Ps that could get a police officer into trouble: prisoners claiming assaults by officers; prostitutes claiming that officers had requested sexual favours; and property held at the station being lost or damaged.

I crossed all the *t*s and dotted all the *i*s to ensure that procedures were strictly adhered to. My fastidious approach prompted some eye-rolling and sighs from colleagues, who thought that I was parochial in my approach. 'County methods,' they would say. This in my book meant doing the job properly, and I could live with that. I was too new to have the confidence to take shortcuts. And anyway, I didn't take any stick: I could hold my own on the job.

I was still able to go on the beat occasionally and I was surprised to learn that in the Met a sergeant could patrol with an inspector. To me it seemed more sensible for someone of supervisory rank to patrol with a police constable, since you could ensure that they were doing the job properly and give them pointers if need be. My partner on patrol was Inspector Elizabeth Neville, an Oxford graduate who had joined the police service three years after me, and who was on the same relief as me. A relief is a team made up of an inspector, two or three sergeants, and police constables who all work their shifts together. At that time, Elizabeth and I were the only two women of supervisory rank at the station. I always looked forward to working with her and I could see why Elizabeth, calm and level-headed, had been selected for the fast-track promotion scheme.

I remember getting a bit exercised one day about a trivial case that hadn't gone our way.

We had been at the magistrates' court after giving evidence against a motorist we had witnessed failing to give precedence to a pedestrian at a crossing. The motorist was found not guilty and walked out of court scot-free. I was not happy.

'We can't say we lost this case at a magistrates' court,' I harrumphed as we headed back to the station. 'It's humiliating to report that a sergeant and an inspector can't convince the court when we had the man bang to rights for failing to give way at a pedex.'

Elizabeth listened patiently, but it was clear from her demeanour that to her it was already water under the bridge – a 'you win some, you lose some' kind of thing. I, on the other hand, felt that my pride had been dented.

Sometimes, Elizabeth and I would visit the local bail hostel in Kew for a cup of tea. Bail hostels, now known as approved premises, were single-sex accommodations for people charged with offences and released on bail with no permanent address to go to, or those who were recently released from prison. As a newcomer to the area, I saw talking to the men at the hostel as a good way of getting to know the faces of some of the local villains and what types of crimes they committed. Most villains I met tended to have a personal signature of a sort relating to their method of crime, and their target. One tenant at the hostel called Terry happily described how he was partial to burglarizing people's houses and even gave details about his method of entry: forcing the sash windows of older Victorian-style properties. Useful to know. I still intended to resume the life of a detective, so it was also a way of building up a network of local contacts. The men at the bail hostel were up to date with the recently released local criminal fraternity: who was into what, and who was doing what.

Alas, patrolling with Elizabeth proved short-lived because the powers that be ruled it unacceptable to have two women of supervisory rank on the same relief – unlike men – so I was moved to a different relief. I wasn't happy about this discriminatory practice but I didn't moan too much because I was the new girl on the block and I wanted to get on.

Elizabeth and I would keep in touch over the years. She would carve out a career in uniform policing, rising swiftly through the ranks to become the second female chief constable ever appointed in the country. She was awarded a Queen's Police Medal (QPM) and subsequently appointed a Dame Commander of the Order of the British Empire by the Queen in 2003. Deserved accolades for a woman I truly admire.

Richmond upon Thames was as twee and scenic as Hinckley was grim, but it was merely a more salubrious backdrop for crime and tragedy. One of the first cases I attended on the beat was on a hot summer's day when a member of the public called 999 to say that a young man had not resurfaced after jumping in the River Thames. He had been part of a group of young people who had leapt from Richmond Bridge after a few rounds of drinks in the pub. I went straight to the scene with a police inspector and the Thames Division, which was the Met's river-police section. There we recovered the dead body of a man in his early twenties and placed him in a body bag. As I stood by the body, the deceased young man's sister saw the commotion on the riverbank and came over. Just as she arrived, a strong wind blew the bag open, exposing her brother's face. 'That's my brother!' she screamed. It was a terrible moment. Any sudden loss of life is distressing at the best of times. That young man had left home for a fun time out with friends and decided to jump in the water to cool down on a hot day without realizing the perils of the fast-moving tide of the Thames. Now his sister was staring down at him in a body bag. A tragic accident; a sad waste of a young life. It was heartbreaking.

Back in 1979, Richmond's popular nightlife hummed, and local pubs would often be heaving. In an era where opening hours were much stricter, the alcohol flowed at pace and fights erupted all too often. Some revellers evidently saw weekends as an opportunity to lager up and spoil for a fight, with officers often seen as fair game. When a massive fight erupted outside a popular pub one night, I was unlucky enough to be passing by on foot patrol as several men knocked seven bells out of each other. They seemed completely out of control, the red mist blotting their minds. The fury in their eyes was frightening, but it was my job to go in and intervene. The minute the brawlers saw me approach, still pumped up, some of them decided to turn their anger on me. It wasn't the outcome that I was hoping for. To my shock, I was kicked to the ground and a rain of blows hailed from all directions as several revellers piled in.

I felt a blow to the side of my head from someone's boot and put up my hands to protect myself in anticipation of more to come. I was helpless and outnumbered. It wasn't until a drinker shouted, 'She's a cop, for god's sake, leave her alone!' that everything stopped. The lull in the violence gave me my chance to radio for assistance. By the time my inspector arrived, the culprits had legged it. I wouldn't have been able to identify them in any event. I was completely dazed. No arrests were made. All I had to show for the attack was an egg-sized lump on the top of my head. A police surgeon checked me out back at the station. 'You'll survive,' he said. Being sent to hospital to be checked out wasn't routine in those days. My inspector was furious that one of his officers had been attacked and sent me home.

As the months passed, I acclimatized to Met life. This was reflected in a favourable performance review in October, six months into the job: 'Leads by example . . . is perhaps not a strict disciplinarian, but gets results . . . totally dependable, will always give her best.' It noted my fastidiousness about 'getting things right', and my desire to return to CID. My gradings were above average across the board. It was encouraging. My first appraisal also noted my ability to get on with people: 'an excellent mixer on and off duty'. Indeed. Work was good, my social life even better.

My life as a gay woman took on an exciting new lease in London. Unlike Leicester, which had 'police clubs' annexed to police stations, Met officers went down the pub to unwind, and I would happily join them to oil the wheels.

My bigger interest, though, was in establishing a social network outside work. I was a reserve goalkeeper in the Met's hockey team, and I was discovering the gay club scene. I loved the fact that you could lose yourself in London, with little fear of being noticed; in Leicester, by contrast, I often felt like a goldfish in a bowl, not helped by driving my distinctive bright-yellow V W Beetle.

Life with Pauline was good and her friends had welcomed me into the fold. It was through them that I met a woman called Sue Weston, who was dating one of Pauline's friends. Sue and I hit it off instantly, and she would end up being one of my dearest and most treasured friends. She had joined the police a few years after me. Tall and slim, with tight curly hair, steely blue eyes and an infectious smile, Sue turned heads whenever she walked into a room.

She made me laugh so much that my sides felt as if they would burst. She loved speaking in Cockney rhyming slang – 'jam jar', 'Barnet', 'whistle' – and her favourite saying when she arrested anyone was, 'Get yer hat 'n' coat, you're nicked!' She nicknamed me FP (favourite person), a moniker I was very glad to have.

We started to hang out at a swanky gay venue called Roy's Restaurant on the Fulham Road, a flashy spot that was a cut above many of the London gay hang-outs at the time.

The gay club scene was one of the undeniable highlights of moving to the capital. As a keen dancer, I didn't have to go too far into west London to find the best dance places. There was a pub with a huge dance floor in Wimbledon which had a gay night on a Tuesday evening and another one in a room above a pub in Hampton Wick.

I loved the anonymity of a club packed with women who turned up to let their hair down, be themselves away from judgemental eyes and have fun, but mainly I was there because I adored dancing. It was a place where I felt that I truly belonged.

My other haunt was the famous Gateways, a popular lesbian club based in a smoke-filled cellar bar at the bottom of a steep staircase. Located at 239 King's Road, on the corner of Bramerton Street in Chelsea, the club was run by two women called Gina and Smithy. Gina was often to be found standing at the bottom of the stairs seemingly watching all who entered, while Smithy was invariably in charge of the bar.

Going into this edgy, underground lesbian club was both a scary and an exciting experience. I don't think I fitted into either the 'butch' masculine lesbian or the 'femme' camp, which seemed to be the two stereotypes for gay women in the 1970s and '80s. I was more of a tomboy and self-consciously dressed that way. Sometimes I met friends down there and sometimes I'd go on my own. Hooking up with a woman that I met in the club wasn't my style.

I particularly enjoyed going on a Sunday lunchtime to catch up with friends over a drink, emerging from the windowless club when it closed to the bright daylight of the afternoon. I never told anyone at the club that I was a police officer, even though I always carried my warrant card concealed in my back pocket, which we were expected to do even off-duty. I knew that some of the women were anti-police due to their experiences: some spoke of police officers hovering outside the club and making homophobic comments as they left or making them feel uncomfortable by staring at them. When I went there with Sue we would pretend that I made corsets for a living – no idea why I picked that – and that Sue was a photographer.

The loud, thumping beats absorbed me and took me to a place where I could lose myself. Gladys Knight and the Pips, Frankie Goes to Hollywood, The Weather Girls, anything by Tina Turner or Diana Ross . . . In those hours on the dance floor, I felt as free as a bird. The song that I particularly relished was Gloria Gaynor's classic: 'I Will Survive'. I would mime the words as I danced, surrounded by friends who would form a circle around me and cheer me on.

Late into the night, I would emerge with my ears still ringing from the music, my chest pounding, feeling exhilarated. Come Monday morning, I would be back in my other persona as a Metropolitan police officer. I juggled the two lives pretty well.

*

I'd been in the Met 18 months when I received a call asking me if I'd like to join the CID. Would I! It may have had something to do with the fact that I'd let my detective ambitions be known to select colleagues, one of whom relayed this to a senior contact at New Scotland Yard who asked me if I'd like to make an official transfer. This telephone call morphed into an interview and, soon after, I was to report to Earlsfield Police Station, southwest London, as a detective sergeant.

With about 11 male detectives, the CID team was smaller than the one at divisional HQ at Tooting a couple of miles up the road. That said, it was pretty busy for its size. Again, it was a case of getting my head down and learning the ropes of being a detective sergeant in the context of the Met. I felt welcomed by colleagues, and well supported. Mercifully, there was no station stamping on my backside this time, although the Met had done this to women in the past. Had they tried it on my older and wiser self, they would have received a less submissive reaction than my colleagues at Leicester got a few years previously.

Three months in, I'd just got to know my new colleagues, the culture and the department's practices when I was called by my DI. 'Can you get down to Brockley Police Station now, Jackie? You're being seconded to be part of the New Cross fire investigation.'

I left the station immediately. That day, 19 January 1981, would prove to be my last at Earlsfield. I was about to investigate one of the most harrowing cases of my career.

CHAPTER 7

THE NEW CROSS FIRE INVESTIGATION

In the early hours of the morning on Sunday 18 January 1981, a party at 439 New Cross Road in Deptford, Lewisham, turned to horror after a serious fire broke out. The event had been hosted by Mrs Armza Ruddock to celebrate the birthday of her daughter, Yvonne, who was turning 16, and a friend, Angela Jackson, who was turning 18. Around 100 guests had been invited by Yvonne and Angela, although many more were believed to have gate-crashed the party, which went on through the night. Many guests had left by the time the fire started. As the flames and the smoke spread quickly through the three-storey house, some people ran out, while others rushed up the stairs and jumped out of windows. Tragically, many were trapped inside. Nine people died at the scene and four of the 26 injured would later succumb to their injuries, including Yvonne Ruddock and her older brother Paul: a double tragedy for Mrs Ruddock. Thirteen Black British young people aged between 14 and 22 lost their lives.

When my DI told me to go to Brockley, I didn't like to admit to him that I'd never heard of the place before. Thanks to my well-thumbed *London A–Z* map, on which I had been relying since moving to the capital, I drove through the maze of south London streets feeling a mixture of intrigue and apprehension. I had enough experience under my belt to realize that this investigation would be huge, given the number of victims involved. Tracking down and interviewing so many partygoers would be a time-intensive task. But I was extremely keen to find out what had happened that night, and to apprehend whoever was responsible if it was proved to be arson.

On arrival at Brockley Police Station, I was sent straight to the incident room, where I met Commander Graham Stockwell, the officer in charge of the investigation and the man who would offer me a blueprint for leadership that would shape the rest of my career. Stockwell was head of CID Area 4, which covered the southeast of London.

Detective Superintendent Joe Bell would be in charge of forensics, and Detective Inspector Henry Dowdswell would act, in today's parlance, as a family liaison officer. Henry was assigned to deal with not only all the families but also the victims. This included the grim task of handling the identification of the deceased. In all, more than 40 detectives were put on the case, plus some uniform officers.

It was our job to discover how the fire had started. Was it an accident or, as many in the local Black community suspected, arson by racists?

Stockwell was calm but firm, with a huge, dignified presence. Refreshingly, he encouraged us to contribute our thoughts and views at the twice-weekly team briefings. I immediately warmed to him and his style of leadership.

I know for a fact that Stockwell had raised concerns with senior officers that he was not the right man for this job because he was aware of ill-feeling towards him by some of the Black community. This was a result of a high-profile case ten years before that had involved the arrests of nine Black activists. Stockwell was a detective inspector stationed at Notting Hill when a series of uniform raids took place on a restaurant called the

Mangrove between 1969 and 1970. Opened and run by a Trinidadian man called Frank Crichlow, the restaurant was famous not only for its delicious Caribbean food but also as a comfortable meeting spot for the Black community.

None of the raids ever yielded anything but, fed up with what customers felt was a targeted attack, the Action Committee for the Defence of the Mangrove was formed and a protest march organized on 9 August 1970, which was heavily policed. Serious fighting broke out and many officers were injured. Of the protesters arrested, nine were charged with incitement to riot. Stockwell was responsible for submitting the evidence from the arresting officers to the Metropolitan Police Solicitors' Department. The charges were dismissed by a magistrate because of a lack of evidence and conflicting police statements, only to be reinstated by the Director of Public Prosecutions. The Mangrove Nine, as the defendants soon became known, were all later acquitted by a jury of incitement to riot, with two defendants representing themselves in court. Four received suspended sentences for lesser offences. Stockwell knew that being put at the helm of the New Cross fire investigation risked sowing distrust in the police's handling of the case. He suggested to his seniors that it might be more appropriate to put another commander in charge of the case, given the history, but he was overruled.

Stockwell intended to tread very delicately. 'This investigation will be highly sensitive,' he told us. 'What I expect from you all is that enquiries will be carried out diligently. Cross every *t* and dot every *i*. I don't need to remind you to be respectful and smartly dressed, because the world's media will be watching you. None of you are allowed to talk to the press and there will be no loose talk in public houses. Bob Cox from the press and public relations department will deal with all media enquiries and, most importantly, remember to conduct yourself with dignity and professionalism as feelings within the Black community are understandably at a high level. This fire is an utter tragedy. Myself and Detective Superintendent Bell visited the scene and the sight of those young people who died is one which I will never forget.'

The vast and painstaking operation involved working with the forensics available at the time, identifying the 13 victims and trying to work out the correct timeline of events that led to the fire. There was a huge amount of work to do to determine the facts.

Our first task was to trace everyone who had been at the party, and to secure their statements. We needed to know who went to the party, what time they left and whether they had returned. Who was in the house when the fire ignited?

Easier said than done. Many had crashed the party. Only a few people came forward to confirm that they had been there, so we relied on others to give names.

The opinion of scientists from the Met's Fire Investigation Unit was that the fire started at approximately 5.45am in the central part of the front parlour – an area that had been designated out of bounds to partygoers.

One of the first allegations to surface was that a white man had been seen at the front door in the early hours, with his arm reaching as if throwing something into the house. The man quickly ran back to his car and drove off.

This individual was a father driving an Austin Princess on his way back from dropping his serving police officer daughter off for her 6am shift at Deptford Police Station.

When he was interviewed by the police, he explained that he drove by the house, saw that it was ablaze, parked, and ran to the house to try to warn the people inside, but the fire had already taken hold. He put his hands up to his face to protect himself from the heat, returned to his car and sped back to Deptford Police Station to report it.

What was clear from the interviews with partygoers was that the usual teenage angst had played out that night: the guys who had a girlfriend but had their eye on another girl; the jealousies fuelled by drinking and maybe a bit of weed. It was the kind of behaviour that of itself was really nothing to worry about. But the prospect of being interviewed by the police in a climate of distrust was unwelcome to many and this proved to be a significant obstacle. Those who perhaps shouldn't have been there in the first place, or who had told their parents that they were somewhere else, were reluctant to admit that they were there that night.

In 1981, we were still operating under Judges' Rules. This allowed us to question and if necessary detain any person we believed could provide useful information – this applied whether or not they were suspected of committing a crime, as long as they'd not been charged with anything at that stage. The interview of any witness under 17 years of age required the presence of parents or guardians or, in their absence, some person who was not a police officer and (for safeguarding reasons) was the same gender as the child.

The working hours were long, the volume of work phenomenal. I was at the incident room by 8am each day, often not leaving for the hour-long drive home to southwest London until past midnight. I would shower and crash into bed before heading back to work a few hours later for another long day. There was no time for a social life of any kind during this period; the compensation was the camaraderie and mutual support among officers working on the case.

What drove me, as I think it did all my colleagues, was the fact that this was about finding answers for the 13 grieving families and those who had been injured that night.

The loss of so many young lives made it the most shocking of cases to deal with, especially for the families and those who managed to make it out alive. The survivors had been through a terrifying ordeal; some were left with awful injuries. The toll on survivors would be dramatically brought home two years later when Anthony Berbeck, who was 18 years old at the time of the blaze, died by falling from a balcony in a block of flats in July 1983. Anthony had lost his best friends in the fire and required psychiatric treatment in the aftermath. At his inquest, the coroner recorded an open verdict.

The interview techniques we deployed were not particularly harsh, but we didn't factor into our approach the emotional impact a trauma of this magnitude was likely to have on the survivors. It was a different era, where the potential psychological effects were not recognized as they are now; trauma awareness, counselling support and trying to create a sense of safety were not considered.

The impact on families and survivors was still acutely palpable 40 years on when the director Sir Steve McQueen made an award-winning three-part BBC documentary on the New Cross fire called *Uprising*, first broadcast in the summer of 2021. Survivors who had been at the party, held on the first floor of the house, described the panic and the confusion as the fire quickly spread from the ground-floor front room and the house became thick with smoke. The electrics went out, the heat intensified and people were screaming and shouting in the dark as they tried to make their way to safety. Some were forced to leap out of windows from the first and second floors, while others made their way down the drainpipe. Parents lost sons and daughters, brothers and sisters lost siblings, and others lost valued friends. A horrific experience.

In the interview rooms back in early 1981, we were focused on trying to establish the facts. As the interviewing progressed, reports began to emerge of an argument between two partygoers, and a group in the hallway near to the parlour. The actual details of what happened were vague. We needed to get to the bottom of these claims, to gauge whether they were relevant to our investigation. Mrs Ruddock, meanwhile, had reported that jewellery and some money had been stolen from her front parlour, where guests were not supposed to be. This could explain why some people were less than forthcoming about where they had been situated just before the fire, and why. We needed to know.

Other allegations surfaced during this period: there was reference to a fight near the seat of the fire shortly before it started, and a knife was mentioned, which had allegedly been used to slash chairs in the parlour. It remained difficult to establish the truth of events. At the best of times, witness accounts will vary to some extent. We needed to clarify the timeline and to prompt people further about the alleged fight to see if it was connected to the fire in any way.

On 24 and 25 February, we were put into teams to re-interview young people who had been named as being in or close to the front parlour at the time of the fire. They were to be interviewed simultaneously at different police stations.

Interview preparation was key. I read all the statements given during the first round of interviews to understand what had been said and by whom, and where each person was just before the fire started. Reading the statements had disclosed contradictions between witnesses and these needed to be resolved.

While conducting the interviews, I adhered to every word of Commander Stockwell's directive and did absolutely everything by the book. Under Judges' Rules, the interviews were recorded in writing contemporaneously, which meant writing down the question we were asking and the reply given to us. At the end, we asked our interviewee to read the questions and answers and to sign each page to confirm that they agreed with it. Commander Stockwell suggested to a senior colleague that the interviews should be tape-recorded in the interest of transparency and to safeguard against any allegation of coercion by witnesses. The tape-recording of interviews was not an established practice in 1981 and it would have required hiring the necessary equipment. The answer from the higher echelons was a firm 'no', on the grounds that this would set a precedent for all future police investigations. How ironic, given that the tape-recording of interviews would soon become standard practice following the introduction of the Police and Criminal Evidence Act (1984).

I was partnered with Detective Inspector Jack Kitchen when we interviewed a male witness over two days in the presence of his mother. His name had been mentioned as one of the group of boys who had been present during the alleged fight at the party. He admitted to us that he had previously lied because of peer pressure.

Jack Kitchen led the interview:

'Why didn't you tell us about the fight when you first made a statement?'

'I don't know. Maybe because I was frightened.'

'Frightened of what?' asked Jack. 'Being connected with the fire?'

'No, because if I was to tell you about the fight, the others would get mad and I was frightened of being beaten up.'

Another witness, in the presence of his solicitor, also admitted that he had been less than honest in his previous interview. He told another officer in the investigation team that he and some friends had agreed beforehand not to disclose that they had entered the front parlour where the fire originated, because they had 'searched out the place a bit'. This was shorthand for searching cupboards and drawers for valuable items.

Deciphering what occurred between the teenagers was proving difficult. Memories were vague as to who was in the front room before the fire started. Amid all this confusion, it was impossible to get a definitive timeline of events.

We were working on four potential theories about how the fire started: the first was that it was the result of an attack by a white far-right extremist; the second, that the culprit was an opportunist arsonist who had entered the house, sprinkled volatile liquid and ignited it; and the third, that a party member had obtained some kind of inflammatory substance and set a match to it; finally, there was the possibility that the fire was a tragic accident. Each one had to be rigorously investigated.

There was no forensic proof of missiles thrown into the front parlour from outside. The front-room windows were covered by a full-length one-piece net curtain and heavy brocade drape, which had been drawn fully. The science suggested that had a projectile entered the house from outside, the fire would have been underneath the curtains – not in the central area of the front parlour, where forensic scientists believed it had started. No receptacle capable of conveying flammable liquid was ever found inside the property, nor could we find any evidence to corroborate reports of something being thrown through the window from outside.

The investigation team was satisfied that the man seen with his hands up around his head then running away and driving off at speed was the father who had dropped off his daughter at work early that morning.

The theory of an opportunist arsonist raised questions. How did they enter the premises? Complaints from neighbours had been lodged during the party about the noise, and environmental officers from Lewisham had attended with police officers on two occasions that night to ask Mrs Ruddock to keep the noise down. Could it be that someone frustrated by the noise had come to the house, snuck in and set a fire?

It was a feasible argument. But an opportunist would nevertheless have had to be in possession of some flammable liquid to commit the arson and no stranger was seen in the house by any of the partygoers. The team questioned closely all the neighbours, and police intelligence looked at all the known arsonists within the area, to no avail.

A metal tube found in the front garden pointed to the notion that someone may have thrown something into the house. The tube, which looked a bit like a cigar container, was found to contain microscopic amounts of sugar and chlorate. A bomb-disposal expert examined it at the scene and described it as an amateurish attempt at making a firework that could have been done by anyone with a basic grasp of chemistry.

The tube was sent to the Army Research Defence (ARD) establishment for a second opinion, but they failed to find any significant trace of sugar or chlorate. After a detailed examination, the theory of an incendiary device being thrown into the house was eliminated from the investigation, since no trace of a similar object was found among the debris inside the house.

While we investigated, bereaved families were waiting for answers. I had met Sandra Ruddock, the young widow of Paul, on several occasions. Despite her immense grief, she pulled together every bit of courage to help us with our investigation. As the weeks passed, it was difficult being unable to go back to her and other families with anything conclusive about what had happened.

Many in the local community were convinced that the real source of the fire was a racially motivated arson attack and were frustrated by our inability to shore this theory up.

Given the backdrop of fraught police–community relations over the past decade or more, activists suspicious of the way police handled crimes against Black people felt that the 13 deaths weren't being prioritized.

Prior to the New Cross fire, there had been far-right activity in the area and arson attacks against community hubs frequented by the young Black community, including the Moonshot Club and the Albany Theatre about three years earlier. Within a couple of days of the fire at 439 New Cross Road, the New Cross Massacre Action Committee was swiftly formed by local Black community groups. Of course, when I was enlisted to work on the investigation I'd known nothing of the racial tensions that existed between the Met and the Black community in this part of London, but I soon caught on.

During my short stint in the Met so far – leafy Richmond and then just three months at Earlsfield – I'd had no occasion to investigate allegations of any racist attacks in west London. Nor had I encountered the particularly poor relations evident between the Black community and the police south of the river.

A planned protest by the New Cross Massacre Action Committee was organized for 2 March, which saw thousands turn out from across the country. The Black People's Day of Action saw placards that read 'Thirteen dead, nothing said' and 'New Cross Massacre cover-up'. The sentiment was clear.

I found the suspicions levelled towards us over the investigation difficult to contend with. There was no reason for the police to cover up those responsible for a fire that had led to fatalities and injuries. I was doing my very best to contribute to solving the case and saw colleagues – not least Stockwell – working equally hard. It proved a challenging time for everyone concerned.

White extremist groups, meanwhile, were using the tragedy as a vehicle through which to spread their viciousness, hatred and cruelty. As a police officer of 11 years' service, I thought that I had seen the depths to which people can plummet, but this took the prize for gratuitous nastiness: anonymous letters expressing vile sentiments and death threats were sent to bereaved families and those with their loved ones still in hospital. As if the families didn't have enough to deal with, they now felt under siege and fearful of attack. All because of the colour of their skin. The police also received a postbag of hate mail.

A bombshell came not long after. The coroner called Commander Stockwell to a meeting to announce that he would be holding an inquest the following month. Usually, the police were allowed a year and a day to investigate a suspicious death before an inquest was held, unless the investigation had been completed earlier. An inquest is a fact-finding legal exercise to determine cause of death. It's no understatement to say that bringing the inquest forward was an unwelcome distraction.

This was a massive investigation with numerous enquiries still to be completed to establish what happened – when, where, why, how and who, if anyone, was responsible. When Stockwell told the team, his frustration at the decision was obvious and everyone in the room felt the same.

To me, the incomplete picture that we had of events meant the jury would be listening to statements, witnesses' testimonies and evidence with many unfilled gaps and no conclusion. Given that some critics believed that a police cover-up was going on, unanswered questions were the last thing needed by anyone – not least the families, who should have been the core consideration.

It would do little to improve the relationship between the police and the local Black community, which seemed to be at rock-bottom. Led by Stockwell, I believe that the team conducted itself impeccably; but looking back, I realize that the profile of the Met did not help – something that I did not fully appreciate at the time. Predominantly white and male, the police service was short on the cultural capital and diversity training needed to help its officers understand all the communities that we were serving in 1981.

Stockwell tried hard to impress on the coroner our concerns about a premature inquest: to hold it within a matter of weeks after the fire and at a time when we were only scratching the surface of establishing what had happened was not helpful.

Still, the inquest was listed for 21 April.

Ten days before the hearing was due to open, riots erupted in Brixton, roughly five miles down the road. Brixton was part of Commander Stockwell's crime command in Area 4. Suddenly, he found himself in the unenviable – and no doubt exhausting – position of presiding over the New Cross fire investigation, organizing a team of about 100 CID officers to be part of the investigation into aspects of the riots, *and* having the administrative burden of preparing for a precipitous inquest. How he found time to sleep during this period is anybody's guess.

For me, the riots signalled the end of my time at Brockley: Commander Stockwell seconded me to the Brixton riots investigation based at Kennington Police Station, which was tasked with looking into the criminal acts committed during the incidents.

I was more than a week into the Brixton riots investigation when the inquest into the deaths resulting from the New Cross fire began at County Hall, on the south side of the Thames. By this time, 40,000 policing hours had been spent on the investigation, and over 700 witness statements taken. Police officers were still engaged in numerous lines of enquiry. No evidence at this stage backed up the theory that the fire was due to arson committed by racists.

Michael Corkery QC represented the Metropolitan Police; Michael Mansfield, Rock Tansey and the late Ian MacDonald – barristers who would all later become QCs – represented the families of the deceased. Many young people who had been interviewed in the presence of their parents told the inquest that they had been pressured by the police to say certain things that were not true.

In giving his evidence, Stockwell laid out his investigation strategy and the four main theories being pursued. The inquest concluded on 13 May; after the summing-up by the coroner, the jury retired for a short time before returning an open verdict on the deaths of the 13 victims. An open verdict is defined by the CPS as: 'where there is insufficient evidence for any other verdict'. The finding could not have been anything else, given that a major investigation was still in progress. It failed to shed light on who was responsible, and whether it was a crime or an accident.

Insinuations that we had put less effort into the case because of the colour of the victims' skin left me feeling bruised. I had been consumed by the investigation, morning to night, week in, week out, with the young lives lost and the injuries of survivors at the forefront of my mind. The fact that, three months in, there were no answers to give didn't mean that we weren't doing our very best. It was distressing to think that some members of the community didn't think we had been working hard enough.

The impact on victims and their families was the paramount concern, and rightly so. Ironically, despite their terrible loss and grief, it was often the victims' families who acknowledged the work of officers who had dealt with them. DC Reg Jones, for example, known affectionately as 'Taff Jones', had, like Henry, worked closely with the community. When Taff died some years later, some members of the fire victims' families attended his funeral. The people directly affected, struggling with the pain of it, took the time out to attend the funeral of one of the investigators.

The investigation into the fire continued for several years. In 1999, the case was fully reviewed, including a re-examination of all the forensic evidence and meetings with survivors and family members of those who died, with the original investigation team, and with community leaders. A £50,000 reward for information was put out, and an appeal for information made on the BBC's *Crimewatch UK*.

Advances in forensics led to new interpretations of the evidence and gave the Metropolitan Police sufficient grounds to apply at the High Court for a new inquest. A second inquest opened on 2 February 2004, at Southwark Coroner's Court, conducted by the deputy coroner, the late Gerald Butler QC, a retired judge.

The purpose was to look at the original judgement and the new evidence established by the second investigation team, particularly forensic evidence. Butler read out the names of the 13 dead but also noted the fourteenth victim: Anthony Berbeck, who died in 1983 'following the trauma brought on by the fire'.

On 6 May 2004, the deputy coroner recorded open verdicts on the 13 young people who died in the fire in 1981. In his summing-up, he said:

i): the fire was not begun by a petrol bomb or other incendiary device, whether thrown from outside or inside the premises. ii): the fire was not accelerated by the use of any substantial, or meaningful quantity of flammable liquid. iii): the fire did not originate in the centre of the floor, its probable place of origin was on or near to the armchair closer to the television. iv): the fire was not caused by an electrical fault or any fault in the gas supply, or gas appliance or have any connection with the rain lamp.

How, then, did the fire begin? I have concluded that the evidence of the witnesses as to the discovery of the fire is too confused and contradictory to permit me to say with certainty where the flames were first seen. This must throw into some doubts any finding that relates to the deliberate application of a flame.

But while it is right that I should mention that there is no direct evidence that at any material time, any person did enter the front room to apply a flame, I must also bear in mind the forensic evidence that if the fire began, not by way of a direct application of a flame but as a result of smouldering from a discarded cigarette some considerable time before the conflagration, there would have been smoke in such quantity, and a smell so foul, that those in the vicinity would have undoubtedly noticed it and commented on it. Yet nobody has said that that was so.

He went on to say:

I have concluded on the totality of the evidence that while I think it probable – that is to say, more likely than not – that this fire was begun by the deliberate application of a flame to the armchair nearer to the television or, perhaps to the curtains, in order to cause a fire, I cannot be sure as to this. Put another way, I am not satisfied beyond reasonable doubt that there was here, an act of arson.

It must follow that I am unable to return a verdict of unlawful killing. But it must follow from what I have already said, namely, that I think it probable that there was here the deliberate application of a flame, I am unable to find a verdict of accident. The result is, that in the case of each and every one of these deaths, I must return an open verdict.*

The deputy coroner added that the first inquest had been held 'too soon after the event', according to a BBC online report. He noted: 'In 1981, many in the Black community, particularly the young, were distrustful of

---

* Commissioner of Police Metropolis v H M Coroner for Inner London South District, https://vlex.co.uk/vid/commissioner-of-police-of-806404725

the police, and did not show that degree of co-operation that has been shown since the fresh enquiry into the fire began.'

So, 1981: open verdict recorded; 2004, open verdict recorded. The deputy coroner could only go with the evidence presented. But for the families, and the wider community – and officers too – the truth about who was responsible for causing the fire that took so many young lives remains unknown.

I've thought about this fire on many occasions over the years. The feeling of pride at having done my very best during my three months on the case is always overshadowed by a feeling of defeat that we weren't able to tell families and survivors who was responsible. Contrary to the police procedural dramas on TV, the truth is not always revealed and the culprit is not always identified. For me, as for everyone else, being unable to give the families answers was deeply frustrating. Imagine if you were watching a police drama that concluded with no prime suspect in the frame. Disappointing, sure, but not a patch on the real-life devastation for families not knowing why their child died and who was responsible.

What could we, the police, have done differently? Perhaps if relations with the local Black community had been less strained there would have been more trust and confidence in our investigation, and those who were less forthcoming with us would have been more so. Who knows.

Commander Stockwell offered us good leadership in the investigation, and I would have followed him to the ends of the earth. But still, nothing can be as unsatisfying as an unsolved case.

Had the fire taken place today, we would have CCTV, social media and mobile phones to turn to for possible evidence, but none of those tools were available then. What we had to work with were the forensic findings of the time and traumatized witnesses trying to remember the exact details of what happened, quizzed by people they simply did not trust. The strong belief held by some that a racist attack was to blame did not stack up given the evidence available. Our job was to keep an open mind and to follow the evidence. There seemed to be no meeting in the middle. I no longer think now, as we suspected then, that a fight had anything to do with the fire.

At the heart of it, teenagers and young adults in the prime of life went to a birthday party to have a good time, and never went home. Their families would never see them again. It doesn't get more heartbreaking than that. Fourteen precious young lives were lost as a result of the fire: Humphrey Brown; Peter Campbell; Steve Collins; Patrick Cummings; Andrew Gooding; Gerry Francis; Lloyd Hall; Rosaline Henry; Patricia Johnson; Glenton Powell; Yvonne Ruddock; Paul Ruddock; Owen Thompson; and Anthony Berbeck.

The tragedy of the New Cross house fire remains one of the biggest unsolved cases in the Met's history.

Years later, I visited Joe Bell, the senior officer who had been in charge of forensics on the case. By then retired and quite elderly, Joe was very ill in hospital. He held my hand with tears rolling down his face as he reflected on the case.

'You know, we did do our best on the New Cross fire, didn't we, Jackie? We did our best.'

He was right. We did our utmost. Joe died shortly afterwards.

My next big case would begin two months later and would prove to be just as haunting.

CHAPTER 8

A MISSING BOY

The hot sunshine of 29 July 1981 was the perfect backdrop to the royal wedding of Prince Charles and Lady Diana Spencer. By this time, Kennington Police Station in south London had been my base for three months as one of the detectives investigating the Brixton riots. The community from the local housing estate had invited us to join them for afternoon tea to celebrate the wedding. There was bunting, little Union Jacks and a spread of food that could have fed an army. It was fantastic to be part of this happy community celebration.

Earlier that day, a solicitor called Vishambar Mehrotra had taken his eight-year-old son, Vishal, and his seven-year-old daughter, Mamta, to watch the wedding procession from his central London office. The family's nanny, Joanita Carvalho, had also come along. They arrived back in Putney, southwest London, by tube in the early afternoon; a tired Vishambar went straight home from the station to have a nap.

From the tube station, the nanny took the children to a newsagent on Upper Richmond Road to buy some sweets. They stayed a while in the shop without buying anything. The nanny decided to go and buy cough medicine in another shop, but Vishal wanted to go home. The nanny watched him cross the road at a pelican crossing on Upper Richmond

Road. Satisfied that Vishal was safely on his way home, Carvalho turned back and walked on with Mamta. It was approximately 2 o'clock in the afternoon. With the wedding celebrations still being broadcast on TV, there would have been few people about.

When Carvalho and Mamta returned home an hour later, Vishambar was asleep and Vishal was nowhere to be seen. The nanny assumed that he had come home then gone out to play, and she and Mamta went for a nap. When they woke up at around 4.30pm, Vishal was still not home. She took Mamta and went to find him, but they couldn't see him anywhere.

By 7pm, it was obvious that Vishal was not out with friends and had lost track of time, so Vishambar contacted the police. It was not uncommon for youngsters to go missing – particularly children in care – but they were rarely as young as this, and not from loving families. An alert was put out.

A missing eight-year-old becomes the main priority for any police officer. Putney police made the usual round of initial enquiries, contacting the Mehrotras' relatives and friends and retracing the steps of the route Vishal would have usually taken. The search went on all night to no avail, and Vishal's disappearance was now viewed as unmistakably sinister. More boots were put on the ground and specialist teams were deployed to do detailed searches.

On Friday 31 July, I was at the station in Kennington when I received a call telling me to report to the major incident room at Putney Police Station. I had just completed a batch of criminal investigations arising from the Brixton riots.

Despite not having stepped foot in Earlsfield station since October, I was still officially part of W Division, which also covered Putney. So off I went.

By lunchtime, I was knocking on Detective Superintendent Mike Smith's door.

'We've got a missing boy,' said Smith. 'We're pulling together a team, and I need you to be the link to the family.'

Smith was the assigned senior investigating officer on the case and briefed me on the run-up to Vishal's disappearance, then laid out what was expected: I needed to get to know the family, pass on anything that I judged of use to colleagues, and update the Mehrotras of any developments.

Before I'd even found my way around the incident room, the superintendent drove me to meet the family in Holmbush Road, Putney, where the Mehrotras lived in the basement flat of a large semi-detached house. Vishambar, a neatly groomed and courteous man, greeted us at the door and showed us into a brightly furnished sitting room with a view of the garden. The home felt warm and inviting. Safe. Despite the circumstances, Vishambar maintained his composure as Smith introduced me.

'This is Detective Sergeant Jackie Malton, Vishambar. We don't want you to have to deal with different detectives who might ask you the same questions over and over again, so Jackie is going to be your main contact. As the SIO, I'll also stay in touch, and come to advise of the lines of enquiry we will be pursuing.'

Vishambar listened sombrely before asking what was happening and what he could do to help. While his demeanour remained calm and measured, he looked dazed and bewildered; the distress and powerlessness he felt was evident in his eyes. He seemed lost.

Essentially, I was going to act as the family's liaison officer, but it wasn't named as such in those days and there was no formal training. I knew how important it was to communicate with the family during the early stages of an investigation of this kind and I had the experience to recognize that my role required compassion as well as investigative skills.

Vishal's mother, Aruna, had arranged to fly over from India, where she had been living since she and Vishambar had separated.

As I left the Mehrotra home that first day, it somehow didn't feel right to shake hands to say goodbye. For the first time in my policing career, I moved towards the troubled father and put my arms around him. As I hugged him, I said to him: 'We will do our very best to find your son, Vishambar.' He didn't say anything, but there was nothing for him to say. I left the house with Mike Smith that day with a heavy heart.

The next day I went back and spoke at length to Vishambar, trying to build a picture of family life and elicit as much information about Vishal as possible. I probed him about his marital breakdown, and Aruna's relationship with her children. In separation and divorce cases where children are involved and parents live in different countries, kidnap by either party is always a possibility. This consideration could not be ruled out at this stage. Sensitive and sometimes awkward questions needed to be asked to understand the family dynamics.

Another possibility was that Vishal had been kidnapped by a stranger wanting money for his safe return. Though such events were extremely rare, a recording device was attached to the home telephone in case a ransom demand came through.

A few years earlier, a 17-year-old called Lesley Whittle had inherited some money from her late father and was then abducted from her bed by Donald Neilson, who made a number of ransom demands for her safe return. Lesley was later found dead in a drainage shaft. With Vishal, we covered every possibility.

I quizzed Vishambar for as much information as possible about his son so that if he walked in the room that very moment, I would feel that I knew him intimately. Both parents had agreed that Vishal and his sister would receive a better education in England. He had not been living in the UK for very long when he disappeared. Where did Vishal go to play? Did he have any problems at school? Was he suffering from any form of anxiety? I quickly learned that Vishal was a very bright and extrovert child who was talented at drawing and loved to watch car racing.

'What would Vishal do if somebody asked him to get into a car?' I asked Vishambar early on.

'Vishal wouldn't go with anyone willingly, I'm sure of that,' he said evenly. 'He's been taught not to.'

The next day, Aruna arrived at Heathrow, where she was met by members of the enquiry team and interviewed before being driven to Holmbush Road. I noticed that she was greeted warmly by Vishambar. Demure and dark-eyed, Aruna struck me in much the same way as Vishambar: highly educated and contained in her emotions. Despite the couple being estranged, they were united in their shared anguish at the disappearance of their young son.

When I asked Aruna in private about her split from her husband, she appeared to have no rancour about the children staying in England with their father. My time with the Mehrotras gave me some small insights into Indian culture and their strong sense of hospitality. Despite their woes, they invited me to eat with them. By this point I was used to working very long hours and often ate on the hoof. Given the trouble taken to prepare the food it seemed churlish to refuse. Through conversations at the dinner table that would extend long into the night, I learned more and more about the family in a way that would have been hard to ascertain from just taking statements or conducting interviews. A relationship of trust with both Vishambar and Aruna built quickly.

Aruna was so devastated about her missing child that it soon became clear to me that she had not instigated his disappearance. As for the idea of someone wanting money in exchange for Vishal's return, no one called the flat.

As I gathered information, an intensive search involving specialist teams and a huge complement of police officers worked flat out to find Vishal before it was too late. The sense of urgency among officers and the desperation of the Mehrotra family were in stark contrast to the nation's celebratory mood following the fairy-tale royal wedding. Sitting with the Mehrotras as they waited anxiously for news, I wanted the world to stop. While people were going about their everyday business, a boy was missing and a family was in anguish. It felt like being in a parallel world. I wanted to shout from the rooftops: 'Everyone stop! Help us find Vishal!'

In an analogue world, without the benefit of CCTV on every street and with no other technological aids available, searching for Vishal was like looking for the proverbial needle in a haystack. The police had next to nothing to work with other than possible sightings of a boy who looked like Vishal and wore the same distinctive blue-and-white T-shirt.

Over 100 officers were enlisted in the operation: detectives, uniform officers, the Special Patrol Group, the dog unit, mounted police and police divers. Police in Delhi were contacted via Interpol and made aware of the boy's disappearance. We made the routine house-to-house enquiries. The details of all the occupants were checked with the criminal records office. Sniffer dogs were deployed to gardens, outbuildings, garages and derelict buildings alongside the River Thames. Officers wearing protective boilersuits and armed with tools such as spades and scythes searched surrounding wasteland for clues. The Met's water division checked every vessel moored in the area and police divers searched along the Thames in Putney and in surrounding reservoirs. Nothing. Where was he?

What had happened to him? Was the fact that the streets were deserted because of the royal wedding the reason that an opportunist seized his moment when he saw Vishal walking home? The questions went round and round in my head constantly.

At one stage, I was deployed in the Met's police helicopter, working with a technician equipped with a thermal heat scanner to detect bodies. We circled Barnes Common, Putney Common, Putney Heath, Wimbledon Common and Richmond Park. A number of hotspots were identified. All turned out to be the remains of dead animals.

'Missing' posters with a photograph and description of Vishal in English, Gujarati, Punjabi and Hindi were circulated.

The case garnered national and international media coverage. In a bid to jog people's memory about the fateful day, a reconstruction of Vishal's journey on Upper Richmond Road was made using a young boy who looked like Vishal, who had been wearing a navy-blue T-shirt with white horizontal stripes, black corduroy trousers and trainers. The publicity generated over 200 possible reported sightings of the missing boy in London. Each report raised hope that the child was still alive; officers checked out every tentative lead, however slim, but nothing panned out.

I would spend a few hours each day at the Mehrotras' and attend briefings at the station; the rest of my time was spent following up leads such as alleged sightings of Vishal by members of the public.

Enquiries were made with the teachers at Vishal's school in Kensington – St James Independent School for Boys – to see if Vishal was troubled by anything. I wasn't the officer who went to the school, but Vishambar had handed over Vishal's school reports, which described him as a bright boy who showed promise. However, as he was a newish pupil there wasn't a great deal of information about him for school staff to share.

Soon comparisons were made in the media with the case of Martin Allen, a 15-year-old boy who had disappeared less than two years earlier on 5 November 1979 and was never seen again. He returned home in Kensington after school, then left again shortly afterwards to visit his brother in Holloway, north London. He never arrived, but his brother and sister-in-law just assumed that he had changed his mind about popping around. His parents, meanwhile, assumed that Martin hadn't come back that evening because he had decided to stay the night at his brother's. It wasn't until 7pm the following evening that the family realized Martin had been missing for 24 hours, and a police search began. One witness claimed to have seen a man with stark blond hair and a moustache holding on to a boy at Gloucester Road tube station in south Kensington, and reported having heard him say, 'Don't run.' As part of an appeal for assistance, the Metropolitan Police released a photo of Martin and a sketch of the man the witness had described. This was to no avail. Martin's body has never been found.

The search for Vishal was a fraught time for everyone. At the daily briefings at Putney Police Station, we explored any other potential searches that could be made and any new leads that could be pursued. Many of the detectives on the case had children of a similar age to Vishal, and I could see the concern etched on their faces at the thought that someone else's child was missing. You could tell that they were all quietly asking themselves, *What if this happened to my child?* With all ideas up for discussion, detectives brought their theories to the table: ascertaining the whereabouts of known paedophiles, making detailed enquiries at a funfair in Wandsworth, which wasn't far from East Putney tube station. The obvious and the obscure. Everything was up for grabs. The more time passed, the less likely we were to find Vishal alive.

I felt powerless watching Vishambar and Aruna's agony up close. Photos of Vishal smiled back at me as I sat in Vishambar's living room. I felt that I knew the little boy without ever meeting him. Switching off at the end of the day was virtually impossible. Vishal was constantly on my mind. As I lay awake long into the night, I pondered possible clues that might have been missed. During the day, with Vishambar, I walked the various routes that Vishal might have taken and imagined him walking home on the day that most people were glued to their TV set watching the royal wedding. The big question was, what happened next? Who took him? Where, how and for what reason?

Vishambar and Aruna were still clinging on to the hope that their son was still alive, but as the time passed, the likelihood of that began to fade.

Five weeks into my liaison role, Detective Chief Inspector Jim Begg, who was second in command on the case, called me into his office. Begg could give the impression of being a bit dour, but he was a decent cop who really cared about others. It was obvious that he, like the rest of us, was intent on finding Vishal.

After a catch-up about the case, Begg got straight to it. 'Who do you know on the Flying Squad?'

It was September and Commander Stockwell had just been appointed head of the Flying Squad.

'Other than Commander Stockwell, no one,' I said.

Begg looked at me a little sceptically. 'You're being posted there in ten days' time. Commander Stockwell has asked for you. Best you finish off any outstanding enquiries on the Vishal case and keep in touch.'

My jaw dropped. 'The Flying Squad? Are you sure?'

'Yes,' he said. 'I've just had a call from Scotland Yard.'

The Flying Squad was a once-in-a-lifetime opportunity that I didn't want to pass up, but my delight at the news was muted by a sense of heaviness at leaving the Mehrotra family. I felt torn but I was aware that the search would soon be scaled down and that all but a few officers would be returned to their stations – in my case, Earlsfield. I visited Vishambar and Aruna to tell them I was leaving the investigation and had been posted elsewhere. They were disappointed because I had been with them from the very start. Saying goodbye was as sad for me as it was for them. I found myself unable to sever ties completely and promised to stay in touch with them. We had forged a connection, having many times chatted well into the night sharing a whisky or two. As I left Holmbush Road that day, I was resigned to the sense that Vishal was dead. Vishal was now such a high-profile missing person it would have been difficult for his abductor to go unnoticed with a young child matching his description in tow. But I wanted to be wrong.

I headed for my new job hoping that being part of the Flying Squad would be a welcome distraction from the helplessness I had felt as I sat waiting for news with Vishal's distraught family.

*

Five months after I left the case, I received a telephone call from the Putney office manager, Detective Micky Parkes. He was usually jovial but sounded sombre.

'Are you sitting down, mate?'

'What is it?' I asked.

'Sorry to break this to you, Jackie, but Vishal has been found dead.'

'Where?'

'In the middle of nowhere. Near Petersfield.'

'Are you sure it's him?'

'It's definitely Vishal. He's been identified by his teeth. The pathologist can't say how he died, though. They've only found the top half of his body, and there are only bones left. I'm sorry, mate. I'm gutted myself. Come and see us soon and I'll buy you a drink to commiserate.'

My stomach dropped as Micky spoke. I felt sick. The news of the discovery was chilling. I'd already feared the worst, but it was still a shock to hear it confirmed. I wanted it to be some mistake and to have the privilege of meeting a smiling Vishal, happy to have been found safe and sound. As I put the phone down, Vishambar and Mamta loomed large in my thoughts – as did Aruna, who was now back in India. What unimaginable grief for them all to suffer.

Vishal was found on 21 February 1982, when two pigeon shooters discovered a skull at Alder Copse, a wooded area of boggy ground surrounded by farmland, near the village of Rogate in West Sussex. In an era before DNA, dental records were the means to confirm identification. Dental features are unique. An x-ray of Vishal's teeth showing one tooth crowding another was used by the forensic odontologist to confirm the skull was Vishal's. An initial police search revealed other remains, relating to the upper parts of the child's body, and a clump of black hair. A more intensive search in Alder Copse ensued, but the lower extremities of Vishal's body were never recovered. There were signs of disturbance by animals, which could explain why the lower body parts were missing. No clothing was found.

A few days after Micky's call, I telephoned Vishambar to convey my condolences, though no words could do justice to the immense loss the family had experienced.

After the deposition site in Sussex had been cleared, I visited the area close to where the remains were found. The main road from Midhurst to Petersfield is the A272, which links to the larger A3 and has a layby on each side of the road. Alder Copse, situated on private land, is accessed by crossing a field some distance away. The location wouldn't be obvious to someone driving along the road unless they already knew of it. Vishal's body would have had to be carried quite some distance from the road to the copse – posing his abductor with a huge risk of being seen.

It seemed to me that the choice of deposition site held the clue. Whoever hid Vishal's remains is likely to have had strong local knowledge; it could possibly have been someone who lived in the locality, or had done so in the past. But who?

Rogate is located between the market towns of Petersfield and Midhurst on the Sussex/Hampshire border, so the murder enquiry was taken over by Sussex Police.

The identity of Vishal's killer remains a mystery.

Every police officer has the cases that stay with them. Vishal is among the names that I will never forget, along with those of the New Cross fire victims.

You don't have to be a police officer to share the frustration felt when the perpetrator of a heinous crime has got away. After being embedded with the family and watching their anguish day in and day out while they waited for news, I felt it most acutely. We stayed in touch over the years, by phone and in person.

In one conversation, Vishambar told me: 'I needed your emotion back then. Thank you.'

'What do you mean?' I asked.

'When I came to England one thing I found difficult was that people didn't show their empathy easily. It was such a different culture to my own. You were different, Jackie. I needed your empathy, your kindness, your warmth and your hugs. You had it. I could feel it coming from you. It wasn't superficial. I knew it was genuine.'

After spending so much time with the Mehrotras, it had been well-nigh impossible to conceal the compassion and empathy that I felt for the family, despite the police culture encouraging a stiff upper lip. To hear from Vishambar that this had made a positive difference to him really mattered to me.

What none of us knew then, or when Vishal's remains were subsequently found, was that the person responsible for killing him would get away with it. I knew that Vishal would always be in my heart and in my mind, and that I would never give up hope that someday the perpetrator would be caught.

CHAPTER 9

THE SWEENEY

It was a case of 'pinch me, I must be dreaming' as I arrived on my first day as a member of Scotland Yard's Flying Squad. My dream job.

Being assigned to the prestigious outfit was a real feather in my cap, not least because I had been working as an acting inspector back in Hinckley only two years before. I felt flattered that Commander Stockwell had asked for me personally and I was determined not to let him down.

As a uniform police officer back in Leicester in the mid-1970s, I'd been one of many avid viewers of the popular TV show *The Sweeney* – with its title that traded on the squad's nickname, based on Cockney rhyming slang: Sweeney Todd – Flying Squad. The show starred the late John Thaw as Detective Inspector Jack Regan and the late Dennis Waterman as Detective Sergeant George Carter. The all-male fictional squad dripped with machismo. I doubt I was the only aspiring female detective noting the regrettable absence of women on Regan's team. After being involved in three major enquiries since January – all necessitating working long hours – joining the 'Sweeney' wasn't the moment for me to sit back and take it easy. This was a big move for me, in more ways than one. It led to the end of my relationship with Pauline – because she knew that the Flying Squad demanded devotion and long hours from its officers, meaning we would have even less time to spend with each other. To me, joining the Flying Squad was a coup and nobody in their right mind would have turned it down. The police was my career, I loved my job and I had many years left to serve. Given that Pauline and I wanted different things, we split up amicably. We'd been good together, and we knew we would stay friends.

We sold our house near Kingston upon Thames and I moved to live on my own in a cottage in a small village near Esher on the outskirts of London.

My new posting had been announced in the Police Orders bulletin sent to all stations to notify Met staff of imminent promotions, transfers, retirements, outcomes of disciplinary boards against individual officers, and new legislation.

It prompted a call from a colleague of mine who was also a detective sergeant.

'Jackie, Police Orders has mixed us up. It's me who's been posted to COC8 [Flying Squad] and you who's going to Croydon.'

'On your bike, Richard! Nice try,' I told my miffed pal. 'Enjoy Croydon!' I understood how Richard felt.

Originally formed in 1919, the Flying Squad was set up as a 'mobile patrol unit' that would be sent out to any area of London to intercept robbers and pickpockets. At its inception the vehicles of choice were two horse-drawn wagons, with spy holes cut in the canvas for covert surveillance and detectives concealed inside ready to jump out and apprehend the offenders. The following year, it became the first unit to be issued with two motor vehicles, known as Crossley Tenders. The Flying Squad's remit developed over the years until it became a dedicated unit investigating armed robberies.

The squad's emblem was a swooping eagle. Many of the detectives were armed. The aim was to catch blaggers (robbers) involved in robberies where firearms or other weapons were used; whenever possible, you'd nick them as they did the deed by 'going across the pavement' – cop speak for capturing armed robbers in the act. Banks, post offices, betting shops and security vans carrying cash in transit from businesses to the bank were the most likely targets. Arresting the blaggers seconds before the robbery was about to take place gave the team enough evidence to charge them with 'conspiracy to rob'. Doing it before that point might only result in a 'possession of a firearm' charge – and leaving it too late could result in the robbery being committed, risking death or injury to innocent members of the public, so it was always a fine line.

When waiting for the guvnor to give the instruction over the radio to 'Go, go, go', adrenalin fuelled by a mixture of fear and excitement flooded my system. My heart raced, my mouth felt dry and nausea would sometimes rise as I prepared to confront armed robbers whose reaction was impossible to predict. The minute the guvnor gave the signal, all that built-up anticipation would unleash and I'd feel I had the strength of Superman; nothing could stop me from the off. My eye was on the target, and I could fly.

There were some women in the Flying Squad when I joined, but it's fair to say they were a rarity. Flying Squad teams made up of roughly 30 officers each were based across four areas of London: Rotherhithe, which covered the southeast of the capital; Barnes in the southwest; Finchley in the north; and Walthamstow in the east. Another mobile unit based at New Scotland Yard brought the total number of officers to around 150. I was the first woman detective sergeant to be posted in the Rotherhithe base, with a couple of women of DC rank elsewhere. There was no specialist training for Flying Squad officers apart from firearms training; it was a case of drawing on experience as well as learning on the job.

I was greeted on my first day by Detective Inspector Stan Finch, a handsome man with a snappy dress sense: smart suit, coloured shirt with a white collar, which was trendy in the day, and black patent shoes. The only other staff present were the office manager and the typist. The system for working was to pair up two detectives with a squad driver. To my surprise, the DI arranged for me to meet my new partner at the Prince of Orange pub across the road from the station at 12 noon.

My new inspector bought me a drink as we waited to meet Phil, who was also a DS.

Around 12.15pm the door to the pub sprung open and in walked a strapping man of about 6ft 3in, slightly hunched with a John Wayne pose, a bent nose and a sullen look on his face. He gave the appearance of someone looking for a fight. It turned out that he was.

DI Finch introduced us. 'Phil, this is Jackie. She's your new partner in the car.'

I smiled at Phil and held out my hand to shake his. Phil looked back and kept his hands by his side. 'Why don't you fuck off, you cunt. I'm not working with a woman.'

I was completely floored but I wasn't about to show it. 'Pleased to meet you too, Phil,' I said.

My disgruntled new partner turned his back on me and walked out. As he left the pub, he muttered in his gruff northern accent: 'See you back at the office.' I think this was aimed at the DI.

DI Finch and I followed Phil with our eyes as he headed out, the pub door rattling from his exit. My senior colleague seemed as shocked as I was.

A brief pause followed. 'I'm sure he'll be OK when he gets used to the idea,' said the optimistic Stan. But Phil never did.

I soon learned from the office manager that my time was going to be tough because the guys on the wider team weren't too keen on having a woman detective in the office either, especially one they didn't know. It was a matter of trust and being able to depend on a colleague if you got in a tight spot on an operation. They dealt with ruthless criminals who were prepared to shoot anyone who got in their way, including the police. Could I be trusted?

I later discovered that it wasn't just about that. As one colleague explained to me: 'If we're on a job, I worry that having you with us is going to be distracting because we'll be worried about you getting hurt.'

'Don't you worry about me,' I said. 'I'll get on with my job, and you get on with yours. I can look after myself.'

It took a while for the message to get through, but they soon saw that I could indeed handle myself.

New officers were always the subject of salacious gossip and fact-finding missions to see if there was any 'dirt' on the recent arrival: what you were like, who you were sleeping with. That kind of thing. It didn't take them long to find out that I was gay, though I think they felt disarmed by the fact that I was comfortable confirming it.

For my part, I strived to be seen as 'one of the boys'. I joined in with post-work drinks down the pub. I avoided doing anything that they might see as 'different', given my perceived dual sins of being female and gay. But part of me didn't expect the men to tackle me quite as hard as they did on the Astroturf when I was the only female playing in the five-aside football team!

Nevertheless, my nickname in the squad was 'the Tart'; this annoyed me, but I shrugged it off because I knew it would be grist to their mill. Everyone got ribbed about something. Phil's jibes towards me, on the other hand, were personal.

'You're not gay, Tart. You just haven't met the right man and had a proper fucking yet.' To complain was out of the question, as Phil well knew.

The culture was to put up or shut up. There was a complaints system of sorts but to say anything officially would have been career suicide.

Many of the detectives on the squad were firearm trained but I declined the offer of training since I had no interest in guns, no desire to carry one and no wish to have the responsibility that came with firing one and possibly killing someone in the line of duty. It wasn't for me. Colleagues presented me with a baseball bat as a form of protection, on which they'd engraved 'Jackie's Bat'. Although I took my trusted bat on all operations, I never used it.

Each unmarked squad car – Granadas, Vauxhalls and the like – had a call sign and ours was Central 884. Flying Squad drivers, like the detectives, were also handpicked: for their experience, their level-headedness and for being cool under pressure. Our driver was called Yorkie, a constable who had 20-plus years' service in the job. He was a man who was shrewd with his money. His working jackets had leather patches on the elbows and the frame of his glasses were fixed with Elastoplast. It never seemed to occur to Yorkie to get his glasses repaired or, God forbid, to buy a new pair. Folded-up *Telegraph* pages would usually protrude from his jacket pocket so that he could pore over the rise and fall of his stocks and shares, which he did daily.

Every few weeks, each team would be on a rota as the 'bank car', which essentially meant being the designated team expected to respond to an armed robbery in the vast geographical area of southeast London. I'll never forget my first trip in a squad car going on a shout with Yorkie and Phil. I was just about to tuck into the fish and chips I'd bought for lunch when we got a call that a robbery had taken place in Tooting.

My fish and chips were thrown all over the car as Yorkie hit the pedal and raced to the scene to the accompaniment of the blues and twos, speeding the wrong way up one-way streets, sometimes mounting the pavement if he could. No one in the car said a word, to avoid breaking his concentration. You could cut the tension with a knife. I quickly learned that the etiquette of being a passenger in a Flying Squad vehicle was to acknowledge the driver's expertise at the end of the journey. 'Nice drive, Yorkie.' It unfailingly was.

Such was the speed of Yorkie's driving that we arrived at Tooting High Street from southeast London before the local detectives, prompting the suggestion that we must have had prior knowledge of the raid. They clearly hadn't experienced Yorkie's superb driving.

Phil was a difficult man to partner. No surprise, given his opening salvo that first day.

I tried to make the relationship work, jollying him along as much as I could, but nothing I did was right in his eyes. The fact that he was downbeat and negative about most things was tiresome enough, but he also seemed invested in trying continually to wrongfoot me.

During my first week in the job, he asked me to be at the office at 6 in the morning so that we could do a reconnaissance of an address for a known robber. I took early starts in my stride. A 6 o'clock start meant getting up at 4, since it was a long journey from my southwest London home. There was no way I'd risk being late. I waited in the office. Phil and Yorkie arrived three hours later, at 9am – the usual start time. I was furious.

'I've been here since 6am as arranged, so what happened to you?' I growled.

'Tough shit,' he replied. 'I changed my mind. We'll do it again Friday.'

And on Friday he did the same thing – no show.

As the newbie on the team, I didn't want to rock the boat; Phil knew that. Stunts like these would continue through our so-called partnership. Even though we were of the same rank, Phil would make sure that I was not allowed to sit in the front passenger seat if he was also in the car: 'Remember who you are, Tart,' he would say. It wasn't worth arguing about. I was no pushover though. When necessary, I would fight my corner. But I wasn't going to get into needless arguments. I just wanted to get on with the job.

Being a Flying Squad officer involved investigating all armed robberies committed in south London. Many of the squad vehicle registration numbers were known to the criminal fraternity. It wasn't difficult for the local blaggers living in our patch to see what vehicles we were using if we were seen driving out of the police station. So our personal cars – in my case a black TR7 – were fitted with a force radio and often used to do surveillance. The challenge was to stay one step ahead.

To catch robbers in the act, preparation was key. Names of prolific robbers would be bandied about in the office and our job was to gather intelligence about who was associating with whom and what vehicles they were using. We did this through a variety of methods, including the cultivation of informants.

As soon as we had a tip that a job was due to go down, observation – which we called 'going on the plot' – became a large part of the work. Targeting armed robbers would often take weeks or months of laborious and tedious observations, be it in freezing cold locations outside or holed up in a vehicle for long stretches of time. Robbers could be unpredictable, despite their best-laid plans. Some hyper-vigilant types looked for signs or omens: a black cat crossing the road in front of them was enough to make one or two decide to do the job another day, as I would learn first-hand from a prison inmate years later.

We could spend hours cooped up in an observation vehicle, waiting for a robbery to take place. It was pretty awkward if you needed a wee. One of the guys bought me a funnel that I could use for emptying my bladder through a hole in the floor of the van. Surprise, surprise, I never used the funnel. This thoughtful gesture confirmed to me that I was now one of the team, though.

The slow points in our operations were quickly forgotten with the thrill of catching armed robbers and getting them off the streets. When we arrested them, some would wet themselves or worse. A far cry from the swagger and arrogance that some would adopt as part of their persona. If they spotted me as a Flying Squad officer in the street, they'd gesture 'wanker' or stick up two fingers, but it never bothered me. They were despicable human beings and an absolute menace to society. I had no time at all for these underworld criminals or the terror they instilled in people. They were men causing misery purely for greed. Their spoils would usually be spent on oversized homes and flash cars, but they didn't have much time to enjoy them since they seemed to spend more time in jail than outside.

*

When by chance a detective spotted a known armed robber getting into a car one day, he decided to check out the number with base, only to be told it was a false plate. The officer decided to do a 'recce' – police parlance for taking a look – and followed the man, called Walker, in his car. When Walker parked and got out of the car, my colleague stopped and followed him on foot. He struck lucky when he saw Walker meet with two known criminal associates who also had form as armed robbers. By complete coincidence a uniform police officer unconnected with the Flying Squad stopped the men and began to conduct a stop and search.

Walker legged it and was seen throwing something over a wall, which turned out to be a handgun. The uniform officer caught him and shouted for assistance. All three men were arrested, and the handgun recovered. The target for the robbery was not known since the constable had unwittingly prevented any robbery occurring. Two stolen vehicles were found nearby. To see if these were connected to the suspects, the forensic team was asked to take fibre swabs from the cars, which were later matched with the fibres of the clothing worn by the three men. The trio was charged with conspiracy to commit armed robbery.

I was asked to oversee the exhibits, which meant that I was responsible for all the evidence and all the items belonging to the suspects relating to the case. It was a particularly busy day when the forensic officer asked me for the car keys so that he could go and take swabs from the car seats.

It wasn't until I was in the witness box giving evidence at the Old Bailey that it was pointed out to me by the defence barrister that I had not logged out the removal of the car keys from the property bag in the charge room. I knew full well that any procedural oversight of this kind would be seized upon to suggest that the lapse was in fact a ruse to plant the incriminating fibre by taking the jumpers and artificially planting them in the car. It's quite easy to panic in these circumstances and say the wrong thing before you have time to reflect on what you're doing. But I knew that to deny my blunder would make things worse and make me appear untrustworthy. No matter how embarrassing it was, admitting the mistake was the only course of action.

'It was a human error,' I said, when pressed by the defence. There was nowhere for the barrister to go with that answer and the issue was put to bed.

I knew from experience of giving evidence in court that barristers were thorough in their preparations and could be incredibly robust in their questioning when cross-examining witnesses. I had learned a lot in the process of listening to them trying to pick the evidence apart during past cases. It had undoubtedly helped me to be a better detective, so my mistake was galling.

As I was giving my evidence, someone sitting in the public gallery stared at me and put two fingers to his head as a warning, a menacing look on his face. He was a known associate of one of the defendants. Intimidation of this kind was often used by the accused's associates or family members to try and scare police officers giving evidence. Threats came with the territory and didn't just happen in court. You learned to put these into perspective and carry on doing your job.

When the jury returned, one of my squad colleagues who had been at court with me was too nervous to sit and hear the jury's verdict. There was a clear panel in the bottom half of the door to the court room, through which he would be able see my feet. 'If there is a guilty verdict, just raise your crossed leg in the air,' he said.

The jury returned a guilty verdict for each defendant, so I slightly raised my crossed leg three times. All three were jailed. To avoid a confrontation with our detractors in the public gallery, we exited by the back of the Old Bailey before heading down the pub to release the tensions of the day.

On his release, Walker continued to be a career armed robber and served long prison sentences. Had he bothered to calculate in monetary terms his winnings against time spent in prison, he would have realized he earned less than the minimum wage.

*

Attending trials to give evidence was a necessary part of concluding a job, but it was far less exciting than chasing criminals or piecing together details about a potential robbery. The added challenge was when we had only partial intelligence.

We were once stymied, for example, when a detective outside the Flying Squad passed on information that he'd gleaned from an informant about a potential armed robbery due to go down in north London. The informant gave the detective the date but not the exact location of where the robbery was going to take place.

The only useful lead was that there was to be a vehicle swap in Hilldrop Crescent, Tufnell Park, with the second car due to take the robbers to the van that they intended to rob cash from. The fact that it was north of the river didn't impede us. The information had come directly to our squad, so it was our case to investigate.

It was always an early start when you went on the plot. I woke up in the middle of the night and drove across London to a nearby police station to meet my colleagues.

The 6am briefing gave us the lowdown on the operation, which included conducting observations above the street where the suspects were going to swap vehicles. The job was a planned haul of cash in transit. But since we didn't know where this was taking place, we couldn't intervene strictly on the plot. Our guv was Detective Chief Inspector Gordon Stepney, who possessed just the right traits for a leader: cool and calm under pressure, skilled at detective work, and able to enjoy a laugh.

Two Flying Squad colleagues had already identified a cash-in-transit van that did a regular route along Camden Road to several premises. We knew the plan for the suspected robbers was to follow the transit van, but we didn't know which one of the locations they intended to attack. This unknown quantity led to the decision to intercept at the point when the blaggers changed vehicles in Hilldrop Crescent. It was too much of a risk to follow them to a target vehicle, in case we lost them or they used counter-surveillance tactics to check that they weren't being followed. One of the suspects was already on the run from the police.

A member of the team was tasked with taking photos from the observation vehicle, as was the norm. The guvnor had also contacted the technical-support unit at Scotland Yard beforehand to set up a surveillance camera from one of the buildings we were using for observation. This was the first time I had worked on a job using filming as a vital evidence aid.

We already knew from information received that the second vehicle was a Mini with false registration plates. My observation plot (OP) was a building in the crescent with a clear view of the street where the changeover was due to take place. We were expecting two suspects. With officers hidden elsewhere unable to get a clear view of what was going on, I was responsible for giving a running commentary and describing the suspects when they appeared.

It wasn't long before a BMW arrived in view and two men got out. One was carrying a sports bag with two tennis rackets protruding from it. All anyone else watching would see was two guys meeting up to play a game of tennis; it would look innocent enough to members of the public. The usual trick of blending in. Nothing to see here. I watched as the two men walked towards the Mini. One man got into the driver's side while the other put the sports bag on the rear seat then sat in the front passenger seat. As this was happening, I confirmed over the radio that the men were in the car. Stepney then gave the order: 'Go, go, go!'

As soon as he said those words, detectives spilled out of the observation van, also parked in the crescent, and other unmarked cars waiting in streets nearby zoomed in and surrounded the Mini to box it in. The two men were dragged out and forced face-down on the pavement as the sports bag was retrieved from the back seat of the car. Inside it alongside the tennis rackets was a loaded sawn-off shotgun. One of the officers took photographs of the bag's contents.

We went to search their home addresses, as is the norm when someone is detained. Some of us went to the residence of the driver, only to find that shots had been fired into the sitting-room ceiling tiles. We recovered the tiles and took them to the forensic-science laboratory for comparison with the gun recovered on arrest. The gun fired into the ceiling was confirmed as the same as the one we had recovered in the bag. Brilliant evidence to present to the court. Or so we thought.

When the case came to the Old Bailey, wily defence barristers turned the tables on us. We thought the gun was unassailable proof of the men's plan to commit armed robbery. One of the defendants' lawyers, however, suggested to the jury that the gun had been planted by the Flying Squad. Their basis for the claim was that there had been a brief moment when the bag was out of view of the surveillance camera. The lawyer tried to argue that one of the detectives had taken the opportunity to slip the shotgun into the bag. As for the ceiling tiles, the defence argued that it was one of us who had gone into the defendant's flat with the gun and shot at the ceiling to cement our case.

These and other queries from the defence raised sufficient doubt in the jury's collective mind to return a not-guilty verdict for both defendants. It was sickening that the jury believed the defence allegations of police planting the shotgun and firing into the ceiling tiles. I couldn't believe how little confidence the public had in our ability to do a good job for the right reasons, rather than to 'fit' somebody up. I had never fitted somebody up in my life.

It was clear that one of the defendants couldn't believe the jury had fallen for it either.

As I gave him back the property that had been seized from his house, he took his possessions and said: 'Fuck me, Jackie, I was going to plead guilty but the defence said, "Give it a run." What a bleeding result.' What a bleeding result indeed.

One of the defence barristers walked by a short while later as I was gathering my things and getting ready to leave. Still fuming over the verdict, I decided on impulse to have my say.

'You know full well we didn't plant that gun. We didn't fire it into the ceiling either.'

The barrister smiled at me knowingly. 'I know, my dear, but I don't defend innocent men.'

The outcome was hard to swallow – not least because we had used camera surveillance for the first time. Two extremely nasty individuals prepared to use a sawn-off shotgun, with deer shot up the spout, walked free. Still, it would be the only not-guilty verdict I encountered during my three years in the Flying Squad.

Our demoralized team headed back to the Prince of Orange to have a drink and swallow our frustration. Drink was a notable feature of life in the Flying Squad: you knocked it back after a bad result, and after a good one. In short, you drank after any old job, whatever the result. As in many other professions of the time, it was common to have a drink at the end of the working day. The occasional formal office lunch was the rare occasion when drinking would trump policing: if an armed robbery occurred during the boozy affair that was a Flying Squad lunch, our colleagues in the Barnes office would deal with it. In return, we would cover for them if a robbery took place on their patch while they were having theirs.

Going to the pub with the team was, for me, more about bonding with them than letting my hair down after a case had finished. The feeling of being an outsider had lurked before I signed the oath, but it became magnified in the context of being the lone female in a specialist team like the Flying Squad – and of being the butt of lewd macho jokes and a slew of misconceptions.

It was at these boozy lunches, for example, that I would receive sex toys from the squad: dildos or love balls because I was gay. Over the years, I received so many sex aids that I think I could have opened my own sex shop. I felt I had no choice but to be a sport, play along and conceal the fact that I felt humiliated to be confronted by their warped notion that gay sex was penetration by an artificial penis. After all, what could I say? To remonstrate at this male pack mentality would invite suggestions that I couldn't take a joke, and distance me further from my colleagues with whom (aside from Phil) I had good relationships. I doubt very much that the men had any idea how their 'jokes' left me feeling.

Some of the men got their share of ribbing too. At one particular lunch, one of the Flying Squad drivers was presented with a slaughtered sheep's back from a Bermondsey butcher with a huge knife in it. The message behind this 'joke' was that some colleagues saw him as two-faced.

These shenanigans were part of the macho squad-room culture. The regular party trick by one officer was seeing how many 10p pieces he could place in his foreskin. The magic figure turned out to be £3.20. I found it embarrassing but I laughed as loudly as everyone else. *Fit in; don't stand out*, I told myself.

As for my partner Phil, things came to a head after six months of working together. It was the day that Detective Chief Inspector Begg – who was still working on Vishal's disappearance – asked to see me to discuss some details related to the case. Given that this was police business, I said to Phil that we needed the squad car to go to Putney. Phil and Yorkie stayed in the car while I went to see the DCI. But 20 minutes into my meeting, the door to the DCI's office burst open. In the doorway stood Phil, looking enraged.

'Come on, you, you've been long enough,' he barked. Before anyone had a chance to say anything, he turned and thundered back down to the car.

A fairly stunned DCI looked at me. 'Who is that?'

Unsurprisingly, Begg was furious that a sergeant had seen fit to storm into a DCI's office in that way. 'Stay put; you're not going anywhere.'

'Yes, guv.'

I wasn't going to take orders barked at me by a fellow DS, but I knew there would be hell to pay later. I stayed until the DCI had finished, then went back to the car. Yorkie and I chatted. A furious Phil did not speak to me for the rest of the day. This was not uncommon. But I'd had enough of his erratic and volatile behaviour, which left me walking on eggshells. I felt like an abused wife. After one too many hostile stunts, one too many derogatory put-downs, one too many unpleasantries, I wasn't going to put up with it any longer.

I went to speak to DCI Stepney, who heard me out. I told him that I couldn't stand working with Phil, and I listed some of the reasons why. Stepney agreed to partner me with an experienced detective called Tony Purdy, who had recently joined the squad from Lewisham. Blessed with a dry humour that made me laugh to the point that I sometimes couldn't catch my breath, Tony was a welcome contrast to the mercurial Phil. The switch meant that I was in another car with a different driver I'll call Jimmy.

Jimmy and I rubbed along OK, but his views on women in the police left me cold. One day, as we waited to do an early-morning raid on a property where the prime suspect was known to sleep with a firearm under his pillow, Jimmy thought he'd fill the time by sharing his views on why women should not be paid as much as men.

I wasn't having that.

'What you don't get is this, Jimmy: we're about to kick the door in on a suspect who is armed. You'll be sitting in the car, smoking a fag and reading the *Sun*. If we get the guy, you won't be writing up the reports, you won't be preparing evidence and you won't be giving that evidence in court. You do fuck all apart from driving a car, so please don't tell me about women and equal pay.'

And before Jimmy could answer, Tony and I were out the car and inside the house to make another successful arrest.

*

Christmas soon loomed, but it would prove to be without cheer. At 12.44pm on Saturday 17 December 1983, the London branch of suicide-prevention charity the Samaritans received a telephone call from a man claiming to be from the IRA to say that a bomb had been placed inside a car parked outside Harrods department store in Knightsbridge, with two more bombs planted inside the store. Two bombs had also been placed in Oxford Street, the caller said, including one in the Littlewoods department store. The message was passed on to New Scotland Yard and police units were dispatched.

Living in London and policing the city at that time were overshadowed by the activities of the IRA. That day alone, there had been 22 calls from concerned members of the public about suspicious items. Litter bins in the West End and other places were removed as potential targets for bomb placement. The Metropolitan Police were on high alert and on receipt of the call instantly started a systematic search of the immediate area. Usually the IRA would give a code, proving the magnitude and danger of a call; on this occasion it could not be authenticated.

Nothing was found in Oxford Street, but at 1.21pm a bomb believed to weigh between 25 and 30lb exploded in a car parked in Hans Crescent, a one-way street behind Harrods. The explosion occurred as some officers were approaching a suspect blue Austin 1300 GT. Sergeant Noel Lane (28) and WPC Jane Arbuthnot (22) were killed instantly. A third officer, Inspector Stephen Dodd (34), later died in hospital following the decision to switch off his life-support machine on Christmas Eve. A female colleague who was stood just inches from Arbuthnot when the explosion went off survived. The IRA bomb also killed three civilians: Philip Geddes (24), a journalist who was in the store with his girlfriend at the time Harrods was evacuated; Jasmine Cochrane-Patrick (25), a young mother who had popped into Harrods to buy Christmas presents; and Kenneth Salvesen (28), a married American citizen based in Chelsea who had a young son. The girlfriend of Geddes, who was just a few steps behind him, survived. Overall, 78 civilians and 13 police officers were injured in the blast. A police dog handler, PC John Gordon, lost both legs and part of a hand. His police dog, Queenie, was so severely injured that she was put out of her misery by an armed officer.

Bombings in London were dealt with by the Anti-Terrorist Squad named CO13, based at New Scotland Yard. Like the Flying Squad, it was a specialist unit working to a specific remit. There had been so many bombings in London around this time that officers were stretched. More were needed to boost the numbers on the team, so the following day myself and colleagues from the Flying Squad were seconded to the Harrods bomb team to assist in taking witness statements.

We were briefed at the offices of the anti-terrorist unit and shown a video of the chilling scene. The bodies had been removed but everything else remained in situ. The roof of the blue Austin 1300 GT containing the bomb had landed on top of a nearby building following the impact of the explosion. Only the chassis of the vehicle remained. The area looked like a war zone, with debris, shattered shop fronts, and clothes blown off the models in the tailor's shop opposite. I can still recall the sound of crunching glass in an otherwise eerie silence as the Met photographer walked slowly to capture the devastating scene on his camera.

I was told to take a desk in the basement of Harrods and to act as the store's police liaison officer, taking statement upon statement from staff who had worked on the day of the attack. Many were still in shock about what had happened, mixed with a relief that they were safe and a desperate sadness for the deceased and the injured. Some had escaped injury simply because they had chosen to use a different entrance than usual. I visited people at home recovering from their injuries, mainly shards of broken glass that had entered their body. One man told me how he was crossing the road in Hans Crescent and was blown into the window display of the tailor's shop by the force of the bomb. This young man, who had just become a father, didn't need me to remind him how lucky he was. I took his statement and left him to enjoy the loving embrace of his family.

Like any major enquiry, the work involved incredibly long hours, often without proper breaks and food. Apart from Christmas Day and Boxing Day, I worked non-stop – 13-hour days, seven days a week – until I had completed the task of interviewing every Harrods staff member there on the day the bombs went off. The horror of it, the fatalities and the casualties, meant that Christmas 1983 was likely to have been a very difficult time for anyone who had been caught up in it.

The IRA admitted responsibility for the bombing by some of its volunteers, but declared that it was not authorized by its army council. In a statement, they said that they regretted the loss of civilian casualties. This seemed entirely disingenuous to me. If you place a car bomb outside one of the most iconic stores in the country at Christmas time, then deaths are inevitable. No one was ever charged.

*

By 1984 I had passed the Metropolitan Police inspector's examination and a subsequent interview. My new rank would mean waiting for a new posting. Aside from my unhappy six-month relationship with Phil, I had loved every minute of my time on the Flying Squad. I was leaving this exhilarating, dangerous, adrenalin-pumping, dog-eat-dog kind of world with a heavy heart. Even my experience with Phil wasn't a complete waste of time. Courtesy of Lynda La Plante many years later, he would be the inspiration for the *Prime Suspect* character Detective Sergeant Otley, played by the late and wonderful actor Tom Bell. After the first programme was broadcast, my phone rang off the hook with calls from former Flying Squad pals. 'We know who Sergeant Otley is!' Experiences, they stay with us.

In 1984, I was promoted to Detective Inspector. I would learn that the higher up the echelons I went, the tougher it became for me as a woman in an institution that was the bastion of white, male privilege. An institution that still resisted the idea that women were up to the job, let alone that they could be at the top of the profession. With few women in senior ranks, the experience could be lonely. And I was about to learn that doing my job properly could leave me feeling more isolated than ever before.

CHAPTER 10
A ROGUE COP

As I drove through the streets of London's West End for my first day as a CID detective inspector on 3 January 1984, I felt excitement mixed with trepidation. My new posting was to be at West End Central Police Station, based in Mayfair's Savile Row – in the heart of London and close to Soho, a hub of subcultures mingling together 24/7. With its theatres and restaurants, Soho was a key destination for people wanting a good time, from out-of-towners to tourists, while the market traders and more upmarket boutiques enticed people with money to spend. I relished the challenge of working in such a buzzy part of London as a newly minted DI. I expected the cycle of crime that took place in this part of London to test my mettle.

West End Central was seen as one of the Met's most iconic stations to work in – and it was one of the busiest too. Stan Finch, my former DI on the Flying Squad, was now my boss as the DCI in charge of the CID, which was good for me since a friendly familiar face always helps. The volume of crime generated in this quarter of London demanded the attention of four detective inspectors. My three male DI colleagues made me feel at home straightaway. They were to be my roommates in a glass-paned side office adjacent to the main CID office situated on the first floor of the police station. The management of CID was shared between the four of us. We were put on rota between the hours of 8am to 10pm, with the one on the late turn being on-call overnight in case night-duty CID wanted to consult a DI over a serious matter.

There were six teams, made up of four or five detectives, each led by a detective sergeant who would report to the DIs. There was just one other woman detective. My responsibilities included liaising with the uniform section regarding the investigation of particular cases and dealing with more serious crimes. But contrary to the way the DI role is often depicted in TV cop dramas, a DI does not spend all her time investigating cases.

As the new kid in the DI ranks, I copped the job of managing all the crime books. These were ledgers in which all crimes were recorded and classified. Each book would cover a category: motor-vehicle crime; beat crimes, such as shoplifting and criminal damage; major crimes, such as burglary, robbery and serious woundings. Too often I would have to chase police officers to ensure that they had filled in the details in full: the name of the victim, what had happened, the investigation conducted thus far and any updates. My job was to check what progress was being made on each case.

Paperwork was the bane of all officers' lives, whatever their rank, but it was an essential part of any investigation. My favourite part of the job was being out and about investigating any major crime that came in when I was on duty and required someone of my rank to attend.

The chief superintendent who ran the station had garnered a fearsome reputation and did not seem particularly well-liked by younger police officers. During my time there, the CS would choose to put some of his energies to questionable use.

In January 1986 a small band of officers formed a freemason lodge exclusively for police officers working in the West End of London; it was christened the Manor of St James, lodge number 9179. This was set up shortly after the then Metropolitan Police Commissioner, Sir Kenneth Newman, had published *The Principles of Policing*, otherwise known as 'the little blue book', which was issued to every officer in the Met. With specific reference to freemasonry membership, the commissioner wrote that

> the discerning officer will probably consider it wise to forgo the prospect of pleasure and social advantage in freemasonry so as to enjoy the unreserved regard of all those around him. It follows from this that one who is already a freemason would also be wise to ponder, from time to time, whether he should continue as a freemason; that would probably be prudent in the light of the way that our Force is striving, in these critical days, to present to the public a more open and wholehearted image of itself, to show a greater readiness to be invigilated and to be free of any unnecessary concealment or secrecy.

Some years later, after I had left West End Central, someone sent me a photograph of the inauguration of the lodge. I recognized about two thirds of the 60-odd men. Most were senior officers. This influential and secretive boys' network was impenetrable to women officers – not that I would have wanted to be part of it anyway. One male colleague who refused an invitation to join the lodge once told me that he was informed that his decision would 'do his career no favours'.

I didn't know the chief super as well as I did Ted Stowe, who was the commander in charge not just of our station but of the other two stations that covered the totality of the West End: Vine Street and Bow Street. (The latter, with its famous white police lamps instead of the regular blue, has since closed and become a police museum.) Stowe was feared by many, but I quickly learned that his bark was significantly worse than his bite and that he didn't seem to mind you answering back as long as you showed him respect. He was extremely protective of his own officers, but less charitable to others who would come in to assist on operations such as policing demonstrations on our patch. Striding through the canteen, Stowe would prowl the room, his eyes lingering on non-West End officers. Any uniform officer with hair that he deemed scruffy or too long: beware.

'We don't do scruffy here,' he would holler. 'This is the premier division of the Metropolitan Police, so we expect hair off the collar, shiny boots and a pressed uniform. You, sonny, can make your way back from whence you came. We don't want your standard of dress here, so please tell your commander that *this* commander, Ted Stowe, sent you back.' And with that, they'd be gone.

Within a few days of joining, I was summonsed to see Stowe for his unique version of a 'welcome to the team' talk.

'Sit down, miss. Let me tell you what I expect from my CID. I expect high standards at all times. If you're caught in a Soho club without permission, you'll be disciplined, sent back to some god-earthly station on the extremity of the Met, directing the traffic. No CID officers will enter a club in this division without prior permission. Got it?'

'I get it, sir.'

'Good to hear it. You're the first split-arse DI we've had here. Welcome to the premier division of the Met.'

Despite this inauspicious start, I grew not only to like Stowe but also to have huge respect for him as a copper: he was a character you couldn't ignore, a uniformed officer through and through. On occasions, he would come to the CID office, grab hold of all the crime books, circle certain entries with a question mark, and write 'MORE INFORMATION NEEDED', as if lower-case letters might fail to get his request noticed. Stowe's queries related mainly to seeking a better description of what was stolen, or a more detailed account of the suspect. But it generated a lot of administrative work for me as well as the fiddly task of chasing the officers who'd made the entries but weren't on hand to fill in the gaps. The mess Stowe made of the crime books that I kept so diligently was infuriating. Administration was all manual – no computers in those days. I once asked Stowe to make a list instead of scrawling across the pages, but it fell on deaf ears.

When Valentine's Day came around, I decided to play a joke on my commander: I found the most obnoxious card possible and sent to it his private office. To my amazement, Stowe proudly displayed it on his desk, causing quite a stir and a few chuckles from colleagues who were in the know. It took three months for the penny to drop.

'I understand it was you who sent me the Valentine's card,' said Stowe one day, after calling me into his office.

'Well, sir, I can't comment on that,' I said. 'But I would say that if it took you this long to detect who sent it, then no wonder you were never a detective . . . Sir.'

'Get out!' he boomed with a wry smile.

*

Not long after my arrival, I was sent off on a three-week inspector's course at Hendon in north London, at the end of which I and another officer were asked if we would like to apply for university scholarships. No doubt this would have improved my chances of getting promoted to the next rank, but the scar of failing my eleven-plus and the disappointment I had caused my parents had not completely faded. What if I failed the degree as well? I didn't want the pressure and the expectations from bosses that would come with doing a Met-funded degree. I wasn't keen to be away from policing for three years either, so I turned the offer down. Sometimes, I was my own worst enemy.

What no one at work knew was that I had already completed a module on women in history with the Open University. A part-time long-distance course meant that I could fit my study around my work and the fact that I didn't tell anyone about it put less pressure on me. Although never one to identify as a feminist, I had picked feminist history because I'd begun to realize that my constant efforts to fit in as one of the boys had made me start to lose sight of who I was as a woman. I wanted to get in touch with my identity and to make sense of why women were treated as second-class citizens by society. Learning more about the lives of women through history made me feel angry at women's lot. Reflecting on the women's department that I joined in Leicester as a 19-year-old, I realized that I hadn't fully appreciated the excellent work that my female colleagues did in their specialist roles with women and children. At the time, I saw that the men's work was more valued within the force, so I wrongly assumed that what we did was therefore less important. I was completely wrong. The course also touched on male power and its violent expression through rape and domestic violence and made me re-evaluate my approach as a police officer.

Being part of a male-dominated institution sometimes made me feel lonely, but I drew on my ability to be a bit cocky and up for a laugh to mask my feeling of not quite belonging. Humour was a useful social skill in my repertoire. It could help to ease the tension in difficult situations and sometimes made other people feel better too. One such instance comes to mind.

One of the nicest pubs in the area – and one that many of us frequented after work – was the Coach and Horses in Bruton Street, a few hundred yards from the nick. The landlady was a feisty, pint-sized Scottish woman called Anne-Marie who stood no nonsense from anyone. With Anne-Marie in charge, it felt like a safe place to de-stress after a difficult day.

Police slang for licensees was 'cock'. I've no idea how this use originated, but as a licensee you were invariably a 'good cock', meaning pro-police, or a bad one. My pal Anne-Marie definitely fell into the 'good cock' category. One evening, I invited her as my guest to a leaving do at Trenchard House, the section house where young single police officers resided: it had a bar where police promotions and retirement parties were often held. Everyone was standing about drinking and chatting until Commander Stowe called the crowd to silence in preparation for his tribute to the departing colleague. He did a double-take when he saw Anne-Marie.

In jest, he shouted across the room: 'What are you doing here?'

I could see Anne-Marie, not normally stuck for words, looking flustered and her face was turning red. I cupped my hands around my mouth and hollered back: 'She's my cock, sir!'

The room fell silent. Then came a ripple of laughter that spread round the room like a Mexican wave until everyone was laughing.

Pointing his finger in my direction, Stowe said: 'You, over here.'

All eyes were on me as I walked across the room, my eyes firmly fixed on Stowe, trying to gauge his response before I reached him. He spun me around to face the crowd.

'This is one of my detective inspectors and a cheeky one at that. Who said you could wear trousers?'

'I'm off duty, sir,' I laughed.

'If you're representing West End Central, the premier division, my *female* officers do not wear trousers on or off duty.'

'Yes, sir,' I said, thinking privately that what I wore off duty was not his business.

It didn't take long for the 'cock' story to spread around the Met.

*

All sorts of cases came my way: murder, arson, blackmail, serious assaults, sexual offences and everything in between. What I never expected was to be working on a case involving rogue officers, but this is exactly what happened before my first year at West End Central was out.

It was November 1984 on a Sunday evening when a uniform colleague I'll call Stella called me at home. She sounded tense.

'Are you on duty tomorrow?' she asked.

'Yes, I am. Why? Is there a problem?'

'I can't speak about it on the phone, but can I come and see you tomorrow afternoon?'

It sounded ominous.

Stella and I knew each other a bit socially through playing squash together a couple of times. She was a good copper who possessed the confidence needed for the cut and thrust of frontline policing and was unfazed by the demands of the job.

I was alone in the DIs' office late the following afternoon when Stella came to see me. She wasted no time getting to the point.

'There's something not right going on with D relief.'

D relief was run by Inspector Smith, who was known as a bit of a maverick. He had recently joined the uniform section at West End Central after working in CID at another station. Stella had joined his team a couple of weeks earlier as an acting sergeant while waiting to go on the sergeant training course after passing her exam.

'What do you mean?'

'On Saturday night we were out on a drugs raid at a club in Greek Street where we did the usual: we crashed in, all the lights went on and everyone who had drugs dropped them to the floor. The drugs that were picked up were all put into a plastic supermarket bag, brought back to the nick and left by Book 66, ready to be booked in.

'When I left the station just before 6.30am the drugs hadn't been recorded yet. So, when I went back on duty the following night, I checked the book again and the drugs still hadn't been entered.'

Book 66 was a huge volume operated by a binder winder, used to record all items seized in a search made under a warrant but whose ownership was unknown. As she was only an acting sergeant, Stella was not allowed to make entries in the book but she could check it.

The bombshell came when Stella explained that she had checked the copy of the warrant used to raid the club, which had been marked up with 'no drugs found'.

'You see the problem . . .' said Stella, looking taut with anxiety.

My stomach sank.

'What quantity of drugs are we talking about, Stella?'

'Small amounts. About half a carrier bag full. Personal use, I'd say – not much more.'

'Are you sure you haven't made a mistake about them not being recorded?'

Stella was emphatic. 'No. I saw them; they were on the counter at the nick waiting to be booked in.'

'What made you check Book 66 when you went to work the next day?'

'There seems to be lots of people coming through the charge room saying the drugs they've been arrested for have been planted. People have claimed that they were stopped by the police in the street and the next thing they know they're being done for possession. You'll always get a few alleging plantings as part of their defence, but there are too many saying exactly the same thing.'

My mind was racing. A bag believed to contain alleged drugs – though the substances had not been analysed – was missing, the inspector in charge said the drugs never existed, and a number of unrelated people had complained of being fitted up that week. This was the first time I'd ever experienced a police officer making a serious allegation of malpractice against a senior officer.

It would be hard to prove whether Smith was guilty of any wrongdoing without finding the bag containing the drugs from the club; but if it was true, it wouldn't have been easy for any officer working under Smith to challenge his instructions. Also, there were probationers in D relief whose policing was being influenced by his leadership.

Our job was hard enough as police officers without the uniform being tainted by a potential scandal. This was not a situation where 'having a word' in Smith's ear – the normal first step – was appropriate. I had no choice. I had to report it.

'Come with me. We're going to see the DCI.'

Stella exhaled deeply; she seemed relieved that she was being taken seriously. We went to the office of DCI Finch. I trusted Stan Finch. As Stella repeated her concerns to him, Finch looked as shocked as I had felt when I first heard them. He left us in his office while he went to check Book 66 to make sure there was no entry for the bag of drugs, then came back and told us the next steps.

'I want each of you to go and write a statement, saying exactly what you've just told me. Do it separately and don't leave the station until you're told.'

CIB2 was part of the complaints-investigation bureau, which was the department that dealt with serious complaints made against police officers.

I wrote up my statement outlining what Stella had told me and handed it to Finch. By this time he had contacted CIB2 officers, who turned up in person later that evening. Finch submitted the statements. I left the station at about 8pm and went home. Things were in motion.

When I came in to work the next day, the atmosphere at the station was palpably different. You could feel the tension in the air. It was clear that word had got around that something serious was afoot.

I had barely settled in when a call came through to say that the uniform chief superintendent wanted to see me. He was not happy. He asked me to reiterate what Stella had told me.

'Why didn't you come to see me first?'

'I reported it to my line manager, sir, which is the correct procedure.'

I got the impression that he thought me naïve for not going to him directly, so that he could deal with it in-house without involving CIB2.

A few days later Stella called me at home. 'Smith and a sergeant took the probationer, Richard, into the police surgeon's room. They were pretty threatening, he said. They told him to say that there were no drugs found on the raid, but he saw them. He told me that he knew what was happening on D relief and wrote everything he saw in his pocketbook in code, so that no one else could read it. Richard's reported it himself. That took some courage.'

Shortly after this incident, Smith, a sergeant and a PC were suspended from duty by CIB2. Suspension involved warrant cards being withdrawn and preventing an officer from carrying on working while the allegations were investigated.

Meanwhile, I was put in charge of the cases surrounding people arrested for drug possession in the week that Stella had identified an unusually high number of people complaining that the drugs were not theirs. Roughly 18 went on to plead not guilty at the initial magistrates' hearing. The fact that they had done so meant that full case files with all the evidence – statements and so on – needed to be prepared for each defendant before trial. I needed to complete the entire batch. Before doing so, I sent a report to the Metropolitan Police solicitors' department in which I suggested that it would be unwise to pursue these cases, in light of the suspensions of the officers and the questions this raised about whether the evidence was safe. In its wisdom the solicitors' department decided that the cases should proceed anyway and told me to appear as officer on the case at each trial. I completed each file but when the cases went to court, the prosecution barrister told the court that no evidence was being offered by the police. Each case was dismissed.

Whether this malpractice had been going on longer than the one week when Stella noticed that something seemed amiss is anybody's guess.

Since the drugs in the bag due to be booked into Book 66 were never submitted, they could not be tested, so Inspector Smith and Police Constable Dell were charged with theft of a plastic bag containing herbal substances belonging to the Metropolitan Police. Alongside a sergeant called Jackson, Smith was also charged with attempting to pervert the course of justice. This was in relation to the incident with Richard in the police surgeon's room.

The job is difficult enough without having bent officers. The pressure to stay silent can be immense. There was a high price to pay for reporting Smith, both subtle and overt. As I walked into the station canteen not long after, all heads turned towards me and then a group of officers stood up and walked out. My stomach lurched and my pace slowed as I took in what had just happened. I couldn't believe it. Colleagues were manifesting their disgust at me for doing my job. It was as if I was the traitor, as if I – and not Smith – had betrayed the uniform. The collective snub from uniform colleagues was a horrible thing to experience and lodged deep. I had completely lost my appetite. I got myself a cup of tea and sought refuge in my office, away from disapproving eyes. It would be my first taste of what was yet to come.

One of my officers told me that graffiti about me had started to appear in the male toilets. I went down to the gents to take a look for myself. The officer wasn't kidding. Someone had scrawled: 'Is the DI a dyke?' on a toilet-cubicle wall. I swallowed hard. My sexuality was common gossip, but I didn't go around talking about it to colleagues, and the graffiti was a clear example of why. I was long used to misogyny and homophobia as part of the work culture; in a calmer and more resilient state I had handled the jibes but the stress of the situation and the hostility I now faced meant that it hit a painful nerve. My sexual orientation suddenly seemed to be weaponized against me: a way of shaming and 'othering' me and making me the problem instead of Smith.

Some uniform colleagues gave me a wide berth, some from discomfort, others with a look in their eyes that seemed to say, 'You're not to be trusted.'

Not everyone joined in with the scapegoating. I have no doubt that Ted Stowe would have supported me, but he had retired by then. Superintendent Trevor Spice was one of the few officers who were very kind to me, as was my Detective Chief Superintendent Michael Purchase. Both seemed to understand the difficulty that myself, Stella and Richard were under and always asked how I was if they saw me in the corridor.

If it was bad for me, I thought, what must it be like for Stella and Richard, who lacked the seniority to protect them from the worst hostility? I wanted to meet with them to ask them how they were doing, but held back for fear of being accused of being part of some conspiracy. I felt as though I was being watched closely, my colleagues waiting for me to trip up. An acute sense of fear started to snowball and paranoia crept in.

I felt isolated at work, and lonely most of the time. I couldn't confide in my parents. I could almost hear my mother, always in fear of anything that would draw attention to the family, saying with a shake of her head: 'You should have kept your mouth shut.'

As the pressure took its toll, my drinking escalated. Less trusting of male colleagues, I ducked team drinks after work in favour of the safe company of women. I would turn up at Anne-Marie's pub and nip upstairs for a quiet drink and a chat away from prying eyes. Nursing a drink seemed to take the edge off my troubles temporarily, so I'd have another and then another. *I can always get a later train*, I'd tell myself to avoid leaving the comfort of the bar.

Sometimes I would arrive at Waterloo Station the worse for wear and descend the staircase to a darkened bar to wait for the next train back to Claygate, the village in Surrey where I now lived. Smoking copious cigarettes, I sat on my own, sipping gin and tonic to drown the misery that I felt.

I remember it well: focusing on the departure board with blurred vision, swaying and feeling like a spinning top. When I stepped onto the train, I would feel the warmth of the railway carriage. With my head resting on the windowpane next to my seat, I would curl my body into a foetal position, hoping to magically disappear from view. A sudden thought about the whereabouts of my warrant card would stir me to unbend myself, hands compulsively checking my coat and suit pockets until I located it. Then I would coil back up into a ball to nurse the shame that engulfed me.

I would wake up dishevelled and disorientated to realize that I was way past my stop and would have to get a taxi all the way back home. These occurrences were never enough for me to stop drinking. Almost exclusively, my life had become work, and drink.

*

My fears for my junior colleagues were spot on. Stella called me to say that she had gone to her car after work to find excreta smeared over the door handle and the tyres deflated. She saw little point in trying to report it.

For me, the cold treatment being meted out focused on my vulnerabilities. I started to hear rumours that Smith's defence was going to try to use my sexuality as a get-out clause by suggesting that Stella and I were in a lesbian relationship and that I had colluded in trumped-up claims to get back at him for some managerial misdemeanour. The word 'dyke' scrawled on the toilet wall loomed large in my mind.

The scab came off old psychological wounds: the reaction of my parents when, aged 30, I'd told them I was gay. Watching my dad cry at the news – though I think this was out of concern about the challenges being gay might pose in my life – and seeing the look of disappointment on my mother's face.

I suspect Mum would have preferred me to fake a heterosexual life, like so many gay people felt compelled to do in the '70s and '80s to avoid being ostracized. But the truth is I never knew what they thought the night I told them, because I was too afraid to ask. I was left with the assumption that my mother was ashamed her daughter was gay; that she wanted her daughter to be 'normal'. I had parked these feelings but now, in the turmoil of what was happening at work, suddenly the sense of shame at being gay felt all-pervading again and proof that I was at fault, somehow wrong.

A few weeks before the trial of the officers, my letterbox rattled at around midnight. I was at home alone. On the mat was a pornographic magazine, packed with lewd lesbian dominatrix images. I felt sick. I ran outside to see if anyone was hanging about, but the coward who had delivered it was nowhere in sight. The following week, another late rattle of the letterbox, another dirty magazine. My paranoia ratcheted up. Things were difficult enough at work and now even home didn't feel safe. My experience did little to encourage any of my gay friends in the Met to come out of the closet.

Increasingly I drank at home to self-medicate, and I soon upped the dose. I just wanted to blot everything out. Hangover after hangover followed. More grist for my shame.

Smith's defence team had been told that Stella, prior to reporting the allegations over the planting of drugs, had received a rollicking from Smith because, in his view, she was taking on more responsibilities than was appropriate for an acting sergeant.

I didn't know whether the defence intended to run with the theory that Stella and I were colluding in some odd act of revenge, but nonetheless, I felt wretched at hearing rumours that my sexuality could be used as a convenient distraction and as an attempt to discredit me and Stella.

My statement would have formed part of the prosecution case when Smith and the other two men were charged, and I expected the prosecution team to call me as a witness. But 12 months later, and a month before the trial, they agreed to hand me over to Smith's defence team to be interviewed. I didn't understand why they did that. For more than an hour, Smith's lawyer quizzed me about what Stella had told me, why she had called me, and the 'exact nature' of our relationship. Were we closer than other colleagues? In other words, were we lovers? It was a fishing exercise, pure and simple.

Later, the defence sent me a copy of my interview to sign, full of inaccuracies about what they had 'heard' me telling them in the interview. In response, I wrote another statement outlining all the anomalies.

On 3 December 1985 I received a letter from the defence solicitor confirming that I would be called to give evidence on behalf of Smith. The trial was scheduled for 9 December, 13 months after Stella made that first phone call to me. I normally enjoyed giving evidence in court. This time, I was riddled with anxiety that my sexuality would be exposed to the public glare. It was one thing for teams I worked with to know that I was gay, but quite another for someone else to tell the world. My main concern was for my parents and the impact this could have on them. My stress levels were off the chart. I smoked even more than usual, lost a stone in weight, struggled to concentrate and endured many a sleepless night.

When the trial finally opened, the three defendants pleaded not guilty. I faced an agonizing wait as the time that I was required to give evidence kept being pushed back. More than once, I could be found hovering over the toilet bowl at West End Central station throwing up with nerves. On the fourth occasion, I received a phone call to tell me that my statement had been accepted and I would no longer be required to give evidence in person. All that worry. For nothing.

Stella gave evidence. She didn't say much about it to me afterwards other than confirming that she'd stuck to her guns. She told me that the defence didn't pursue its speculative revenge theory after all. Richard also took to the witness box. Smith was found guilty by the jury of stealing a police bag containing a herbal substance and conspiring to pervert the course of justice. He received a 12-month prison sentence. PC Dell was also found guilty of the theft of the police bag and received a six-month sentence suspended for two years. Sergeant Jackson was found not guilty of conspiring to pervert the course of justice. Judge Lymbery QC praised Stella and Richard for coming forward to highlight the malpractice in the first place. The judge would not speculate about where the drugs were going and told the defendants: 'If it was for some kind of corrupt purpose, then the sentences would have been substantial indeed.'

I was in the canteen buying a cup of tea when a uniform inspector approached me and looked at me in disgust. 'Smith. He's gone to prison. A married man with four kids. Hope you're pleased with yourself.'

He turned his back on me and walked away. Other than the catering staff behind the counter, no one else was around. I put my cup down, went back to my office, grabbed my coat and left the building. I had to get out of there.

The cold December air was just what I needed to clear my thoughts. I walked up Savile Row to Regent Street, smoking a cigarette, with the familiar sound of Christmas carols in the background. Festive lights illuminated the West End and the scent of hot chestnuts pervaded the air, but joy was the last thing I was feeling. Tears rolled down my face as I thought of Smith boxed in a narrow cubicle in the back of a prison van on his way to begin his sentence. It was grim, and it was sad, not least for his family. But he had made a choice, one which let him, his family and the Metropolitan Police down.

I couldn't get my head around the attitude of some colleagues who seemed to believe that warranted officers who committed wrongdoing should be protected from facing the music. We were trained to follow the rules and uphold the law. We arrested and charged fathers and mothers, sons and daughters every day. Many of them ended up in jail. But it seemed that when it came to our own behaviour, different rules were supposed to apply.

It had been 13 hellish months of anxiety and I was relieved that it was now over. By the time the case ended, Richard had passed his probation and transferred to a different unit, but I heard that he left the service not long after. Stella, meanwhile, moved on to a new posting as a sergeant. On arrival, she was told by her peers that there was a 'trust' issue as a result of her reporting a senior colleague. Hopefully, they said darkly, she would never be in a position where she needed to call for 'urgent assistance' on the streets because there wouldn't be any forthcoming. Stella had the courage to stick it out. Like all gossip in the police, life moves on, as do officers, and the memory of the story eventually fades.

My annual appraisal for 1985, written by Superintendent Spice, acknowledged that I'd had a 'difficult year' but had got on with the job regardless 'in the manner we have come to expect of her'. In his view, I had, he wrote, 'absorbed the pressures well'.

Not as well as Spice seemed to think – but then again, I hadn't confided in him or anyone else at work about how tough I had found it, for fear that this would be viewed as weakness on my part. It had been the worst experience of my entire life. Yes, I had coped, like the proverbial swan paddling furiously beneath the water line – but only just. I was skilled in stuffing down difficult emotions that I should have paid attention to; but as my stress increased, alcohol became more of a prop than ever before, though I hardly noticed it at the time. A glass (or two, then three) of something strong became the default route to numb the feelings and hold it together. It didn't occur to me then that I was storing up trouble for myself, nor that the traumatic time I had experienced and tried to bury would lurk within me for years before finally surfacing.

My other coping strategy was far more beneficial: I applied to join a women's group called Network, which had been founded by a businesswoman called Irene Harris after a frustrating experience at a servicemen's club. She and Odette Hallowes, the French wartime resistance heroine, were refused a drink at the club bar because they weren't with a male companion. Fed up that there were no clubs for women in senior management to network in the way that men did, Irene created one.

Network enabled me to meet some fascinating women, many of whom could relate to the sense of being isolated in their profession simply because they were women: barristers, doctors, dentists, journalists and businesswomen. We were all in the same boat.

I was the only senior Met officer in the mix, which I later learned had initially raised suspicion. Some members wondered whether I was there to spy on them and report back to the Met. They soon realized that I was one of them. It was refreshing to be among like-minded women operating in the male-dominated senior echelons of their respective professions. No one cared that I was gay, no one side-lined me for it, nor made me feel uncomfortable. It proved a valuable resource during those grey days and helped me to take stock of my situation: I wasn't going mad after all.

CHAPTER 11

DIPPERS, HOOKERS AND BLACKMAILERS

The case with Smith had severely blighted my first posting as a DI and felt like a far cry from my hopes when I had first arrived at West End Central. I had to keep it together and get on with the job, but my emotions had taken a real battering. Thankfully, the range and number of offences that landed on our watch served as a useful distraction.

Working in the heart of the capital city brought with it a variety of criminal activity in an area surrounded by designer stores, street markets, pubs, restaurants and theatres. The Crime Squad, which was the route for trainee detectives, was constantly busy working the streets on the lookout for pickpockets, known as 'dippers', and store thieves, some of whom would fly in from European countries and South America to work the West End for a few days and then fly out again. Dippers flooded to Oxford Street to steal from the pockets of unsuspecting shoppers. Professional shoplifting teams known as 'hoisters' would descend on the stores to steal the most expensive items they could find – designer handbags being a popular choice. It wasn't just central London they 'worked'; they could be in Oxford Street in the morning and caught in another store in St Albans in the afternoon.

The West End was also home to the 'seedier' sides of life, involving prostitutes and rent boys (as young male sex workers were then known) operating in the vicinity of the Wimpy bar in Piccadilly Circus – an area crudely referred to by the station as the 'meat rack'. There were a couple of pubs nearby known to be frequented after work by ostensibly straight men hoping to pick up gay men for sex before going home to their wives and family. The irony of society's homophobia was never lost on me.

A dedicated Clubs and Vice Unit, separate to CID, policed the Soho clubs to make sure that they were compliant with the licensing laws. The unit was staffed by a team of officers from the uniform section, although they worked in plain clothes. CID officers, on the other hand, were not allowed to enter clubs in the West End to deal with any matters regarding licensing. This came under an edict passed following some notorious historical incidents of police corruption in the 1960s and '70s, when a few high-ranking CID detectives ended up on the payroll of a Soho kingpin. Commander Wally Virgo was sent to jail before his conviction was later quashed on a technicality. Ken Drury, the head of the Flying Squad, also ended up in jail.

The long-ago sins of disgraced detectives were not forgotten and, rightly or wrongly, officers from the uniform section were seen as less corruptible. The Clubs and Vice Unit also policed the prostitutes and pimps operating in Soho. If a detective needed to enter a club to investigate a crime, we would have to seek permission from the Clubs and Vice Unit first.

A common crime committed by the working girls was the practice of 'clipping'. This involved asking a potential customer for money up front to secure a room where they could go and have the sexual encounter. The sex worker would ask the client to meet her again a few minutes later and would turn up as arranged, to assuage any doubt that she could be trusted. Lo and behold, she would then say that she needed more money because the landlord had raised the deposit. The punter, believing that this was the final hurdle before getting his end away, duly handed over more money. Cue the woman disappearing into the alleyways of Soho, never to be seen again by her unwitting victim.

Reports of this would surface at the station on a pretty regular basis. I was amazed by the lack of shame the men had in coming forward to report it. Part of me thought that being short-changed was all they deserved. I remember a victim being called by the Crown Prosecution Service all the way back from Australia to give evidence against a woman charged with clipping.

It was on the morning of 17 April 1984, not long after I started at West End Central, that a uniformed officer came running into the CID office shouting that a female police officer had been shot in St James's Square. I ran downstairs to book out a police radio and raced to the square, less than a mile away, thinking of all the female officers at West End Central and wondering who the victim might be. When I arrived, the area was blocked off by cordons. I was told to wait until the mobile control vehicle arrived. I could see a number of police hats lying in the road, including the white-topped style that WPCs wore at the time.

An armed officer already on the scene told me that there had been a small demonstration held that morning outside the Libyan People's Bureau – previously known as the Libyan Embassy – and that shots had been fired from the windows of the building onto the demonstrators, 11 of whom were struck. WPC Yvonne Fletcher was shot and fell to the ground. She was rushed to hospital.

An eerie silence now pervaded. All streets surrounding St James's and beyond had been closed off to traffic and pedestrians.

The mobile police control van arrived a few minutes later. Police had taken over a bank on the corner of Charles II Street, which was to become the main HQ. The officer in charge of a major incident is named 'Gold', and that morning it was Ted Stowe, as commander of the West End. I reported my presence to him. By this time, we had learned that WPC Fletcher had died on the hospital operating table. Stowe's usual confidence was replaced by a deflated expression, his face on the verge of tears after the news came in. WPC Fletcher was just 25 years old.

'It's going to be a long job,' Stowe told me. 'Hostage negotiators and D11 Firearms will manage the terrorist situation. I'd rather you get back to the station and look after the CID.'

I felt a huge sense of powerlessness but Stowe was right in his assessment: there was nothing for a divisional DI to do here. This was the job of specialist officers and experts in terrorism. As I headed back to the station, I wondered what the officers from Bow Street Police Station were feeling at the loss of one of their colleagues. The death of Yvonne Fletcher made me sick to my stomach, and I didn't even know her.

When I returned to the station, a heaviness hung in the air. A young officer killed in the line of duty was devastating. She was one of us. It was a chilling reminder that this could happen to any of us as police officers. Despite the dangers of the job, nobody goes to work expecting not to return home. It was terrifying.

The news media later revealed more details about what happened that day. Around 70 anti-Gaddafi protesters had turned up outside the embassy, as had rival protesters who supported the Libyan leader. Uniform officers from Bow Street had put up barricades and policed the event. WPC Yvonne Fletcher and her work partner PC John Murray had their backs to the embassy building as they faced the rival demonstrators. The hail of bullets came from sub-machine guns pointing out from the embassy windows.

The late filmmaker Michael Winner wrote to *The Times* newspaper, suggesting a memorial be erected in Yvonne's memory in St James's Square.

'It would serve to indicate that not everyone in this country takes seeming pleasure in attacking the Police in the execution of their difficult duties, but that most of us regard their conduct and bravery, under a whole series of endless and varied provocations, as demonstrably noble and worthy of our thanks,' he wrote, according to the Police Memorial Trust, which Winner set up the same year.

On 1 February 1985, a stone memorial was erected in St James's Square with the inscription: 'Here fell W PC Yvonne Fletcher 17 April 1984'.

In 2015, a man called Saleh Ibrahim Mabrouk, a former minister in Gaddafi's government, was arrested by the police in connection with WPC Fletcher's murder. Two years later, the Metropolitan Police said it was not possible to bring a prosecution against Mabrouk for conspiracy to murder because national security matters had prevented evidence held by the intelligence services from being handed over. Mabrouk was released without charge.

A police statement reported in *The Times* on 17 May 2017 said:

We believe our investigation has identified enough material to identify those responsible for W PC Fletcher's murder if it could be presented to a court.

However, the key material has not been made available for use in court in evidential form for reasons of national security. Therefore, without this material, and following a review of all the evidence that was available to the prosecutors, the Crown Prosecution Service – who we have worked closely with throughout – have informed us that there is insufficient admissible evidence to charge the man.

No one was ever charged for W PC Fletcher's murder.

PC John Murray, who had held Yvonne as she lay dying, had vowed to get justice for her and fulfilled his promise in 2021. Murray, who experienced post-traumatic stress disorder following that fateful day, decided to take a civil action against Mabrouk in the High Court for assault and battery. The burden of proof in a civil claim is based on the balance of probabilities, rather than the higher threshold of 'beyond reasonable doubt' required in a criminal case. A High Court judge ruled that Mabrouk was a 'prime mover in the plan to shoot the anti-Gaddafi demonstrators and, if necessary, any police officer who was in the way'.

In his judgement, Justice Martin Spencer said:

> I am satisfied on the balance of probabilities that there existed a common design to respond to the planned anti-Gaddafi protest by using violence, and specifically by firing shots at or in the direction of the protesters. Witness statements and statements made by Mr Mabrouk demonstrate not only his knowledge of the common design, but also his views of the inevitability of that response.

He went on to say:

> Coupled with his position as one of the few leaders of the Revolutionary Committee controlling the People's Bureau, it amounts to confirmation of the common design to fire upon the demonstrators, in which he was an active participant. On that basis, I am satisfied that on the balance of probabilities the defendant is jointly liable for the shooting of WPC Yvonne Fletcher on the doctrine of common design.

Murray claimed only a nominal £1 in damages, which he was awarded. His aim had been to find those responsible for the shooting of Yvonne.

Mabrouk, who did not to attend the hearing, denied any involvement in the shooting.

The nature of the job meant that none of us had much space to reflect on traumatic events such as the death of a fellow officer – or indeed anyone else. Crime didn't stop for our benefit, or the public's.

*

You never knew what you were going to be dealing with next as a police officer, but even I was surprised to be approached by the Met's press bureau to work on a TV series. The brief was to liaise with a production team at Thames Television for an episode of the popular ITV police series *The Bill*. First broadcast in 1984, the show gave a very realistic representation of station life, with good attention to detail, which I soon found out was due to the use of police advisers to help make things as authentic as possible. I loved watching *The Bill*, so I was delighted to be asked.

The storyline involved a rape, so I provided them with a sexual-offences kit – a brown box that contained swabs, blood vials, two combs to take hair samples, and the brown sheet of paper to collect debris from clothing. I also spoke to the writer to ensure that the script and the handling of the rape victim by police officers was true to life. *What a great way of reaching the public about what we do and how we do it*, I thought then. A very senior colleague didn't agree.

'I don't think that you should be helping a TV company like this,' he said. 'It's fiction. It's a waste of time.'

'With all due respect, sir, I don't think it is,' I retorted. 'I was adding accuracy and authenticity to the storyline, so that what people see is closer to the way that we actually do things. And millions of people are watching this.'

Away from the world of fiction, real policing was keeping me occupied.

When a call came in alerting us to a serious stabbing at a shoe shop in Bond Street, I ran to the location to find a young man lying in the entrance being treated by paramedics. Steven Hindley was dying in the doorway of the shop. Uniformed officers arrived on the scene soon after. Steven's colleagues said that a man had come into the shop to complain about shoes that he had bought the week before. They were hurting his feet, he'd claimed. He wanted to return them. Steven explained that as the shoes had been worn, a return was not possible. The irate customer responded by producing a knife concealed in the sleeve of his coat and stabbed him fatally in the neck. The killer was quickly arrested at a bus stop in Piccadilly. His name was John Wooder, a US army veteran of the Korean War.

Steven's parents lived outside London and rushed down by train but by the time they arrived their son was dead. They were devastated. I drove the father to the mortuary to identify his son. For me, watching the shock and grief of someone having to identify their loved one was the most distressing part of the job.

Steven was wearing a gold chain on the day he died, which was broken during the attack. I went to a jeweller to get his chain fixed so that I could return it to his parents. Of course, what they really wanted was their son back. The sadness on their face as I handed them the gold chain was heartbreaking.

Steven had left home that morning fully expecting to go home to his parents that night, as he did at the end of every working day. Instead, his young life ended brutally and abruptly at the hands of a military veteran scarred by what he had witnessed at a time of war. Wooder's defence team successfully showed that he was suffering from a mental disorder; a plea of manslaughter on the grounds of diminished responsibility was accepted and he was sent to Broadmoor.

*

It was during my time at West End Central that I encountered my first case of blackmail. A wealthy businessman turned up at the police station to report that his mistress had received a bunch of photographs through her letterbox. The pictures were of a sexual nature. The man spoke to two detective colleagues but gave a false name, refused to give further details and then left. He came back to the station a couple of days later after receiving photographs at his office, and this time spoke to me and my colleague D C Roger Glass. His name was Mr Ogilvy, and his mistress was a Ms Vine. The photographs of them together had been taken at a flat that Ogilvy had rented to conduct their affair. He could date them to their last encounter a week before. He knew this, he said, because Vine was wearing lingerie that she had not worn before.

Ogilvy told me that this had been followed up by a telephone call on his private line at work, a number that only a few people knew about. The man on the call demanded £100,000 in used notes and threatened Ogilvy: 'If you don't pay, we'll tell your wife, children, newspapers and all your friends. If you pay, you'll get the prints and negatives back. Get this money together and we'll ring you on Wednesday with arrangements.'

A hundred thousand pounds was a vast sum in 1985 – the equivalent of around £273,000 today. While the businessman was rich, most of his wealth was invested and he couldn't lay his hands on that sum immediately. It seemed evident to me that the mistress was part of the conspiracy. Ogilvy didn't want to believe she was involved, though; it was too much for him to bear.

Ogilvy's relationship with Vine had begun a few years before when he contacted an agency that provided 'high class' women escorts. Ogilvy had requested her regularly and eventually persuaded her to give up the escort work by promising to support her financially. He paid the fees at her children's private school and often took her on expensive business trips.

Ogilvy had evidently fallen for the woman hook, line and sinker. He was sensible enough to come to the police to seek advice, but was in two minds about whether to proceed with a formal complaint – without which it was impossible for us to proceed.

But the questions we asked made him start to suspect her. After all, the 'love nest' was supposedly known only to the pair of them. And how did the blackmailer know both the address and his telephone number, since few people knew about the latter?

We pointed out the obvious pitfall if he chose to go ahead without police involvement. 'If you pay up, you'll never know if she was involved or not,' I told him. 'And it will be on your mind every time you see her.'

That did the trick. Ogilvy decided to officially report the blackmail. I arranged with the technical-support unit at New Scotland Yard for a tape recorder to be placed on his private telephone line at his office. I asked him to make arrangements to meet his mistress and tell her he had negotiated a price for the return of both the photos and the negatives. Fitted with a body tape recorder, Ogilvy told Vine that he had told the blackmailer he could only obtain £25,000 cash from the bank, and the blackmailer had agreed to this reduced sum.

A couple of days later, Vine telephoned him to say that she'd received a phone call from the blackmailer with instructions to place the money in a bag and leave it inside her car, which was parked outside her north London home. Ogilvy agreed to deliver the money to the vehicle later that day. In the meantime, cash was placed inside a briefcase fitted with an alarm and a body tape put on Ogilvy once more. I gathered together an arrest team from the office and called for a surveillance team from New Scotland Yard to follow Ogilvy's car to Vine's address. Surveillance teams were made up of highly trained specialized officers who rarely got involved in the arrests but kept observations on criminals, many of whom were 'surveillance aware' and would make certain manoeuvres to check if they were being followed. In this case, surveillance would provide continuity of the bag's journey. Everything was in place.

Ogilvy turned up at the appointed time of 5.30pm, placed the money in the car boot and left. We watched the house for several hours – so long I became desperate for the loo, but as the leader of the team I couldn't afford to go anywhere in case the alarm went off. Five hours passed. It wasn't until 10.30pm that Vine came out of her house, went to the car, retrieved the briefcase and took it inside. Shortly after, the alarm was activated. Someone had opened the case. It was all units go!

I knocked loudly on the door.

'Who is it?' said a woman's voice.

'Police.'

Vine opened the door. Shock was etched across her face as she let us in. I showed my warrant card.

'I'm DI Malton from West End Central station, and this is DC Roger Glass,' I said. 'We're investigating an allegation of blackmail. I understand that you took possession of a briefcase containing money this afternoon?'

'Yes, I did.'

'Where are the briefcase and money now?'

Vine regained her composure. Cool and collected, she said: 'The briefcase is in the bathroom and the money is in my handbag. A note was pushed through my door earlier, telling me to remove the money from the briefcase and put it in a bag.'

We'd been watching the house since Ogilvy had made the drop; not one person had come to her door.

'Can I see the note, please?' I asked.

'I burned the note and put it down the sink.' *Fast thinking on her part*, I thought.

I instructed one of the team to dismantle the sink in an effort to retrieve the note, which I knew didn't exist.

'I understand you have some photos?'

Vine went to her bedroom with me following close behind. She lifted the mattress and retrieved an envelope containing a number of photographs depicting her and Ogilvy having sex. She handed them over to me and I arrested her on suspicion of blackmail.

We had to make arrangements for someone to be with her children while we took her back to the police station for questioning. By this time, it was well after midnight. While Vine waited in a police cell, I went to my desk and reviewed all the evidence we had to date to prepare my line of questioning. The interview, which I conducted with DC Glass, began at 1.20am and ran on until 6.45am, with breaks. Vine stuck to her story throughout: she denied that she was one of the conspirators and insisted that she was a victim. I drove home at 7am for some brief and restless shut-eye. Vine, meanwhile, still holed up in the cell, used the time to mull things over.

When I returned to the station to interview Vine again at lunchtime, she had changed her tune. She confessed to setting up the blackmail sting with a male friend, an out-of-work actor who was in need of cash. He had taken the photographs and made the calls to Ogilvy. Vine insisted that she had only agreed in order to help the actor out of his financial mire. She personally wasn't interested in the money, she said.

I arranged for the actor to be arrested. A rather pompous character, he claimed that the blackmail plot had germinated from an idea that he had for a film script. As usual, the phrase 'as thick as thieves' bore no reality to how criminals behave when caught: each blamed the other and minimized their own part in the crime. Vine claimed that she had not expected Ogilvy to fall for it and certainly hadn't believed the idea of setting up a blackmail sting was serious. This from the woman who had taken the money from the boot and opened the case. She had no doubt witnessed first-hand the stress that Ogilvy had been put under as a result of the calls and the mail drop.

As for the victim, he was devastated by the confirmation that his beloved mistress had betrayed him in this way. Ogilvy had placed hope against hope that his hunch was wrong. Given the secrecy of his affair, he had no one to talk to about it, not even his friends or relatives.

He sought me out several times so that he could talk about it over a meal. My own sense of the situation was that it was a simple story: a trade gone wrong. Vine wanted the finer things in life and Ogilvy was her route to them: the first-class travel, five-star hotels, the clothes he paid for, the school fees. As for Ogilvy, he clearly loved her.

At the end of the trial at the Old Bailey, I called Ogilvy from the court to tell him the result.

'They got two years each.'

'I know,' he said.

'How could you know? I'm still at court.'

'I was in the court, sitting in the public gallery above,' he said. 'I dressed up with glasses and a cloth cap. I had to be there . . . It's like going to the theatre watching a play act out and not knowing the end.' Some theatre.

The case generated a lot of interest. The cartoonist JAK in the London *Evening Standard* worked up the image of a couple signing into a hotel with the caption: 'That'll be £50 for the room and £100,000 for the photographs!' I called the newspaper and asked if JAK would be kind enough to sign a copy for me, which he did. It was a bit of a coup if one of your cases inspired JAK.

I would have missed out on this and some other unusual cases if I'd taken one particular opportunity that came my way not long after the court case with Smith and the other two officers. I had received a telephone call from a detective chief superintendent who asked me if I was interested in having my name put forward to be bodyguard to the young HRH Prince William, as he was about to start nursery school. My mind flooded with possibilities. Could my sexuality draw press attention and become a distraction, interfering with the low profile this job required? Spending all day at nursery school didn't appeal either. All things considered, I declined politely. I have no regrets about this decision.

In my private life, I continued drinking to the same extent that I had done during those stressful 13 months when the trouble with Inspector Smith was going on. Somehow a switch had been flicked that I couldn't turn off again. Deep down, I knew that I had become increasingly dependent on alcohol as an emotional prop, but I couldn't stop. It helped to blot out the unpleasant feelings that lurked. At home, when I picked up a bottle of gin, it wasn't a pub measure that I was pouring; by now it was the equivalent of half a glass, topped up with a bit of tonic. As it went down, I felt its warmth on my throat like soothing honey and a pleasant kick in my brain that turned off the inescapable stress. A sense of completeness would wash over me temporarily, and I would top up my glass when it began to subside. The following day I would wake up with a dry mouth, a heavy head and an even heavier heart. I vowed that I would cut down or stop. The days that I didn't drink I felt good; the days that I succumbed I would feel ashamed. I no longer felt in control of alcohol. No one at work had a clue that I was struggling personally – and to be fair, I hardly ever admitted it to myself.

I felt a dis-ease that I couldn't quite put my finger on. You would have thought that the confidence I'd gained by meeting with likeminded women at Network would have improved my self-esteem sufficiently to make me feel more grounded in myself as a woman. Instead, I just felt more of a fraud. After the fallout of the Smith incident, I was ready to do anything to avoid experiencing that feeling of social isolation at work again; but deep down I was more conscious than ever of not being my true self. My persona at work relied on the idea of me as someone who gave as good as she got and could handle the heat of the locker-room culture. I thought that this was the only way to survive in the job. Admitting how I really felt was not something that I could bring myself to do. I feared that it would smack of weakness, of losing my bottle.

*

Two years into my time at West End Central I was seconded to Paddington Police Station to work as the deputy senior investigating officer on an arson in a five-storey Georgian building in west London. Two people who were trapped in a top-floor attic flat had died. During the investigation, a senior officer asked me if I would speak to a woman who wanted to talk in confidence about something sensitive. Her name was Louise and she was the wife of a police officer stationed elsewhere in London. Although I'd never met him, I was aware of who he was.

Louise explained that her husband was wielding excessive control over her: burning her arms with cigarettes and leaving her a minimal amount of money each day to feed her and their baby. The woman showed me the burn marks. 'I've got a child to think about. We live in a police flat; I've got nowhere else to go. I don't know what to do.'

She was in a terrible state. Here was another dispiriting case of a cop perpetrating a crime. This was in the days before domestic-violence units were set up to tackle this endemic problem. I checked whether her husband had been the subject of any police complaints in the past. Sure enough, a complaint had been made against him by a suspect who claimed that the officer had assaulted them when they were in station custody by burning a cigarette upon their arm. It was this person's word against the officer's and the complaint could never be substantiated through independent evidence. Louise was clearly terrified and felt that she couldn't press charges against her husband. This was not uncommon in abusive relationships, but it meant there was nothing that we could do formally. I was concerned for her, but also by the fact that a pattern was emerging regarding her husband's behaviour at home and at work. I didn't want to leave it there.

Louise was too afraid to leave him and seemed to want us to have a word with him instead, but unless she made a formal complaint our hands were tied. In the course of our meeting, she told me that her husband was intent on becoming a detective and saw joining the freemasons as his route to success. The only thing that I could do was to write a report about her allegation that would ensure there was a permanent record of it on his file, which he wouldn't get to see. Any further complaints from whatever quarter would then hopefully be taken more seriously. And senior officers would see it when he was considered for another position. I learned a little while later that he had resigned from the police force. I didn't hear from Louise again.

As for me, I returned to West End Central after the inquest of the two fire victims. Though we had a prime suspect for the fire, we were not able to prove he was responsible. My experience was that arson attacks were the least rewarding cases to deal with. They were the hardest to prove. One can only hope that nowadays, with CCTV and more elaborate forensic tools, it is not such an uphill task as it was then.

In 1987, almost three years after arriving at Savile Row, the time had come to move along. My experience with complex cases and my ability to handle them boosted my professional confidence. I entertained the idea of a posting to Counter Terrorism or Criminal Intelligence as my next step.

My deliberations were interrupted by a call from Commander Stockwell, who suggested that I join the Met's Company Fraud Squad, based in Holborn, where he had recently worked. He saw it as a good move for my CV. I wasn't terribly keen, but I valued Stockwell's advice, so I packed up my things and headed to a world where men in smart suits would be the prime suspects.

CHAPTER 12
UNUSUAL SUSPECTS

The Company Fraud Squad, better known as S06, was spread across a huge office block in Lamb's Conduit Street adjacent to Holborn Police Station in central London. Below us and quite separate was the 'Aliens' department, a rather astonishing term then used to describe immigrants who were required to register their London address with the police.

The Fraud Squad was staffed with police officers from the Met and the City of London Police working out of different offices to investigate the myriad manifestations of fraud. 'Long firm' fraud, for example, once routinely used by organized crime gangs in the 1960s, involved setting up a trading company and legitimately placing a large number of small orders; the invoices for these orders would be paid promptly, thus aiding the new company's credit rating and its credibility. Once the firm was established as a reliable outfit to do business with, the criminals would place large orders on credit and disappear with the goods.

Another team investigated advance-fee fraud – a confidence trick that persuaded businesses or individuals to pay an up-front fee on the promise of receiving expensive goods and services of a greater value. Often these kinds of fraudsters appealed to investors in search of a bargain, who were promised huge returns on their investment. The saying 'If it looks too good to be true, it probably is' is right. As in all frauds, the only loser was the investor left significantly out of pocket.

The team that I joined dealt with multiple share fraud relating to the privatization of some state-owned companies by Margaret Thatcher's Conservative government during the 1980s. British Telecommunications had been the first in line and in 1984 just over 50 per cent of shares were sold to the public as ordinary people were encouraged to become shareholders for the first time. I joined the squad in December 1986, the same month that the state energy firm British Gas was floated on the London Stock Market. A massive advertising campaign – with the famous slogan 'Tell Sid' – was launched to persuade the general public to buy shares in the company, making many first-time shareholders. The scheme had high visibility through an advertising blitz via billboards, newspapers and television.

The minimum allocation of 100 shares was priced at 135 pence per share, and you could apply for up to a maximum of 5,000.

While the sales prospectus categorically stated that each individual could submit one application for an allocation of shares, many ignored it and made multiple share applications regardless. This was despite clearly written warnings that doing so was a criminal offence under Section 15 of the Theft Act 1968. As the new detective inspector, I was tasked with investigating every multiple share application.

Touche Ross, a huge accounting firm based in High Holborn, was brought in by the government to 'police' the flotation of British Gas following lessons learned from the sale of BT shares. For the first time, computers were used to cross-check names and addresses to reveal possible share-dealing rings and individuals. Suspicious applications began to come through in early 1987.

The firm allocated a huge room to the investigation, filled with boxes containing 'suspicious' applications with cheques attached that revealed multiple addresses. The applications where fraud 'rings' were suspected were put in piles. For each stack of suspicious applications, Touche Ross would prepare a schedule outlining the number of applications, names and addresses plus payment details, which they would hand over to us.

The job took me and my partner, Detective Constable Trevor Rawlinson, all over the UK. A tall, slim, self-contained man with a dry sense of humour, Trevor was a real perk of the job. He had more years than me in age and service, and was a meticulous and conscientious detective for whom I quickly developed huge respect. Usefully – for me, at least – he barely drank and offered to do all the driving cross-country.

The main task was to identify the ringleaders, who would invariably have many accounts in their names at a number of banks. We looked at groups of applications that were made under different names and registered at different addresses, but that were all financed by only one or two individuals. In other cases, some people would make more than one application from their home address, using different names. Sometimes, the perpetrators used the names of their budgies, cats and dogs. Trevor grouped cases together based on their geographical location. He loved to plan the journey, book the hotels and make the appointments with the relevant banks.

We checked out all the listed addresses for applicants and bank accounts, then returned to London with the evidence gathered. We would invite the prime suspect to attend Holborn Police Station for interview. By and large, the majority of culprits we came across were middle-class professional men who were intelligent enough to understand that they were breaking the law. They seemed to think that the law did not apply to them. They were mistaken.

Without exception, witnesses and suspects assumed that Trevor, being the man, and older, was the detective inspector. I got used to it. Trevor would pause, take one step back and gesture to me with a deferential sweep of his arm in my direction. 'This is the detective inspector,' he would say. It happened with such regularity that Trevor put in an increasingly polished performance.

Like any good detective, a Fraud Squad investigator needed to be thorough in the preparation of files to present a case: laying out clearly every step of the investigation and every piece of evidence gathered that led to charges being brought.

When it came to the interview stage, I would push the share prospectus across the table and flick the pages one by one. 'Can you see there, where it says, "Only one application can be made"? Look, it's on every other page. Which part of that didn't you understand?'

More often than not, the answer revealed a particular line of thinking: 'I saw the warning but I thought that they just had to put it in there but were more interested in the selling of the shares.'

A stockbroker named Stuart Johnson allegedly masterminded the submission of 166 applications for hundreds of thousands of shares, using the addresses of several properties in southwest London that he owned. He also roped his cousin Tom in to help him.

This was a biggie and I wanted to secure the best evidence before we questioned the two suspects. It required Trevor and me to make a vast number of enquiries: checking out all of the addresses listed, taking statements from some of the occupants and making checks on the account holders at the respective banks.

To avoid the two men talking to each other, we needed to make the arrests simultaneously. I arranged for two arrest teams to go to the suspects' homes with a search warrant. Johnson seemed to be the driver of the alleged fraud, so I went with the team to his house only to be told by his father at the door that he had left the country for business in the States. We went in and searched anyway.

Tom was arrested and brought back to the station. He was very forthcoming, admitting his part in filling out the false applications using the addresses of a number of properties owned by his cousin. He had been paid handsomely by Johnson for his efforts. I charged Tom with attempted theft by deception. After Tom pleaded guilty in court, I was asked to give the antecedent history of the defendant, together with any criminal history, and confirmed that this was his first offence. He received a large fine equivalent to the money he'd received from his cousin.

The problem was that the bigger fish had swum away. I circulated Johnson's name and details on the police national computer as a suspect wanted for interview over alleged fraud should he ever return to the country. It was the first and only time that we were unable to interview a share-fraud suspect.

It was some years later before I heard of Johnson again, by which time I had moved on to pastures new. In 1993, I was contacted by a firm of solicitors in the US acting on behalf of a major company seeking an injunction to block Johnson's battle to wrest control of its board by replacing the existing chairman. The solicitors had discovered Johnson's failure to report to the Securities and Exchange Commission that he was subject to a criminal investigation back in the UK.

They asked me if I would fly over to New York to confirm in a federal court that Johnson was wanted back in the UK, so that he could be interviewed for his alleged part in a multiple share application dating back to 1987.

After a flurry of exchanges between the American solicitors and the Metropolitan Police, I was given the green light to go. The federal court seemed far less formal than the Old Bailey and other London Crown

Courts I was used to. From my seat, which was parallel to the judge's, I could see that he was wearing jeans and white trainers under his formal black gown.

I explained to the judge that the police were keen to speak to Johnson because he was suspected of being the major figure in a share ring involving numerous applications. The judge seemed delighted to have a Scotland Yard detective in his courtroom. Smiling, he picked up on the fact that I had planned the raid on Johnson's house for 5 in the morning.

'That's the middle of the night for me,' he quipped. 'If you raided my house at that time, I'd be fast asleep.'

He seemed an affable man with a sense of humour, so I thought I'd run with it.

'Exactly, your honour! I rest my case.'

I heard later that the federal judge blocked Johnson's bid to take control of the company and ordered an injunction. There were times when my job felt pretty surreal. Had I known during my time in SO6 that it would lead me across the pond some years later I'm not sure I would have believed it.

Back in the UK, we continued to deal with a range of cases big and small: from fraud rings to the people who chanced their luck. There was a wealthy individual in the agricultural industry who, like many before him in the interview chair, believed that the administrators would turn a blind eye to what he was doing and was devastated to be called in for police questioning. Deeply embarrassed, he was completely open about the applications he had made. Here was a man of huge repute about to be charged with a criminal offence for the first time in his life. He received a large financial penalty.

On the other side of the social spectrum was a case where it appeared that almost everyone living on a sprawling council estate just outside

London had applied for British Gas shares. The masterminds behind the operation were two savvy working-class men I'll call Tony and Ray. They were both in their early thirties and had worked brilliantly as a team. Tony, well-known in the area through his involvement with the local football team, persuaded locals on the estate to receive share-acceptance letters at their home addresses and hand them over to him in exchange for £10. Ray, the quieter of the two, seemed to be the one with the more financial nous. He organized the logistics and the writing of the cheques for each application. The fact that all the cheques were financed by only a few bank accounts registered in either Ray or Tony's name was what triggered the computer to alert us to a suspected share ring.

You had to take your hat off to the duo for their efforts. As I started to prepare the case against them before the arrest, I could see that they had worked extremely hard to fill in hundreds of application forms purporting to be residents from the estate. Once we had logged all the cheques and secured statements from some of the estate residents, we coordinated swoops at the homes of the two suspects in the early morning. Tony and Ray were described as likeable characters by some of the residents they'd roped in to help and I formed the same impression of the pair when we interviewed them. The case went to court and both received a prison sentence.

*

We came across some very unusual suspects at times. There was a schoolteacher who generated a large volume of fraudulent applications using the names of pupils at his school. His motive was to support his daughter through university. Unfortunately, when someone who holds a position of trust in their employment is convicted of a crime, the police have a responsibility to report their conviction to the relevant authority. In this case, I had to report his conviction to the education authority, which resulted in him losing his job – a high price to pay indeed.

As we worked our way through the British Gas cases, I was still failing to get a handle on my drinking. Trevor knew that I liked a drink after work. He rarely stayed for Friday-night team drinks, but I did. When we'd catch up on the following Monday morning, and I would tell him about having knocked back too many and waking up on Saturday with a banging headache, he would roll his eyes at me. 'You just can't say no when I'm not around, can you?' He didn't realize that whether I said 'yes' or 'no' to a drink depended on how I felt about myself on a given day. When my resolve collapsed – as it routinely did – pressing the 'fuck it' button felt like a release. The thought of having a drink seemed exciting – exhilarating even – but this feeling would soon be replaced by shame and remorse in the cold light of day. I would look at Trevor with envy over the way that he could take a drink or leave it. Alcohol had a power over me. I hated my need of it. Perhaps Trevor noticed more than he said, but he chose not to pierce my carefully constructed persona of a woman who could handle anything.

I experienced a jolt when a new detective inspector joined the team in preparation for the sale of British Airways. It was none other than Phil, my nemesis from the Flying Squad. On his first day, wasting no time picking up where he had left off, he told everyone in the office that I had been known as 'the Tart' on the Flying Squad and that I was a 'lezza' and not safe to be left around other people's girlfriends.

I pulled my chair back noisily and stood up looking squarely at Phil: 'You. Outside.'

He looked a bit taken aback and followed me to the corridor. A good foot smaller than him, I stood up on my tiptoes to gain height, with my index finger pointing in the direction of his nostril.

'I'm the senior DI this time, sunshine, and I'm not taking any more of your bullying shit. If you try it, just once, I'll be in the commander's office like a ferret up a drainpipe and I'll get you shipped out. Do you understand?' Shaking with anger, I was almost frothing at the mouth. Phil backed down.

'OK, OK . . . keep your hair on, I've got it. You'll get no trouble from me.'

From that day on, he never put a foot wrong when it came to our working relationship. If only it could have been like that back in our Flying Squad days. I'm glad that I had a chance to see the better side of Phil, if only rather late in the day. When I heard through the grapevine many years later that he'd died at a relatively young age, I felt a twinge of compassion.

By 1989, after two and a half years of investigating suspected fraudulent applications, I could have done the job in my sleep. I'd been a detective inspector for almost six years and I felt confident about stepping up to the next rank, so I applied to become a detective chief inspector.

The day of the promotion-board panel came and, thanks in large part to Trevor's support, I was well prepared. Always the kindest of men, Trevor ensured that a working trip to Scotland not long before my interview involved stay-overs in hotels with no bars. Knowing my tendency to keep drinking once I'd started, Trevor strategized to ensure I didn't have the opportunity to have my first one. He was spot on, of course: without the tempting distraction of a licensed bar, I would go back to my room and do my research after dinner each evening.

As I left the interview, I sensed that I'd done myself proud. But as I waited for the news, doubts about my performance on the day began to creep in. I mulled over my answers and decided they had fallen short. *I bet I haven't got it*, I concluded.

Eventually, I was put out of my misery when the commander phoned to congratulate me. Trevor took me to lunch to celebrate. I felt so happy, mixed with a flicker of sadness at the thought of leaving my valued friend and colleague for the next step on my journey. Trevor and I kept in touch, and the last time I saw him was to say goodbye when he was dying of cancer. He was a truly wonderful man.

CHAPTER 13

A LIFE-CHANGING MEETING

One day in early 1990, I arrived at a stunning home in southwest London to be greeted at the door by a striking petite woman with a fabulous smile and a cascade of red curly hair, an Irish Wolfhound by her side.

'I'm Lynda. Do you like dogs?'

'I love dogs!'

'Well, that's a good start,' she smiled.

It would prove to be an auspicious meeting, sparked by a call that had come out of the blue when I was still in my first year of working as a DCI in Hammersmith CID. The call was from a former Met colleague who was now working with Lynda La Plante as a police adviser. La Plante happened to be writing a new police-procedural drama with a female DCI as its lead character. 'You need to talk to Jackie Malton,' he'd told her.

'How would you feel about meeting Lynda to talk about your job?' he had then asked me.

'Happy to,' I said. 'Just tell me where and when.'

Lynda La Plante was a familiar name. I was an avid fan of her fantastic early-1980s drama *Widows*, about the wives of armed robbers who had died committing a security-van robbery who decide to finish the job themselves. I'd met the wives of a few armed robbers during my time on the Flying

Squad. They tended to be a no-nonsense band of tough women. As I watched the show it was obvious that Lynda had done her research. I was excited at the prospect of meeting her.

Lynda's house had a lot of character, with stone floors, colourful rugs and wood-panelled walls. We chatted in the kitchen for a while. Her interest in senior female police officers in the Met had been piqued while watching the BBC's *Crimewatch UK* where serving police officers appealed to the public for any useful knowledge and leads relating to a live case. What struck Lynda was that the police officers talking about murder cases onscreen were invariably men. Were women never in charge of murder cases? she'd wondered. She made enquiries at New Scotland Yard and learned that there were only three female detective chief inspectors in the entirety of the Metropolitan Police. I was one of them.

Lynda led me into a large sitting room where she handed me a script with the words *'Prime Suspect'* typed across the front page.

I sat down on one of her comfortable sofas with a glass of wine in one hand, an ashtray by my side, and began scanning the script.

Lynda's writing laid out a compelling plot about the gruesome murder of a sex worker. I was hooked from the off. The storyline reminded me of the Yorkshire Ripper murders committed by Peter Sutcliffe. The fact that the lead investigator in the case was a female DCI made it particularly interesting for me. I resolved to be as helpful as possible to Lynda's endeavour by using my first-hand experience of being the lone female detective in a team.

Eventually, Lynda came in to say that supper was ready.

'Well, what do you think?' she asked.

'You've got a great story here, Lynda,' I said as I watched her serving up the pasta. 'The bit that doesn't ring true is what it's like for a female in a senior rank, and there are elements of police-procedural stuff that aren't right – but I can help you with all of that. Everyone seems to think the police have far more powers than they actually do. *Prime Suspect* is a great title, by the way. I like it.'

'I don't know where the title came from,' she smiled. 'It just popped into my head as I was talking on the phone to the script editor Jenny Sheridan at Granada.'

I did most of the talking over dinner that night as I filled Lynda in on my experiences as a female detective. Out it all poured, while Lynda listened, both of us drawing on our cigarettes.

She was visibly shocked as I told her that female police officers were classified as either a 'bike' or a 'dyke', and that my nickname on the Flying Squad was 'the Tart'. I recounted in detail what female officers had to put up with to survive in the job, including the humiliating CID initiation by male colleagues. Lynda's surprise made me realize that the behaviour I had come to accept as normal was not every woman's experience at work.

It was late when I stepped into the cold night. I'd really enjoyed the evening and gave Lynda my number as I left: 'Anything else, just give me a call,' I said.

*

When I first joined the Met, women police characters in UK police dramas were still token at best, with little to say and even less to do. The police-procedural *Z Cars*, which began in 1962, showed no progress on *Dixon of Dock Green* and *No Hiding Place* in terms of the representation and visibility of women police. Nor did the macho but exciting police drama *The Sweeney,* which hit the TV screens in the mid-1970s. But then came 1980, and with it two police dramas with female leads: *The Gentle Touch*, which portrayed Detective Inspector Maggie Forbes, and *Juliet Bravo*, about a uniform inspector called Jean Darblay, who was replaced after three series by another character called Inspector Kate Longton.

The character of Forbes, played by Jill Gascoine, was the first lead female detective in a UK police drama. What's more, the series focused on her character. The representation of a female detective of DI rank was inspiring and motivating – similarly so with *Juliet Bravo*. It was fantastic to see a woman in charge.

The cop show that I particularly loved was *Cagney and Lacey*, the US import about a partnership between two female New York police detectives called Christine Cagney and Mary Beth Lacey; one single, the other a devoted wife and mother. *Cagney and Lacey* showed the strong camaraderie and friendship of two colourful female characters. I loved Cagney – a fun, feisty, mischievous and complicated character. I wasn't alone: all the gay women I knew – most of them fellow police officers – were big fans. These three shows were manna from heaven for someone like me. I identified most with Cagney's character: single-minded, ballsy and unafraid to say what she thought.

It never occurred to me as I left Lynda La Plante's home that first time that I would end up becoming deeply involved in another defining television series depicting a female detective as the lead. Since someone was already working as an adviser on the project, I didn't expect to hear from Lynda again. Some weeks later, I did.

Lynda told me that she wanted my help creating the perspective of a female detective.

'I need someone with the inside track, someone who is currently in the job.'

I was more than happy to help.

And so began almost weekly meetings to talk about policing in general and my experiences in particular. Over the ensuing months, I relayed everything that I thought might be relevant: the dynamics of a male-dominated policing culture ridden with bravado and male camaraderie; my experience of feeling like an outsider; my efforts to blend in. I knew my story wasn't likely to be very different to those of many other female officers serving at that time.

What was less common was a female officer being called 'ma'am', since few women had progressed to a rank that warranted it. 'I don't like being called "ma'am",' I told Lynda. 'I find it archaic and a bit stiff. So I always tell my junior colleagues: "Call me "boss" or "guv", but don't call me "ma'am"; I'm not the bloody Queen." It usually makes them laugh.'

I talked, and I talked, smoking cigarettes as I focused on the memories. I described how I conducted myself at work, down to the way that I presented myself to be taken seriously: how I always wore expensive skirt suits for work – never trousers – and a smart 'detective' coat to look the part even if I didn't always feel it. I recounted how all too often witnesses or suspects would presume a junior colleague was in charge merely because he was male. I described a life dominated by the job, with personal relationships taking a back seat.

Lynda was interested in learning about the police culture to give colour to the script. I stressed to her that I had chosen to play the game of being one of the boys in order to be accepted; how I was always present for the drinks down the pub; how I fielded the banter as best I could.

Some doors were of course firmly closed: the all-male boxing nights to which I would never be invited. Frequented by police officers having a night off and a good time with colleagues, these dinner-jacket bashes, fuelled by booze, helped the men to bond as well as to raise money for charity. Then there were the freemason lodges, a source of power and influence seen by some as a shortcut to promotion.

When I told Lynda about Phil, my first Flying Squad partner, she looked at me aghast. Unbeknown to me, her mind was whirring. It was through these conversations that Lynda came up with the character of DS Bill Otley, who would channel the misogynistic vulgarity of the squad room. Otley's dialogue would include calling Tennison 'that tart', 'that bitch' and uttering the quip: 'Who would fancy that skinny-arsed dyke?'

A woman working in a man's world was only part of the story. Lynda and I would spend hours talking about the realities of policing and the procedural elements that had to be followed. I wanted to do my part to make Lynda's drama as realistic as possible while keeping the entertainment value high.

I laid out the long hours that detectives routinely work and explained that detecting serious crime involved painstaking attention to detail: the house-to-house enquiries; the tracing of a car from part of a registration number, or the make of a tyre from a mark left at the scene; the forensic examination of the crime scene regarding fingerprints, blood splashes and footprints.

Lynda also showed great interest in cases that I had worked on, so I spent many an evening reciting the more notable ones from start to finish. When I paused to take a breath, another thought would spring to mind and I would preface my next anecdote with, 'Ooh, and another thing. . .' before going off on another long rant.

Lynda never interrupted, and she absorbed everything. She didn't take down a single note, but much of what I told her would end up in the drama in one form or another, like the Leicester prostitutes' bittersweet banter from our car rides home, for example.

I kept a keen eye on how the realities of police procedure could serve the plotline and build dramatic tension. Whenever I spotted a flaw in the way Tennison and her team were operating, I laid out how someone in her shoes would be likely to go about it, or how they could circumvent obstacles. Far from being fazed by the feedback, Lynda would simply go back to the drawing board. She would show me her script rewrites and there would be more conversations, more changes. The script began to take firm shape.

What I didn't realize was that Lynda was studying me too: my tendency to smoke my Silk Cuts intensely, my unconscious tic of running my hand through my short hair. She was also, I learned, a great mimic. I'd thought I'd lost my Leicestershire accent, but listening to Lynda I realized I hadn't so much. I never stopped laughing when I was with Lynda. She was fantastic company.

Over time, Lynda fleshed out Jane Tennison into a fully formed, credible character. I didn't lie to her about my drinking or the way that it had escalated since the tough time I'd had at West End Central. Lynda made Tennison a hard-working, hard-drinking cop. At some point in our discussions, Lynda had bravely suggested that Tennison should, like me, be gay. Nice idea, I thought, but no.

'Why not?' she asked.

I shook my head. 'The British public isn't ready for that. It would be a distraction from watching a female DCI making her way.'

I didn't think, at that time, that an audience would empathize with what it was like to be gay. That said, I was touched that Lynda had raised it.

*

As the process went on, doubts would sometimes surface in my mind about whether I was betraying the police, but the other voice in me affirmed that I wasn't. I was being truthful about my own experiences, honestly felt. I loved my job, but the fact remained that the work culture was challenging for anyone who did not fit the straight, male prototype. And I had already told the Met's press department that I was helping a writer with a script. I had played it by the book.

I sought permission for Lynda to come with me to Hammersmith and experience the 'feel' of a busy detectives' office. I introduced her to the murder-incident room – the hub for an investigation – and she met colleagues of both sexes who were willing to chat to her about their working lives.

With her exuberant personality and genuine interest in policing, Lynda was a real hit. Meeting officers of more junior ranks also helped her shape other characters in the drama – WPC Maureen Havers, for example, the uniform officer who joins the murder squad and proves to be a loyal and supportive ally the isolated Tennison can confide in. Played by Mossie Smith, Havers was a great narrative device to depict the tensions and the isolation that women can feel in a room of men.

Later Lynda visited the Metropolitan Police Forensic Science Laboratory near Lambeth Bridge to meet experts. I also took her to a mortuary to see the identification suites where the next of kin identify their loved ones, and where post-mortems take place. I never got used to post-mortems, I told her. I hated the smell and could never dissociate the body on the slab from a previously living, breathing, human being. The fact that the body was once someone's brother or sister, father or mother, daughter or son would never be far from my mind.

Lynda listened intently as the pathologist explained what his job entailed. He would start with a description of any clothing, including any blood stains or cuts to the material. Each item would then be handed to a police exhibits officer, who would bag each one up separately in a labelled evidence bag. The pathologist would then examine the naked body closely, making notes or speaking into a Dictaphone to give a detailed description of all that he observed: wounds, lacerations, bruises, scars and marks. Then he would make the first incision of the body.

Lynda's interest was palpable and she wouldn't waste anything that she had learned. Armed with questions for everyone that she met, she was keen to listen to those with first-hand experience and to let go where necessary of what she had in mind originally, such was her desire to bring maximum authenticity and integrity to the storytelling process. When I ended up working in TV myself later, I would learn that not all writers immerse themselves in the research process in the way that Lynda did. What fascinated me was Lynda's ability to take away these experiences and weave them so creatively into the script.

At the end of several months, Lynda had shaped a wonderful story with a twin narrative about a woman managing a complex investigation against a backdrop of an institutionally sexist environment.

Once she had submitted the final script, I was invited to lunch with the executive team at Granada Television – all women. It was a delight to chat with them about Tennison and the overlap with my own life.

Not long after that, Lynda called me to say that they had found an actor for the lead.

'They've cast Helen Mirren to play Tennison. I'd like you to meet her.'

'I've never heard of her,' was my honest reply. A quick bit of digging told me that she was an accomplished actor with a background in stage and film. I was impressed.

Lynda invited me to supper to meet Helen. I'd spent so much time with Lynda talking about my experiences that I felt very attached to the Tennison character, but it was Helen who was going to bring her to life through her own interpretation of the role.

Slim, attractive and blonde, Helen had a presence that made me feel a little awed when we first met. I felt nervous, whereas she seemed very composed. The three of us chatted over dinner. Given that I was doing most of the talking, I felt a bit hyper; drinking and smoking too much didn't help. Part of me was saying to myself, *Shut the fuck up, Jackie,* but I carried on like a runaway train as stories about my work poured out of me. My pause for breath would be my chance to top up my drink.

A little later, Helen invited me to have dinner with her at a restaurant. One of the areas that she was interested in was how I presented myself at work. I told her: 'I try to avoid giving mixed signals with my body language, and I never show my vulnerability or let my guard down at work. You never cry in front of the men. If you feel the need to do it, you lock yourself in the loo so that no one hears you and no one sees you.'

At the end of the meal, Helen expressed an interest in doing her own research and I set up some introductions to oblige.

The cast was a friendly bunch. I attended the read-through of the script with them at a location in London. I tried to broker meetings for those playing police-officer roles with real-life equivalents by rank and gender, such as for the late John Benfield, who played Detective Superintendent Michael Kernan.

Soon, the drama was in production. Despite the show being set in London, filming took place in Manchester. The large part of my role was done, but I took some time off to be available on set to advise in the early part of shooting. The days were long, with a lot of waiting around between scenes. Actors would ask me the odd question and set designers were also keen to know whether the details on the set were right.

It was a surreal experience, watching a character shaped and drawn from my experiences, my life, uttering some of my quips. It hadn't occurred to me until then how the character would be seen by others. Tennison manifested many of my experiences. Soon everyone would see it – a thought that invariably set off a flutter of butterflies whizzing around in my stomach.

I liked the depiction of Tennison as a flawed character: steely, cool and smart on the one hand; sometimes tactless, obsessive, intense on the other – traits that I recognized in myself. She invested her energies in being able to win around her male team by joining in with the macho culture, but her obsessive drive to solve a case and make her mark resulted in a trail of failed personal relationships. Tennison was authentically complex.

And unusually for prime-time TV, the show cast a middle-aged actress to play a middle-aged character. This was drama, but the crime plot aside it was in so many ways true to my life, which is why I felt so unsettled when an actor cast in the show told producers that his police mates thought the script was a 'load of bollocks'. It fuelled misplaced fears within the executive team that the female protagonist wouldn't resonate with the audience and the programme would bomb.

I was really impressed by Helen's portrayal of Tennison. She was a class act and did tremendous justice to the role that Lynda had created. What was difficult to admit to myself at the time was that I saw in the character a confidence, a self-possession and a certainty that I strived to feel, but with mixed success. Somewhat ludicrously, I felt that Tennison seemed a more credible DCI than I did.

It wasn't until the day of the preview at the British Academy of Film and Television Arts (BAFTA) in Piccadilly that I knew with certainty that I had been right to speak up about my experiences – not just for me, but for other women too. My nerves jangled; I had to remind myself that it wasn't me on the screen, but a character interpreted by the talented Helen Mirren. I took Bob Sherwood and a couple of other friends from work to the packed theatre to watch the first two-hour episode projected onto a big screen. The loud applause at the end told me that I needn't have worried. I was pleased that my work with Lynda was reflected when the credits rolled, with me being named as 'police adviser' on the series.

*

I was glued to the screen when the first half of the four-hour mini-series was shown on ITV, even though I had already seen it. Viewers witnessed the reaction of an all-male detective squad angered that Tennison had been put in charge: the sulky silence in the room, the arms crossed, the brows furrowed. The release of the show had a particular poignancy: Alison Halford, the assistant chief constable of Merseyside Police, who at the time was the most senior-ranking female officer in the country, was in the process of suing for sex discrimination after unsuccessfully applying for promotion nine times in three years. Her case would be heard in an industrial tribunal the following year, and a financial settlement was reached.

Lynda had created a prime suspect who was handsome, affable and charming. Played by John Bowe, George Marlow is a devoted son and the sort of fellow you could simply not imagine raping, torturing and killing women.

Crime scenes were portrayed graphically and camera close-ups of the body were used in the post-mortem scenes; photos of the murdered victims were shown rather than merely alluded to and the forensic science that offered clues to the investigation was relayed through dialogue. It was a testament to Lynda's ability to apply her research to good effect. 'Such moments of forensic realism, while ground-breaking in 1991, have since become de rigueur in TV crime drama,' wrote Deborah Jermyn in her book about the show for the BFI *TV Classics* series.

Unlike my experiences of dealing with post-mortems, Tennison is completely unfazed when studiously watching the pathologist at work.

'S'cuse me, where's the toilet?' she asks the male pathologist.

'Oh, feeling a bit queasy?' he asks expectantly.

'No, but I think he is,' says Tennison, looking at her male colleague.

As far as I was aware, such a vivid portrayal of a pathologist's work was the first of its kind in a UK police drama.

A strong script was delivered by a talented cast of well-crafted and interesting main characters. My favourite scene was Tennison and members of her team in a police interview room with a solicitor and Marlow's common-law wife, Moyra Henson, played by the formidable Zoe Wanamaker. Initially refusing to look at the photographs of the victims, Moyra eventually glances down with a suppressed look of shock on her face as she recognizes the torture marks on the bodies as familiar. She asks that all the men leave the room. Tennison says nothing, holds Moyra's gaze and waits. It's a powerful moment. She watches silently as Moyra finally cracks. Marlow had tried to shackle her by the hands too, but she hadn't liked it. She weeps as she realizes that she has been living with a serial murderer. Tennison has a dawning realization of her own as she knows for sure they have nailed their suspect once and for all. She turns to look at Havers, and the pair give each other discreet, knowing smiles.

The morning after the first episode was broadcast, I smiled all the way to work as I tuned in to people on the tube talking about it and speculating whether Marlow was guilty or whether Tennison and her team had the wrong man in the frame.

I had quite the reception when I got to work. My Monday was punctuated by knocks on my office door from colleagues asking me to put them out of their misery.

'Did he do it, Jackie?'

'You'll have to wait and see,' I smiled mischievously.

When the second part of the series was transmitted that night, one of the last scenes showed Tennison trying to find her team after Marlow's confession so that she can take them out to celebrate. It's left for PC Havers to tell her they've all gone home. A despondent Tennison walks into the squad room, only to find her entire team waiting for her with a big bunch of flowers and bubbly to toast their success under her leadership.

I don't know if it was a case of life imitating art or pure coincidence, but a few months after the first series aired, a similar thing happened when I invited some colleagues for a drink to celebrate my fortieth birthday and everyone said they already had plans. My superintendent came to the rescue and said: 'I'll take you for a drink, Jackie.'

'Thank you. I'm glad someone cares,' I replied.

So off we went to a pub in Hammersmith, where I followed the super into a separate room only to be met by my whole team. They had even taken the trouble to order me a cake. You could have blown me away. It was all drinks on me.

*

After the show was broadcast, I received many letters and phone calls from female police officers who said the depiction of Tennison echoed their own working lives.

What was pleasing to me was that men as well as women had found it absorbing viewing, despite it being a drama from a female officer's point of view. The only detractor to raise viewer dissatisfaction was a female police officer that I knew from another station, who took the trouble to call me at home to offer me her unsolicited review not long after the series had concluded.

'I thought it was the biggest load of bollocks I've ever watched,' she said.

'Well,' I said, 'there appear to be millions of people in this country who thought differently. Thanks for your call anyway.'

A male police commander, meanwhile, confided that watching *Prime Suspect* had made him feel uncomfortable.

'Why was that?' I asked.

'Because it was so obviously true.'

This validation from a senior officer pleased me enormously. A TV drama had more powerfully conveyed my experience of being a senior policewoman in the Met than if I had sat him down and tried to explain myself.

Thankfully the press reviews were overwhelmingly positive. Peter Paterson wrote in the *Daily Mail* : 'As a well as a gripping, high-class murder story, this was also a tale for today, with a woman struggling for acceptance in a male-dominated world.'

Perhaps surprisingly, there was no backlash from the Metropolitan Police. Indeed, my annual appraisal of that year noted as a positive that 'she was used as the role model for the *Prime Suspect* series on TV . . .'

Lynda wasted no opportunity in interviews with the press to speak up for female police officers. 'Sure, there is prejudice against women jostling to keep on top,' she told the *Daily Telegraph*. 'If two detectives are on a case, the man will open the car door for the woman – very polite – but it'll be the rear door so he can sit in the front, where the power is. That sort of thing. And of course a squad of young detectives will be especially hostile to a woman if she replaces a much-loved guv'nor, as I had happen in my script.'

She added of police officers generally: 'You have to remember the insane hours they work, the pressures they are under, not being able to talk to their wives and kids about the nasty sights they see. A woman has got to be strong to survive in such a world, stronger than the men, but she mustn't lose her feminine insights in the process . . . that's why I had Tennison reproved by one of her lads for not giving the murdered girl's father a chance to grieve alone.'

As the inspiration for Tennison, I was also the subject of press coverage. At no point did I out myself as gay. I didn't want to embarrass my parents by discussing my sexuality in public. I remember telling one journalist that I thought Tennison was a harder character than I was, but I loved what Lynda had done.

The show was a massive hit. It drew 14 million viewers and garnered several nominations at the BAFTAs the following year. I wore a black and silver evening gown for the most glamorous evening of my life so far and arrived at the venue by taxi with Lynda and her then husband Richard. We walked up the red carpet to flashing photography, and joined a table of Granada executives along with some of the team and cast from the show, including Zoe Wanamaker and Helen Mirren.

When it came to 'Best Drama Serial', *Prime Suspect* was up against Alan Bleasdale's excellent *GBH*, the period drama *Clarissa*, and *Coronation Street*. As the celebrity came on stage to read out the shortlist and winner, I turned to Lynda excitedly and said: 'You've won!'

Lynda looked a mixture of amused and confused as she asked: 'How do you know I've won?'

There on stage was Sharon Gless, one half of the double act from *Cagney and Lacey*. I somehow doubted that Gless was about to give Bleasdale the award. And I was right. I clapped so hard as I watched Lynda go on stage with the show's producer, Don Leaver, and director, Christopher Menaul, who each received a BAFTA. Equally deservedly, Helen won the 'Best Actress' category.

By then a second series of *Prime Suspect* had been commissioned. I talked to Lynda as she worked up the storyline for *Operation Nadine*, as it was called, then worked with Alan Cubitt, who was brought in to write the script, which explores racist police attitudes to the Black community and to fellow Black officers.

In the opening scene, Tennison is seen interviewing a Black suspect arrested for rape. As the tense exchange comes to a climax, the interview is stopped by another DCI and we realize the interview was a role-playing exercise filmed as part of a police training course. The suspect in the hot seat is in fact Detective Sergeant Bob Oswalde, with whom Tennison has a fling on the course.

Meanwhile, the remains of an unidentified female are unearthed in a back garden in a residential area with a large African-Caribbean population. Previous incidents have left the community distrustful of the police. As a police adviser to Lynda, I drew on my experiences and observations on the New Cross fire and Brixton riots investigations to highlight some of the tensions that I had perceived at the time. Oswalde, played by Colin Salmon, is brought in by Tennison's boss as an 'antidote' to the racist officers in Tennison's team, notably one who antagonizes local residents. Unhappy about working with Oswalde because of their fling, Tennison reacts by initially side-lining him on the case. The show portrays the overt and the subtle forms of police racism experienced by the local community, and by Oswalde as the only Black officer in the squad.

In preparation for the show, I put Alan Cubitt, members of the production team and Colin Salmon in touch with DCI Mike Fuller – who would go on to become chief constable of Kent – to talk about his experiences as a Black police officer in a predominantly white force.

I worked with Lynda more closely again on *Prime Suspect 3*, when she wrote the script for a plot that foregrounds police homophobia and child sex abuse. Whereas Lynda had her plot worked out for Series 1 before we had met, on this occasion I could tell her about work experiences that could help inform the story. We discussed the conviction of Frank Beck, who was sentenced to life imprisonment for sexually abusing young boys in his care while manager of a succession of residential homes in Leicester. Seen as upstanding in his work in dealing with the emotional and behavioural issues of vulnerable boys, Beck managed to hoodwink authorities for years. I had also touched upon the case of a senior male police officer whose name had come on my radar in relation to the use of rent boys. I had forwarded the information, received through an unrelated case, to CIB2, though the officer concerned died before he was ever investigated.

The show sees Tennison heading up the Vice Squad when she come across the case of a rent boy burned to death. The prime suspect that emerges is a well-connected man called Edward Parker-Jones who runs an advice centre for vulnerable children and young people. Tennison and her team also find evidence of the involvement of a recently retired senior police officer in a paedophile ring, but she soon realizes that her bosses are surreptitiously trying to stop her probe straying beyond the murder. When she is finally told directly to back off the case and 'bury everything else', Tennison requests a promotion to superintendent. The now retired police officer in her sights kills himself. With insufficient evidence to charge Parker-Jones, Tennison leaks his case file to a journalist so that he is exposed. The series won 'Best Drama Serial' category for a second time at the BAFTA awards ceremony in 1994.

Lynda left after the third series while I went on to work as a police adviser on *Prime Suspect 4*, which consisted of three self-contained stories involving around five hours of drama. Personally, I preferred the original format of the show. Series 5, 6 and 7 returned to the original longer mini-series, but sadly I wasn't asked to be the police adviser. I understood the need to keep the series energized with new ideas, but I won't deny that I was disappointed to no longer be involved in a show that I had invested so much of myself in. The seventh and final series, *The Final Act*, was first broadcast in 2006.

In the first scene, we see Tennison waking up dishevelled on her sofa, looking hungover, her telephone off its receiver. Breakfast is a glass of vodka. She is weeks away from retirement. Her drinking is affecting her work and her professional judgement is impaired as she investigates the case of a missing 14-year-old girl who is later found dead. Her boss urges her to seek help with her drinking and go off sick until her retirement date, but Tennison insists on seeing through her last case and claims that she is attending Alcoholics Anonymous. She learns that her father is dying of cancer, and she struggles with loneliness. She eventually starts attending AA meetings. There she meets her old nemesis, Bill Otley, who offers her support at her lowest point and is later killed trying to protect her in a shooting incident. When Tennison finishes the case, colleagues organize a leaving do for her, but she leaves quietly without even saying goodbye – the inverse of the celebratory party in the first series at the end of the Marlow case. I thought that it was a sad ending, but the fact that we see Tennison attend AA offers the viewer some hope for the iconic female character's future.

In 1992, the first series of *Prime Suspect* was broadcast on the PBS Mystery! channel in the United States to a good reception. 'Without preaching, *Prime Suspect* does the best job I've seen of showing how men belittle women in a small multitude of ways, how we use sidelong looks and inside humor to screen them out of the action,' James Wolcott wrote in *Vanity Fair*.

I took some annual leave and was flown out to Washington first class by PBS to be interviewed on their channel as well as other media outlets about my experiences as a detective. It proved to be another very glamorous affair. My accommodation was a corner suite in a luxury hotel; my transport was a black limousine with a driver who took me to various TV and radio venues over three days.

The show produced more than 22 hours of drama over 15 years – with a seven-year lull between *Prime Suspect 6* and *7*. It was transmitted in 78 countries, reached an audience close to 200 million globally for some series and garnered numerous awards internationally, according to *Justice Provocateur* by Gray Cavender and Nancy C. Jurik.

When I first spoke to Lynda, I could never have imagined how popular the show would be worldwide. Lynda bravely raised important social topics such as misogyny, racism, homosexuality and child abuse in a prime-time show – no mean feat. Working with her had been a privilege and I was proud to have made my contribution by sharing my personal and professional stories.

In one interview, Lynda would explain that at the outset she was met with resistance to the way that she had portrayed Tennison, by those who thought the character 'was too hard, too unemotional, she smoked too much, she was an unacceptable woman'. Lynda said that she fought to keep the character as she had written it, 'because I knew the woman the character was based on, and I didn't want to insult her. I wanted her, at the end of the series, to be able to say, "Yes, this is what my life is about."'

*

And I was, for which I am eternally grateful to Lynda. *Prime Suspect* gave voice to my and many female officers' experiences and would open many doors for me. But I still had a job to do as a DCI at Hammersmith, which kept my feet firmly on the ground and my mind fully occupied.

CHAPTER 14

THE NEXT RUNG UP
THE LADDER

The woman sitting in my office in Hammersmith looked like a Sunday-school teacher. Visibly distressed, she refused to give her real name. She behaved like the prime suspect of a crime, rather than the victim of a serious sexual assault. Earlier that day, men working in the shop below her bedsit had heard her screams and rushed to the rescue. They caught the perpetrator before he could get away and called the police. The officers gathered from speaking to the shop owner that the woman might be a sex worker, since he often saw men going in and out of her flat. But the woman wouldn't tell them anything, not even her name.

It was late 1989, roughly six months after I had arrived at Hammersmith in my first posting as a detective chief inspector.

Sitting in front of me was a prim-looking, attractive and well-spoken woman in her thirties. She wasn't giving me any eye contact. I needed to engage with her. I was judged for being different, so I wasn't about to do the same to her. I just wanted to get to the bottom of her refusal to talk.

'My name is Jackie, and I'm the detective in charge. We have a man in custody for an alleged sexual assault on you and we need to know what happened.'

The woman's eyes remained fixed to the floor. Something was clearly afoot. I recognized it instantly.

'I think I understand,' I said finally.

The woman looked up. Encouraged by the flicker of a response, I took a deep breath. What I was about to do next was a risk, but it was a calculated one.

'I'm gay, which is not an easy thing to be, particularly in the police. It's used against me at times, and every time it is I feel shame. Is that what you're feeling? Shame about something you do? Is that why you're not talking?'

Sometimes, my instinct told me that I might yield better results by speaking as though I were talking to a friend in a coffee shop, rather than as a detective interviewing a victim. A silent pause followed as she turned over my words. Then she spoke.

'Thanks for sharing something so personal about yourself. Yes, it's the same; sitting here right now, I feel ashamed, but I do what I do for my son.' Contact had been made.

'What's your name?' I asked.

'My name's Jane. But I'm not giving you my surname unless you can promise me you won't tell anyone?'

'I can't promise you that, Jane. But I will see what I can do to protect your anonymity in a court room. How about that?'

Out it poured. She was living a double life. A married mother of one who had been employed as a nurse in the past, she was pretending to her husband that she was a bank nurse working night shifts at various hospitals across London. She'd chosen a peripatetic job as her cover to deter her husband from ever calling her at work, since she was not actually there. She was a sex worker; the pokey bedsit where she was attacked was the rental she used to ply her trade, far from her family home at a smarter London address. She was doing it, she told me, to put her only child through private school. She usually screened clients by asking them to make a call from a phone box opposite her flat so that she could see what kind of person they were before allowing them up. If in doubt, she would turn them down. This time she had made a huge error; the man looked 'normal', she said, so she agreed to let him into the flat. As soon as he came in, he attacked her. She was mad at herself for being a victim, she told me, because if this seedier side of her life came to light her family life would come crashing down. It was a powerful motive to stay silent.

It would not be until 1992 that all victims of sexual assault had lifelong anonymity under the law. Without a statement, this perpetrator would walk, and that simply would not do, so I proposed a way forward.

'I'm going to give you a pseudonym that will be used in all court papers, so that there is no possibility of your real name and life being known to anyone except me. There will be no trace of your real name on any documentation. I will make all the necessary checks to verify that you are who you say you are, and I will give assurances to the prosecution that I know your true identity. But what we need from you now is a full statement about what happened.' Jane agreed and I was true to my word. The gentle touch had paid off.

I wasn't working in Hammersmith by the time the case came to court, but I heard that Jane had to give evidence because her attacker pleaded not guilty. Luckily, the jury didn't buy it. He was found guilty and jailed for two years.

Years later, our paths would cross again, this time in the smarter surroundings of Joe Allen's, a restaurant near the Royal Opera House in Covent Garden. I spotted Jane having supper with a male companion. She didn't look much like a Sunday-school teacher now: she was sophisticated, glamorous, classy.

I said hello to her as I walked past her table as I was leaving the restaurant.

Jane smiled and introduced me to her companion as a friend. I chuckled inwardly: he had no idea that she was talking to a detective who knew full well how she made her living. Jane and I exchanged numbers, and she called me a while later. She was an escort now. The sex was still part of the deal, but now it was in smart hotels and the clients she entertained were exclusively professional middle-class men. I was pleased that Jane had moved into this relatively safer line of work, though of course there were no guarantees. Selling sex is always risky work for anyone to do, but Jane clearly thought that submitting to a strange man's desires was worth it for her son. And who was anyone to judge her for that?

*

I had arrived in Hammersmith as a newly minted DCI in April 1989 with a few nerves and qualms. A DI for five years, I was ready for the more onerous role of DCI. Hammersmith was the biggest and busiest of the three stations in F Division, the others being Shepherd's Bush and Fulham.

This was the first time I'd worked within a police station since my time at West End Central, and I was excited to be back on a patch. I liked being connected to a community, fostering good relations and engaging with a variety of serious investigations. Working in specialist operations SO6 (the Fraud Squad) had been a more disconnected affair, since my job there had involved dealing solely with suspected fraud anywhere in the country.

As DCI, I was in charge of the Hammersmith CID as crime manager. The role was less operational than that of a DI and required me to take an overview of cases investigated by my teams. Ultimately, I was accountable for the way they handled cases, their results and their clear-up rates (the number of cases solved). The job involved sitting in more local meetings, whether to discuss departmental budgets or targets, detection rates or team performance, as well as area-wide meetings.

The Met in 1989 was divided into eight areas, each with a mini-headquarter led by a deputy assistant commissioner. Hammersmith was part of '6 Area' and DCIs from different divisions within it would meet regularly at an area crime group, where local DCIs could ask for additional manpower to help us address a particular problem in our backyard: a spate of sexual offences, for example, or a high volume of burglaries. It was also a chance to share local intelligence and find out if similar patterns of crime were happening on other turfs. At those meetings, I would be the only female DCI in the room – but it was good to see that the commander of 6 Area was also a woman, Jane Stitchbury, who would later become chief constable of Dorset Constabulary.

My rank gave me the potential to have greater influence, not just in the way the CID worked cases, but also in creating a more inclusive culture within the teams that I managed. Over the years, I had noticed that some detectives could be pretty disrespectful to uniform colleagues of the same rank. As a result, some uniform officers could look positively nervous stepping into the detectives' den. Not on my watch.

F Division was infamous throughout the Met as the site of the 1966 murders of three police officers: Detective Sergeant Christopher Head, Detective Constable David Wombwell and Police Constable Geoffrey Fox. The policemen had been patrolling in Foxtrot One One – an unmarked police car called a 'Q' car – in Shepherd's Bush, when they approached a car parked in Braybrook Street, near Wormwood Scrubs prison, to check the driver's documentation. The three officers were shot dead by the car's occupants: Harry Roberts, John Witney and John Duddy. The trio did a vanishing act but were all eventually arrested, charged and sent to prison.

Roberts, who killed two of the officers, was released in 2014 after serving 48 years. Social media was awash with comments from both sides regarding whether he should ever have been released, but the decision to allow Roberts to return to society didn't go down at all well with police officers. Were he to be convicted today, Roberts would no doubt receive a whole-life order, meaning that he would never see freedom again. The truth is that he was a 78-year-old man when he left prison – an environment where everything was done for him – and had to stand on his own two feet again, with almost five decades of societal change to contend with. It seemed to me that this was penance in its own right.

Situated on Shepherd's Bush Road, Hammersmith Police Station was a couple of doors down from the famous Hammersmith Palais, a dance hall that first opened in 1919 and remained a popular venue for decades. When working late, I would often see from my window a long queue outside it, with bouncers ready at the door. You could almost bank on a fight breaking out at some stage in the evening, and revellers ending up in the charge room instead of on the dance floor.

My spacious office was located above the Metropolitan Police coat of arms on the façade of the station. It seemed far too grand for a DCI. I would notice with a smile that the higher the rank, the better the furniture and the nicer the quality and colour of the carpet.

My window looked out to the main road between Hammersmith and Shepherd's Bush, and the vista, it has to be said, was dull in contrast to other stations I had worked at before. I would leave the greenery of my village for a panorama of grey concrete in built-up Hammersmith, which was quite shabby in parts. Office buildings lined up across the road, with the main shopping area in nearby King Street. The beautiful Hammersmith Bridge and the River Thames snaking its way towards the heart of Westminster offered some compensation, as did Ravenscourt Park.

Like any new boss might expect, I had some of the more dyed-in-the-wool detectives testing how easy-going I might be with their requests for overtime, overnight stays in hotels when enquiries had to be taken outside London, and so on. They soon learned that I had the experience to know when someone was pushing their luck, but you had to hand it to them for trying.

When I was growing up, my father had told me about the value of a 'walkabout' on arrival at his newspaper office. Now I took a leaf out of his book, and I did the same at the beginning of each day to ensure that I was abreast of everything I needed to know should a senior officer raise any matter with me. I would usually have a chat with the canteen and cleaning staff while getting my tea. Coat off, and a cup of tea in hand, I would stroll over to the control room, where all the calls from the general public and beat officers were directed. I would then pop my head into the charge room to see how many prisoners had been detained overnight and were awaiting CID-led interviews, and then go on to the front office to check the missing-from-home register to ensure that all the requisite enquiries had been made. Onwards to the property room, and to the collator's office, the intelligence hub.

At first, I found it difficult to acclimatize to my new rank and the big job of presiding over the entire outfit. My two detective inspectors nudged me on this point early on. I was stepping on their toes and interfering too much with the teams.

'You're acting as if you're still a DI, guv,' they told me. 'But you're the chief now. Let us do our job.'

Enough said. Now I was a DCI, I had to trust my capable DIs to do their job. My focus needed to be on the bigger picture.

*

The CID was made up of six detective sergeants, each with a team of four detective constables. Two of my detective sergeants would end up becoming lifelong friends.

Bob Sherwood and I had our first exchange when he approached me to check that I would not block the study time that had been signed off by my predecessor so that he could pursue his law degree. I had lived to regret my decision not to take up the offer of applying to study for a degree after my DI course, so it didn't take long for me to give Bob my answer.

'I'm not going to stand in your way,' I said. 'I think what you're doing is great.'

And there began a beautiful friendship.

Reliable, honest and diligent, Bob was one of the hardest-working detectives I had ever come across. He was unfailingly supportive; I could pick up the phone to him any hour of the day or night and benefit from his wise, cool head.

The other gem that I met at Hammersmith was a whirlwind called Sue Hill: a bundle of energy, enthusiasm and drive. Sue was a straight talker blessed with a knack for making people laugh. Her savvy nature and charismatic style made her one of the most able detectives around.

Sue and I would do our utmost to prepare the young officers on the crime squad, which was a sort of apprenticeship for uniform officers hoping to become detectives. I would support their application to go before a board for selection if I deemed them suitable. My focus was exclusively fixed on people's capabilities. Sue and I would prepare them for interview by role-playing a mock board and lobbing questions that candidates could expect to be asked. We even told them to bring in their chosen attire for interview so that we could offer an opinion on the impression they would make. We didn't have one failure.

A few months after the case involving Jane, Sue came to see me about another sexual assault. The alleged victim was a young woman I'll call Amanda. 'I dealt with her when she was raped last year, and her rapist was convicted,' Sue explained. 'She says she's been raped again, by someone else, but something doesn't seem right to me. Can you talk with her and see what you think?'

Amanda was brought up to my office and eventually admitted that, as Sue suspected, this time she had made her story up. But why? Amanda told me that she was lonely and feeling very low. She thought that if she came to the police as a victim, she would have more of the care and attention that she had received the last time. She had felt supported and heard, something that she had never experienced before.

We could have charged her with wasting police time, but what would be the point? Amanda was suffering enough. What she needed was looking after; she'd just gone about it in the wrong way. We referred her to adult social services and mental-health team services, which were best placed to help her in the long term. Fortunately, instances of women making false allegations like this are rare.

Being a police officer often meant dealing with human frailty and vulnerability, but I had always had the sense that we operated in a culture of disbelief where rape was concerned. When I joined in 1970, we were told that challenging the rape victim's story was a way of seeing whether they would stand the test when grilled by the defence in a future court case, but I have my doubts as to whether this was the real reason. We weren't encouraged to treat victims of other crimes in this way.

The tide began to turn in the 1980s after an episode of *Police,* a BBC fly-on-the-wall documentary series about Thames Valley Police by the late Roger Graef, aired in 1982. The episode, called *A Complaint of Rape*, showed a woman alleging that she had been driven to a flat by two men she didn't know who then raped her. Filmed with her back to the camera to protect her identity, she was interrogated cynically and without any sensitivity by three male detectives. As the camera rolled, one detective said: 'Listen to me, I've been sitting 20 minutes, half an hour, listening to you. Some of it's the biggest lot of bollocks I've ever heard. I could get very annoyed very shortly.' He added: 'Now stop mucking us all about.' Another detective told the distraught victim that he believed that she had been a willing party and that her account was 'a fairy tale'.

I watched this in utter disbelief, as I imagine did many of the 12 million other people who saw it that night. You could well understand why women were reluctant to report sexual assaults if this was the barrage of aggressive questioning they faced after the trauma of rape, I fumed. I had no idea that some victims alleging rape were being treated in this way. The officers concerned were bullies. Totally unprofessional. When the programme was first broadcast, I was a detective sergeant and had I witnessed anyone on my team conducting themselves like that I would have immediately instigated disciplinary procedures against them and sent them for training on handling sexual assaults while they waited for their case to be heard.

The documentary was the subject of much discussion in the canteen the next day. Women officers who took statements from alleged victims were stunned. In fact most police officers I spoke to seemed to feel as shocked as me. I could not believe that some colleagues were treating women in this way.

When Graef later discussed the making of the programme, he said that when he attended Hendon Police College while working on the documentary he witnessed 'young coppers being told that 60 per cent of women who claimed to be raped are making it up'.

The documentary was a masterclass in what not to do, and led to the establishment of a week-long training course for detective inspectors on handling cases related to sexual offences. *A Complaint of Rape* was shown during the training. I did my course when I was a DI at West End Central and was the only woman in the class, but the men were as appalled as I was after watching the film.

'This is what you can't do,' a senior detective told the class when the episode finished. 'You need to believe the victim until proven otherwise.'

My irritation got the better of me: 'With all due respect, sir, some of us have always listened to women's stories with an open mind.' We were all being tarred with the same brush as those officers on the film, and I wasn't having it.

Within a few years of the programme's release, and under pressure from other quarters, new measures relating to women reporting rape and sexual assault were brought in. In 1984, a four-week Sexual Offences Investigative Techniques course (SOIT) was introduced to train detectives – in particular female detectives and some female uniform officers – in dealing with rape victims more sensitively. Officers were taught about rape myths, for example, and rape trauma syndrome, which led to a variety of symptoms being exhibited after a sexual assault (anxiety, shock, anger, fear, shame, self-blame, depression, a tendency to act out distress – or, conversely, to behave a little too normally, as if nothing out of the ordinary had happened). This era also saw the early incarnations of rape examination suites away from police stations, where complainants could be medically examined in comfortable surroundings; though initially there were just one or two of these facilities. One of the first was at St Mary's Hospital in Paddington. Detective inspectors became the senior investigating officers in rape cases.

Sexual assaults are only part of the picture of violence perpetrated by men against women. Even by the early 1990s, the force was pretty ignorant about domestic violence. The police found it frustrating when a woman called them up to report domestic violence only to later withdraw her complaint.

It was widely believed in those days that if a woman was unhappy in an abusive relationship she could simply walk away and leave him. If only. The police force was slow to understand the many ways in which women could be victims at the hands of men. Back then we knew nothing about coercive control, gaslighting or harassment. We didn't understand that a woman might stay in a relationship because she still loved her abusive husband and hung on to the misguided hope that things would improve if only she behaved more as he wished her to.

Also overlooked was the fact that the prospect of homelessness was a deterrent to leaving, especially if the woman had children. For some, of course, the violence was so extreme that they had to leave. Sadly, this doesn't always stop the perpetrator. Domestic violence, at its worst, can escalate to murder.

The widespread attitude that dealing with domestic incidents between husbands and wives was more trouble than it was worth pervaded for decades within both the police and broader society. The idea that police saw this issue as 'nothing but grief' and 'best well left alone' is reflected by John Sutherland in *Crossing the Line*, his book about his 25 years of service. Sutherland, who joined the Met in the early 1990s and rose to become a chief superintendent, concludes that domestic violence is 'a disease of pandemic proportions and the single greatest cause of harm in society'.

This was a realization that I reached myself through my own years in policing and through speaking with victims. The obvious shift needed was education within the police to change its mindset about and approach to violence committed against women by partners or ex-partners.

Now that I was a DCI, I wanted to do something to improve our response to domestic-violence incidents and to victims. My rank gave me more clout to make things happen and I wanted to use it. As luck would have it, not long after I arrived at Hammersmith, a report into the way local agencies responded to domestic-violence victims was published following an eight-month study. Commissioned by Labour-run Hammersmith and Fulham borough council, the research included interviews and surveys from women who had experienced domestic violence. Coincidentally, one of its authors was a Dr Liz Kelly (now a professor) whom I had met a few years previously when studying with the Open University.

The report found that police and social services were two groups that women were not keen to approach. The police response was seen as relatively ineffective and the penalties for violent men too weak. Victims wanted the police to focus on removing abusers from the household where the violence was being perpetrated.

What I envisaged the police doing was collaborating with local agencies dealing with the impact of domestic violence so that they could help us establish a better service for victims. The trouble was that my experience of the police thus far was of a defensive institution constrained by an insular and rigid approach to tackling problems. Another hurdle was the Met's antipathy to collaborating with outside agencies on an equal footing. The Met tended to expect to be in charge of the show. This point was reinforced by the incumbent uniform chief superintendent, who was suspicious of the local authority-run community-safety unit (CSU) and told me to avoid working with its members.

The CSU was a crime-prevention scheme to help people feel safer in their homes by looking at measures to reduce problems such as (for example) domestic violence, antisocial behaviour, burglary, robbery and car theft. Initiatives included improving street lighting or helping to fix windows or installing stronger front doors so that people felt more secure.

For the first time in my career, I decided to ignore an instruction from above and made an appointment to see what we could do together. I met with the two local-government officers leading the CSU: David Cutler and Robyn Holder, a dynamic Australian woman interested in developing community-safety projects for women. It was a fruitful conversation and they agreed to support me in my efforts to set up a domestic-violence unit (DVU).

My next piece of good luck was the appointment of a new chief superintendent who was open to the idea of working with others outside policing.

I arranged to meet with Jacqui Burrows and Becca Thackray, the two female police officers who in 1987 had pioneered London's first DVU, in Tottenham, to learn from their experiences. They stressed the need to educate police officers on the issues that lie behind domestic violence and to operate a standardized approach to dealing with incidents.

Jacqui and Becca gave me the impression that senior police officers had taken the lead in the multi-agency discussions. I resolved to avoid a top-down approach looking for black-and-white solutions that fitted with our usual way of working; I wanted to listen and to learn and to see where that led us.

One of my officers, Police Constable Stephanie Knight, had a keen interest in working on the project, so I appointed her as the dedicated officer to build up the DVU. I wanted Stephanie to be based within CID to raise the profile of domestic violence as a serious crime. The brief was to develop a victim-focused approach. We knew that we had our work cut out trying to change hearts and minds within our ranks. Stephanie attended a domestic-violence workshop at the local women's refuge to learn more.

Soon, the Hammersmith and Fulham Domestic Violence Forum was established with a view to offering women and children experiencing violence in the home better protection by the police and more tailored support from local agencies.

Trying to change our ways involved a lot of time spent listening to victims to understand what they were going through and why they were so often reluctant to press charges. The criticism levelled at the police included our failure to make arrests when called to incidents, and the insensitive line of questioning when interviewing victims. Instead of asking why women didn't just leave abusive relationships, for example, we needed to ask what made them too afraid to do so.

The conversations deepened our understanding of the need to ensure that domestic violence was routinely recognized as a crime rather than a tolerable part of married life, as many people believed. There was to be no more of the 'Well, do you want to press charges, love, or don't you?' attitude.

One aspect of our work was to earn the trust of organizations who were suspicious of the police because of their past dealings with officers whom they'd felt to be short on compassion, empathy or understanding.

I couldn't blame the scepticism of charities such as Women's Aid and other outfits that dealt with the fallout of violence against women. Similarly, Stephanie and I needed to put aside our preconceived ideas. With efforts from both sides, and a few constructive arguments along the way, stronger alliances emerged and attitudes began to shift. I was invited to join the management committee of Shepherd's Bush Women's Aid refuge.

The discussions led to us introducing a number of changes, many of them similar to those pioneered in Tottenham: domestic-violence training for uniform officers within the station, for example, and a positive arrest policy whereby any evidence of an assault automatically led to an arrest. Other changes included logging all domestic incidents – whether as a crime, where there was evidence of violence, or notifying the DVU of any call to the police of a domestic incident, even if no offences were committed. This meant that every incident was now recorded, allowing us to monitor escalating levels of aggression in the home, whereas previously an incident was recorded only if further police action was taken. Nothing was swept under the carpet and everything was on our radar. I also assigned the responsibility of overseeing domestic-violence cases put before the court to one of the detective sergeants within CID.

Women referred to the DVU were invited for a chat at the station and, where appropriate, officers would refer them to other support services, be it for the mental-health issues triggered by the violence, help finding somewhere to stay, or the group setting that would help the victim feel less alone in their plight. Where the violence was more serious, we gave women mobile phones so that they could contact us directly if the abusive partner tried to return to the family home.

A charity called the Riverside Trust offered us office space for a weekly drop-in service for domestic-violence victims; this was run by Stephanie and quickly turned into a support group. Stephanie also helped women apply for injunctions against their violent partners.

In parallel, a scheme to support perpetrators to change was run by a man called Neil Blacklock. The Domestic Violence Intervention Project (DVIP) offered support with anger management, and group and one-to-one counselling for men willing to change their ways. Over time, the DVIP evolved to work with women as well: encouraging them to place the responsibility for the violence with their partners, rather than seeing themselves as to blame.

The collective community response to domestic violence in Hammersmith was crime prevention at its best. Police officers told us that they felt more knowledgeable and more supported in dealing with domestic-violence incidents, notably with repeat victims.

The project absorbed quite a bit of my time in the first couple of years. It was gratifying to have this work recognized nationally when I was invited onto BBC Radio 4's *Today* programme and *Woman's Hour* to lay out our approach.

My first live radio interview was nerve-racking. A wonderful broadcaster on *Today*, the late Brian Redhead, put me at my ease while I talked by rolling his finger in the air as if to say, 'Keep going, you're doing fine.' My media experience was short-lived, however: a more senior police officer from area headquarters decided that he would be the voice of policing domestic violence, because 'the detective chief inspector rank is too low'.

It didn't matter. I had ignored a direct order from above and eschewed the usual top-down and rigid mindset of the Met, which always thought it knew best – and this decision had paid off. We had worked in collaboration. We didn't assume we knew it all or that our way was always the right way, and we acknowledged that we had much to learn from those at the receiving end of policing. The setting up of the DVU was noted as a 'successful venture' in my annual appraisal later that year, but knowing that we had improved our service to victims of domestic violence was my real reward.

*

'Where's the DCI?' I heard the urgency in the officer's voice on the police radio system as I sped to the scene of an explosion that had occurred at 6am at Norland House, a block of flats on the Edward Woods Estate in Shepherd's Bush. One person was dead. By the time I arrived as the on-call CID officer, the area was already cordoned off and the explosion was designated a major incident.

With no clear idea of what had caused the explosion, the main concern was the safety of the other residents. Around 170 flats had to be evacuated to a community centre on the estate by police officers and firefighters. I sought out the duty inspector from Shepherd's Bush station, Alan Wiggins. I already knew Alan and that morning I found him to be his usual unflappable self.

Standing in the square below, we looked up at the charred flat on the eighteenth floor, its windows blown out where the explosion had gone off, with fire damage to some of the flats above visible. My eyes scanned down and across to a parked car that had the frame of one of the blown-out windows embedded in its roof. Nearby on the pavement lay a body, face down. I winced at the bloody sight.

Alan explained that on his way down, the victim had collided with the top of a rental van parked in the square, ripped off half his leg in the process, then bounced off and hit the ground. Whether the victim had jumped or been blown out by the force of the explosion was not clear at this stage.

We had to establish the identity of the deceased; speak to the next of kin; determine the cause of the explosion via the London Fire Brigade and a team from the Met Police forensic lab; liaise with the council and their services; and take statements from witnesses and neighbours.

Alan said that the occupant of the flat was from Ireland. Given that London was so often a target of the IRA, we needed to check for any political affiliations or connections.

I stood in the flat where the explosion had taken place and saw that the room was burned out. The smell in rooms consumed by fire is invasive. I left with the odour of smoke clinging to my hair, my skin and my clothes for the rest of day.

A reconstruction by the two fire-investigation teams showed that the gas had deliberately been disconnected by the occupant and something like a spark coming from the fridge must have triggered the explosion. I couldn't get my head around the force of the explosion being so powerful that it jettisoned a man out of the window. He had no chance of surviving.

The fire brigade and local council officers who were making safety checks in the building beckoned me to another flat, where the resident who had their gas disconnected after failing to pay their bill had simply reconnected it to a gas fire in the sitting room using a garden hose. The flat could have blown up at any time. Such a risky DIY effort was shocking to see. The flat was immediately condemned as unsafe.

With no obvious crime having been committed, the DCI would usually leave the investigation to the duty inspector. Since I was on call all weekend and back in the office on the Monday, I carried on working on the case for the next few days to take the pressure off my uniform colleague.

I accompanied the sister of the deceased to make a formal identification of the body, and then took a detailed statement from her about her brother. The victim, who was only 39, appeared to have been a man with few friends; he rarely contacted his family and was depressed and a loner. It was a brutal ending to what sounded like a sad life.

A few months later, I was one of 16 police officers to receive a Chief Superintendent's Commendation. Mine was for leadership. Eighteen other officers from Shepherd's Bush received commendations from the deputy assistant commissioner. I felt proud of the work we did. Every time I drive along the Westway, I look up to the block of flats and think of the officers that I worked with so seamlessly that week, and of the lonely man whose life ended so dramatically.

*

My first stint as a DCI coincided with a modicum of social progress: in 1990, the first formal and recognized staff-support association for gay officers was formed. The Lesbian and Gay Police Association was set up to give gay officers a voice within policing and to create a more inclusive and tolerant workplace. It was sorely needed. During my years in the Met, I had come across several gay female colleagues who chose to keep their sexuality quiet at work. Not surprising, given the grief it could generate. Most of the people who joined the association were of constable and sergeant rank, and most were male. There was only one other woman present when I attended my first meeting, and she was a police constable. The association seemed to me more relevant for younger officers; worried that my status as a DCI might intimidate junior colleagues, I decided to attend the odd meeting as a lay member rather than put myself forward for a committee position.

At this point in my career, stuffed to the gills with responsibilities, there was even less time than before for a private life. It was probably just as well, since my absolute commitment to the job did not make me the ideal girlfriend to have. I was not available enough, and when I was present my mind was often on work-related matters. My problematic drinking created a barrier to intimacy. I just didn't realize it at the time.

Far from trying to make more space away from work, I was always on the lookout for new opportunities to widen my skill set. I chomped at the bit when I spotted a notice in the 'Police Orders' – an in-house bulletin – for a two-week hostage-negotiation course. There was a dearth of female negotiators, and female applicants from DI or DCI rank were encouraged to apply. *I'll have a bit of that*, I thought. I was one of two Met candidates put forward. The rest of the group was made up of officers from other UK forces and from abroad, all equivalent in rank. I was the only woman.

There was a lot to learn on the course, held at the Hendon detective training school. Strong communication skills and the ability to be a quick thinker were essential requirements.

I learned about Stockholm syndrome, whereby a hostage can develop a psychological bond with their captives; de-escalation techniques; the importance of patience and staying calm; the need to keep the hostage-taker engaged to gather as much detail as possible, and to avoid making false promises or telling them lies. If a hostage-taker asks you if the area is surrounded by armed officers, for example, admit it rather than palming them off with a, 'No, it's just me out here.' It was fascinating stuff.

The days were long, and by the time we'd had a debrief and drinks afterwards, I would often roll into bed past midnight.

We took part in a spectrum of role-play scenarios, be they a terrorist incident on a plane, or a domestic incident. I remember playing the role of negotiator in a scenario at the firearm training unit at Lippets Hill in Essex. Wearing headphones, I talked to the 'hostage-takers' to try to bring the situation to a peaceful conclusion while my classmates watched. Suddenly, there was a loud 'boom' followed by shouting. It was only when I took off the headphones and turned round to ask one of my colleagues what had happened, that I realized that there was only me still in the room. My audience had left to watch colleagues storm the building. I was so busy concentrating that I hadn't noticed.

Another role play was to persuade a 'depressed detective' not to kill himself. The officer playing a man on the brink was on the other side of a closed door, which made trying to connect with him a little more challenging. It wasn't hard to engage him on the stresses of being a detective, but I was chuffed all the same to receive praise from the course instructor for my efforts.

We were also privileged to hear from speakers with first-hand experience of a hostage situation, notably PC Trevor Lock – the diplomatic protection officer taken hostage at the Iranian Embassy in 1980. Trevor paced the floor and sweated profusely as he relived the experience of surviving six days with 25 other hostages held inside by six armed men who were members of the Democratic Revolutionary Front for the Liberation of Arabistan. Their demands were autonomy for a region in the south of the country, and the release of a number of prisoners.

Knowing what we do now about post-traumatic stress disorder, I very much doubt that Trevor would be asked to relive his experiences to a room full of people today, but the policing perspective that he offered us was invaluable. He recounted how the terrorists had patted him down but failed to find the gun strapped to his torso. Trevor kept his coat on at all times to keep it concealed. He would ensure that he would be the last one to go to sleep and the first to wake up, with his police cap always on, so the hostages had the reassurance of a British police officer in their midst. When one of the hostages was about to be released after being taken ill, he briefed the individual on the details of the firearms and ammunition the terrorists were holding so that they could relay it to the police. I was captivated by Trevor's account of his experience, which served to underline that lives are often at stake when a hostage negotiator is called in.

The course was the most testing that I have ever done. There were times when I wondered whether I would make it through. But after two weeks of extremely hard work, I was an official hostage negotiator for the Met, and I was added to the 'on call' list at New Scotland Yard.

The first time that my services were called upon was when an armed robber was seen running into an apartment block near Shepherd's Bush Green. No one knew which flat he'd gone into and there were fears that he might have taken the occupants hostage. An hour earlier when the call came in, I'd been almost home after leaving the station. I pulled into a nearby police station to request a marked police car to drive me all the way back through rush-hour traffic, using the blues and twos.

I arrived at the scene to find it steeped in silence. All the flats were searched. The suspect had somehow got away, so that was that. The officer who had driven me there had kindly waited for me and drove me home in a more leisurely fashion.

Still, there were other opportunities to flex the new techniques I'd acquired. There was the time when I was called to deal with a naked man threatening to jump from the top of a block of flats one summer's evening. As I arrived, kids below seemed to be enjoying the drama and were cruelly urging the poor man to 'jump, jump, jump'. Uniform officers were already at the scene and had cordoned off the area below the building. My stomach flipped as I looked up to see a man with his feet just inches from the roof ledge, staring outwards into the open space.

I learned from his desperately worried mother, who was watching helplessly, that his name was Jake and he was experiencing a psychotic episode. Jake, who was in his mid-thirties, usually took medication to manage his mood, his mother said, but he had been feeling so much better of late that he had convinced himself he didn't need to take it anymore.

As I went to the top of the building and onto the roof, Jake seemed to be in conversation with an imaginary person. My job was to talk him away from the edge and get him to retreat into the safety of his own home. Being a negotiator takes enormous focus, although uniform officers behind me provided back-up. Standing to one side of Jake, I talked calmly to try to connect with him. This went on for an hour, with little success. Trying to connect with someone when they are a danger to themselves or others is draining, and the tension is mentally exhausting, but I persisted in my endeavours to bring him to safety.

Jake refused to even look at me. The time passed, then suddenly, he turned and faced me:

'Don't you ever shut up?'

A breakthrough. 'I'll shut up when I see that you are safe,' I replied and gave him an encouraging grin.

Not long after, Jake stepped down off the edge. He ran into the flat where my colleagues pinned him to the ground. He was then led to a waiting police van, which took him to a mental-health hospital so that he could be sectioned and receive treatment.

My next call didn't take me to a rooftop, but to the corridor in a block of flats. A man called Tom had taken his girlfriend Janine hostage when she told him that she wanted to leave him, triggering a row that spiralled out of control. Tom couldn't accept that she had ended the relationship and had pulled a knife out of the drawer and was threatening to kill her and himself. Sitting in the stairwell, flanked by firearms officers, I talked to the man through a closed door, trying to convey empathy. He felt wronged by his partner, and trying to challenge his thinking required me to tread carefully, to avoid making him feel that I didn't understand. *Better to let him sound off to me until it burns out*, I decided. I monitored my voice to make it calm and soothing but mostly I listened, occasionally looking over to my armed colleagues positioned close by in case things went belly up. Slowly, the emotional temperature dropped on the other side of the door. After about 90 minutes, Tom came out and released his girlfriend, unharmed. He was taken to the station, where he was remanded in custody until his appearance at the magistrates' court. As a negotiator, you don't get involved in what happens after the crisis situation is over. Once the victim was released and safe and the offender arrested, my job was done. As I walked back to my car, feeling utterly drained, I remembered Sergeant Cyples telling us as police rookies that talking was 95 per cent of the job. I much preferred that to holding a firearm – though both are obviously necessary when lives are at risk. Hopefully for Janine, this was the end of the matter.

*

As a DCI during my two and a half years at Hammersmith, I had plenty of work arrive on my desk – but as much as possible I made time to put myself forward to cover the acting superintendent role. The superintendent is the person who can authorize the use of certain powers under the Police and Criminal Evidence Act 1984 (PACE), such as further detaining a person arrested for a period of up to 36 hours to preserve evidence relating to his arrest. Given that it's a 24/7 position, the three chief inspectors at the station were expected to share the responsibility so that the superintendent could have time off in the evenings and at weekends. Since I wanted to accrue as much experience as possible in readiness for climbing the next rung, it made sense for me to cover whenever I could.

At the end of the 1980s, the police started to undergo some changes. The Met commissioner Sir Peter Imbert initiated reforms to improve both public perception of the police and the quality of the service. Sir Peter, who had previously served as the Met's deputy commissioner, had been concerned about the image of the police following the year-long miners' strike in 1984, and the Wapping dispute between Rupert Murdoch and the print unions in east London in 1986. The Met was seen as a defensive organization that suffered from a poor public image on several fronts, not least in its relations with people from ethnic-minority communities. Not long after being appointed commissioner in 1987, Sir Peter asked a firm of corporate-identity specialists called Wolff Olins to look at what was needed to make the service more user-friendly and accessible. As well as concerns over relations between the Met and the general public, morale among his staff was an issue. Major changes in policing that had taken place in recent years had proved unsettling, for example, and many police officers felt under siege by the level of scrutiny by the media, which was often hostile.

The focus was on the Met's identity: what the Met stood for, what it did and how it was seen by its own staff and by the public. The findings and recommendations were published in a report called *A Force for Change*.

The report led Sir Peter to rebrand the force the Metropolitan Police Service. He introduced a number of changes designed to turn the Met into a more open and transparent organization. As part of his mission, he initiated the PLUS programme: working parties were set up across the

Met, and seminars held for all 44,000 police and civilian staff as well as team meetings at area and station level.

I for one thought it was a brave move by the Met chief. The danger of institutionalization is always there, so pausing to reflect on why we joined, what the job was about, and how we conducted and presented ourselves seemed a good idea to me.

I put myself forward as a representative of the PLUS programme. A frank exchange of views led to useful discussions about how we represented ourselves and our own attitudes towards others. I admired the honesty in those meetings. For many, it was the first time they felt heard.

Freshening up the interiors of police stations and making their reception and waiting areas more welcoming, comfortable and accessible was seen as a good first step, along with improving the way officers spoke among themselves and to the general public, right down to their telephone manner. Out went the slow pick-up of calls and the sometimes gruff one-word responses, and in came a more professional welcome.

As for improving morale in the station, I suggested tongue in cheek that we lift the mood by choosing a nice shade of pale pink for the canteen. The colour scheme meant that the canteen was soon nicknamed 'the creche'.

What Sir Peter, later Lord Imbert, did for the Met was to underline its key mission: to serve the public. Sadly, not all my colleagues embraced the ideas he tried to instil, but I still believe that it influenced many, like me, who wanted to improve trust with the public. After all, we couldn't do the job without them.

CHAPTER 15

ONE DRINK TOO MANY

The evening of 29 December 1992 was a real peasouper. Staring out into the cold, foggy night in miserable silence, I watched the lights of the London traffic flash by from the back seat of a car heading for Walton-on-Thames. Two men sat in front: one of them I barely knew, the other not at all.

An hour earlier, I had watched them pour every fluid ounce of alcohol to be found in my house down the drain. John and Eric had listened as I wept and confessed my behaviour like a guilt-ridden suspect. I felt complete and utter shame.

When we reached our destination, I emerged from the car into the blur of the evening. John ushered me across the threshold of a community hall. I stepped into the unknown, heavy with a sense of defeat and despair as I joined a room full of women and men just like me. 'My name is Jackie and I'm an alcoholic.' I was 41 years old.

The truth is I never really liked the taste of alcohol, but I began to drink in my late teens to be sociable. I soon found that alcohol triggered a feeling of confidence within me: it stroked my ego and it made me like myself more. I quickly learned the other payoffs too: drinking alcohol soothed and it numbed. After becoming a police officer, the odd glass of wine or half a pint down the pub helped me to swallow the feelings that would sometimes lurk after bearing witness to the misery caused to victims. But I could take a drink, or I could leave it. It wasn't a big factor in my life. Then slowly, and at first imperceptibly, I began using it as a crutch.

Alcohol pushed back the awkward thoughts and feelings that intruded with increasing frequency from my mid-thirties onwards. The person I showed to the world was a ballsy, fearless character, always up for everything, never shy to confront; a straight talker; a real street fighter. The truth was that it was more complicated than that.

Gin, which eventually became my drink of choice, morphed into a panacea for all ills. As soon as alcohol hit my nervous system, it washed away all my worries and gave me – if only briefly – the sense of normality that I craved. It made me feel like I belonged – accepted, and acceptable.

By 1992, I knew without doubt that I was in trouble. On the surface, I had plenty to be happy about: by then I was in a new post in Kensington and Chelsea, working in community liaison as a DCI, which I thoroughly enjoyed; my involvement in *Prime Suspect* had led to plenty of media attention the year before, and I was now working with the scriptwriter on the second series; I also had a good group of friends. Looking in from the outside, I had it all. Looking out, it was a different story.

Away from prying eyes, I harboured a closet full of insecurities. Not good enough; not clever enough; not normal enough. Feelings of shame, of being an impostor in my career, of seeing myself as utterly inadequate as a person – and frankly, of just *feeling too much* about everything.

Instead of basking in my recent successes, I felt my sense of being a fake in my own story rocket to an all-time high. This was to the point that

I thought, rather ludicrously, that the fictional character Jane Tennison was more of a real copper than I was, even though the character was largely based on me. Madness. While my heart knew that I'd done the right thing by talking to Lynda about my experiences, my mind still occasionally tussled with whether I had betrayed the Met by doing so. I had exposed some of my own vulnerabilities in the process. For as long as possible, I hung on to my identity as a strong, capable woman who could cope with anything, but it was proving increasingly hard to do.

The deepening sense of despair that I felt had been building over years, but the cracks had widened and were now impossible to ignore.

I remember turning up to an address in Hammersmith to be met by two completely devastated parents. They had found their baby daughter dead in her cot earlier that morning. The mother asked for a photograph to be taken of her with her child before the baby's body was taken away. I was there to investigate, and it was evident that this tragedy had all the hallmarks of a cot death. The parents' intense grief was affecting. I left the scene to attend a senior management meeting. Sitting with colleagues discussing budgets felt surreal. There was no space and no time to process. It would be ten hours later, as I sat in my car, that the floodgates opened as I thought about the dead infant and the parents' unimaginable grief. Arriving to my empty house, I went straight for the gin and poured myself a generous glass. And then another.

I hid the traces of my reliance on alcohol pretty well – or at least that's what I like to think. Such was my paranoia that people would twig that I was struggling with drink, I alternated my visits between the off-licences in my village to avoid suspicion.

Over time, I needed more refills to achieve the same numbness. The more I tried to suppress my feelings, the more they fought to surface for air, and the more often I drank. Alcohol changed the way that I felt about myself, and it promised the oblivion that I ached to achieve. Too many times, a drink with friends down the pub became drinking in a pub alone after missing my train, or at home alone. At work and with friends, I felt slightly removed. Distanced. Detached. I opted for denial about my problem drinking, but it eventually gave way to a growing desperation to understand what was happening to me.

My increasing dependency on the bottle whittled away my self-esteem and my sense of self as a moral, upright person. I began to do things that I had never imagined: waking up in a state of dread in anticipation that I may have said or done something unguarded in a drunken stupor the night before; fretting about whether I had paid the fare when I rolled out of the cab that brought me home. The abandon of alcohol meant undignified behaviour that would make me cringe as I sobered up the next morning. I would take a deep breath, heavy of heart and of head, and pick up the telephone to apologize to the person I might have offended in my inebriated state. What a way to start the day. My anxiety levels ratcheted up and became a permanent fixture. I didn't like myself at all.

I feared losing my job. I feared causing an accident. I feared ending up on a park bench. I feared losing my friends. Yet I would wake up each day and repeat the drinking, somehow expecting a different result.

If I drink today, I'd tell myself, *it won't be like last week*. And of course, it was indeed just like the last. I lost my dignity and cultivated regrets. Seeing other people – in train carriages, in the street – I yearned to feel like they looked: confident, it seemed to me, and unburdened. But I felt stuck.

My shame at what I had become was complete the day I watched myself splash whisky into my early-morning cup of coffee before heading off to work. As I sat in my car at traffic lights later that morning on my way to the office, I looked at other drivers in their cars pleadingly, as if urging someone to come and rescue me from myself. A hopeless thought. At work, I managed to keep my professional face. Letting the mask slip was out of the question.

Confiding to anyone at work about what was going on was not an option. Admitting that I was struggling with my mental health was career suicide. It would, I feared, be seized upon as proof that a woman couldn't cut it in senior ranks, so I kept quiet.

The easier option, bizarrely, was to fantasize about being hauled off to a psychiatric unit to escape from my own life. Still, I didn't speak. I continued drinking. It was about to get worse.

When I received a call from an inspector called Kate in early 1991, I didn't realize that what would happen next would lead me to the edge of a precipice. Kate had a dilemma and wanted to talk. A female officer had alleged that she'd been raped by a colleague and Kate wanted to support the woman to report it. She was weighing up the consequences of ignoring a senior officer who warned her off from getting involved.

'Can you talk to me about what happened to you at West End Central when you reported an officer?' she asked.

I swallowed hard.

Kate hoped that hearing about my experiences at my old station might better prepare her for how to deal with the hostility she anticipated getting for supporting her female colleague.

I felt duty bound to help. 'Bear in mind that it was seven years ago,' I said. How naive was I?

I arranged to meet Kate at 11 o'clock in a Polish café on the Brompton Road, South Kensington, for a chat. A chat that would trigger an unravelling.

I told Kate what happened and as I talked, I experienced a strange sensation of not being in the room. My heart raced, and I felt lightheaded. I looked at Kate with a sense of disconnect. 'I just need the loo,' I said. Once I got there, I was physically sick. I went to the sink and splashed water on my face and then stood in front of the mirror trying to calm myself down.

I returned to the café table, made my excuses, told Kate to call me if she needed anything else from me, and left.

As I walked along the Brompton Road, my head reeled. I held on to a nearby railing trying to catch my breath and flagged down a cab to take me back to the office. As I sat at my desk, my body went into uncontrollable spasms and my anxiety soared. Colleagues called an ambulance and I was taken to hospital.

Doctors ran tests but found nothing. The conclusion was that the physical reaction was a panic attack caused by hyperventilation. At the time I didn't connect the attack to talking to Kate about a difficult time in my life. I had no idea that the turmoil of those awful months at West End Central still had so much power over me.

The panic attacks would continue for 13 months. In the cinema I would sit at the end of the row to avoid feeling trapped. Walking down Kensington High Street one day, I froze on the spot, unable to go backwards or forwards. I just stood there. A colleague from work had to come and fetch me. *I'm going mad*, I thought. Pills prescribed by the doctor to ward off attacks were gratefully received.

I tried to police my own drinking as best I could: putting myself on call more frequently than necessary to stop me having a drink after work; volunteering to drive people to parties and committing to not touch a drop if I was behind the wheel. The strategies worked to a point, but the grip that alcohol had over me remained. I was desperate to stop; I just didn't know how. The months rolled by, and my desperation grew. Then I remembered John. I had met him a few months before, when he had turned up to Kensington and Chelsea's police consultative group. John had been invited to give a presentation about Alcoholics Anonymous as part of the organization's outreach to the public. He talked about his descent into alcoholism and his recovery through AA. My interest was purely professional. As he talked, I wondered to myself how we in the Met could help signpost the organization for the many people who ended up in 'drunk tanks' – police cells used then to allow drunks to sleep off the intoxication.

'What would you like the police to do?' I asked. My 'rescue' role in full throttle. 'Would it help if we put A A posters up on the ceilings of cells so that people see them when they wake up feeling like shit?'

'Why don't you come to a meeting and see what it's like so that you can have a better sense of alcoholism and how alcoholics recover?'

Not likely. I was affronted by the question. I didn't give any thought as to why.

'I would,' I said, not so genuinely now, 'but I'm afraid that it would be hard to find the time to do that.'

John wouldn't have it. He insisted, gently; I gave way, reluctantly.

The room at the World's End Community Centre in Chelsea was thick with cigarette smoke blended with the smell of urn-made coffee. I added to the fug by lighting up as I listened to speaker after speaker describe their slide into alcoholism. Most contributors at the well-attended meeting talked about the way their lives had spiralled out of control until the point where they couldn't cope anymore, with or without drink. There was only ever one positive turning point, and that was the day that they quit alcohol – one day at a time. *These poor souls*, I thought.

'Did you identify with anything that was said in there?' John asked me afterwards.

The question made me bristle. What an odd thing to ask me. 'It's very sad, listening to these people's stories. It must be hard for them,' I said. 'Very tough.' *Them and us* . . .

I didn't think about it much after that – not consciously anyway – but many months later, on that late-December day, I woke up realizing that I had reached my fill of being sick and tired of being sick and tired. I wanted my dependency on the bottle to end. I knew there was something better within me, but I just didn't know how to reach it. I knew I had to call John.

'Hi, John. My name is Jackie. I don't know if you remember me. I'm that cop who came to your meeting. I think I'm one of you.'

'OK,' he said. 'How about I come around to see you?'

That evening, John came with Eric and they drove me to my first AA meeting.

Mortification was the predominant feeling as I sat waiting for the meeting to start. *Look at me now*, I thought glumly. *I'm sitting in some poxy hall with a bunch of alcoholics*. It's not a sentiment that I'm proud of. I knew that I was drinking too much, but nobody wants to admit out loud to others – or even to themselves – that they are an alcoholic. No one imagines that when they grow up, their character could become disfigured through drink; no one wants to concede that their life is out of control.

The people at the meeting were mainly drawn from the middle classes: men and women who on the surface had all the trappings of the good life, yet were drowning in alcohol. I listened properly, this time without an air of detachment. They had found what AA describes as the 'gift of desperation' – being so fed up with their situation that they were willing to contemplate change. I had come to that point too.

I had made that phone call to John knowing that I never wanted to drink again. And here I was now among people who seemed happy, healthy and hopeful. It was such a relief to hear them talk about how AA had helped them find their way out of the mire. Could I ever feel the same as they did now?

As the meeting came to a close, several people said of the AA programme: 'Keep coming back. It works if you work it.' And I kept coming back, a few times each week to different venues. At work, I would meander through Portobello Road Market during my lunch hour to attend an AA meeting at the Salvation Army hall, then return to my desk with no one any the wiser about where I had been.

A A meetings are about 'experience, strength and hope': people are encouraged to talk about their past drinking and its effects, and about their life in sobriety. The A A provides a 12-step programme that members use to look at their own behaviour and to take responsibility for themselves.

Despite all the advances in science about the brain and about addiction, the 12-step programme has never changed since it was developed in the 1930s. I started to contribute to meetings, which involved introducing myself as an alcoholic – a declaration that made me feel overcome with shame at first. But the meetings are confidential, and people listen without judgement or comment about what you say.

It took a while to find my feet, but I was getting myself back on track without anyone in the job knowing that I had been struggling. I found a female sponsor to guide me through the programme; fellow members gave me their phone numbers to call if I ever needed a chat.

I went to therapy and saw a counsellor who, ironically, had their base opposite the Polish café where I had experienced my first panic attack. The therapist's view was that events at West End Central had locked in as post-traumatic stress, a sort of ticking time bomb waiting to explode. The trigger had been talking to Kate about it.

The therapist encouraged me to revisit my experiences at West End Central – and when I finally did, the words tumbled out and released the fear and the pain. That day, the panic attacks left me for good. It didn't mean that the experience at West End Central hadn't left a permanent mark, but it no longer had a grip on me.

My life until joining A A had been one of trying to be what I thought other people wanted me to be: first my family, followed by the police force; – two institutions with set norms and expectations of how one should act and behave. At some cost to myself, I had tried to fit in to stop feeling like an alien who might one day be whisked to another planet that would finally feel like home.

Opening up to others on the AA programme about my difficult feelings and experiences turned out to be liberating and fortifying. It released me from the shame and allowed me to accept that I, like everyone else, had vulnerabilities.

West End Central proved the breaking point; my recovery was the turning point. It placed my life on a new axis. Every day since that foggy December night I have felt gratitude for my sobriety, because 29 years is a hell of a long time to live a decent life, one day at a time.

CHAPTER 16
LAST RITES

August Bank Holiday, 1992. The Notting Hill Carnival was about to begin – a popular annual street festival that celebrates Caribbean culture and usually runs over three days. With its colourful costumed parades, steel bands and the blaring of Caribbean music from static sound systems, the event drew enormous crowds, and still does to this day. It took a huge amount of preparation and planning, with both police and stewards present. The carnival would prove to be one of the highlights of my new role as community liaison officer at the Royal Borough of Kensington and Chelsea, just next door to my old manor of Hammersmith. The switch of role was unusual for someone with so much detective experience, but I had applied because I thought it would offer me useful career development.

My role spanned the whole of the borough, which was made up of three police stations: Kensington, Chelsea and Notting Hill. Being a CLO was still on the frontline, but with a twist: instead of catching criminals, the focus was on working with local agencies to reduce crime.

I had joined the carnival organizing committee when I arrived in post in the spring of 1992. The committee representatives included police, the carnival management committee, representatives from the Royal Borough of Kensington and Chelsea, the emergency services and agencies such as the Arts Council. Meetings would take place throughout the year in the run-up to the event; as soon as it was done and dusted, discussions about the next one would begin. The onus was on trying to accommodate the needs of the festival organizers without compromising safety. When the carnival kicked off, my job was essentially to act as a go-between for the organizers and the senior police team should there be any concerns.

I arrived at the site early on the Saturday morning as van drivers unloaded equipment and people bustled as they set up stalls and wired up the sound systems. Some houses along the route were boarded up, their occupants vacating the area for the duration. As the carnival started to get in full swing, the aromatic scents of Caribbean food from the street vendors would hit my nostrils and, despite my best efforts, my hips would start to sway to the music blaring from the sound systems set up along the route.

Briefed on which street vendors and sound systems were authorized, I would refer any breaches to the stewards, including any floats creating a backlog by going too slowly along the route. The days were long, and my feet ached from walking the streets, radio in hand, but the party atmosphere was electric. I loved it. Uniform officers welcomed the extra money for working the Bank Holiday, but not everyone was a fan. The decibels were too much for some, while others were unhappy with the long days and the unappetizing food served up by the Met's catering team. An officer called Bill Lamb, now departed, was among the enthusiasts: he knew everyone involved and was seen by the organizers as an ally of the carnival.

The carnival was just one strand of my responsibilities. Based in a building in nearby Earl's Court Road, I led about a dozen officers in the youth and community section (YACS) team. The agencies I worked with were notably those that tackled disaffection and supported vulnerable groups. I wanted us – police officers – to be more understanding and to work in partnership to tackle problems because, in many instances, the police could not do it alone. In some small way, I felt that I finally had a chance to achieve this and to do my bit to improve relations between the Met and various communities within the area.

Most of my time was spent out of the office and, very occasionally, out of London. I vividly remember turning up to join YACS colleagues for a couple of days on an outward-bound-type course in Dorset for children from deprived backgrounds. Torrential rain was the order of the day. A lot of soothing was needed as drenched kids whimpered, 'I want my mum, I want my mum . . .' They weren't the only ones! The aim was for officers to spend time with youngsters doing things that would broaden their horizons, to engage them and give them a little hope and aspiration. I wonder where those kids are today.

Building bridges with hard-to-reach groups allowed me to focus my sights on women from Black and ethnic-minority communities who didn't seem to come forward very much to report crimes committed against them. I had never forgotten the Asian woman back in Leicester who doctors were certain was the victim of a machete attack, despite her insistence that she had fallen down the stairs. It seemed to me that women not coming forward was possibly symptomatic of a cultural resistance to going to the police about domestic problems, and a general distrust of the police. I arranged visits to an Asian women's centre, a Muslim women's centre and a refuge safehouse for Black women to talk to them about the service provided by the Met's domestic-violence units. The response was positive, and I could only hope that the visits would encourage these women to reconsider approaching the police when they needed to.

Sometimes, my focus wasn't about crime prevention at all. For example, we spoke to colleagues about avoiding arresting drug addicts who were attending chemist's to use the healthy-needles exchange, a programme that helped to prevent the spread of HIV and other blood-borne infections.

Streetwise was an outreach service for rent boys operating within Earl's Court. Hot showers, food and sex education were part of the package of support offered, with a long-term view of trying to get these vulnerable youngsters off the streets. It was a world away from my time in the Flying Squad and CID, but I saw it as just as important. Some might think that this shouldn't have been a priority for a police officer, but it was about tackling the undercurrents of crime and sometimes saving lives.

During my time at Kensington and Chelsea, my bosses recommended me to apply for the superintendents' assessment, which was a series of tests to gauge your suitability for the next rank. Frustratingly, I scored well above average on almost every component, such as decision making, resilience and leadership/influence, and got top marks for awareness/ strategic thinking, but I fell down on numeracy, for which I scored only a grade 2 out of 5. This meant an automatic fail. I was, quite frankly, pissed off. I had run my own budgets for several years and had never gone into the red. But I brushed myself down and resolved to try again at the earliest opportunity.

I continued as a CLO until the end of 1994. This role hadn't always made my life easy, not least because it involved trying to engage the interest of colleagues who were more focused on the arrests side of the job. But by the time I left Kensington and Chelsea, attitudes towards collaborating with agencies outside policing had shifted significantly in the Met; there was more awareness that the police could benefit from working with others.

*

My next posting was back in CID. A previous offer of joining the C11 Intelligence Unit, based at New Scotland Yard, had not appealed. I liked being at the coalface and part of the station buzz. What's more, being a crime manager – the senior detective in charge of CID – played to my strengths. On reflection, staying in my comfort zone was an error: working from New Scotland Yard could have provided a network that opened doors for my career.

By then, I had notched up two years of sobriety and was regularly attending AA meetings. Colleagues who had known me for a long time didn't have a clue, other than the fact that I didn't drink anymore. I didn't feel the need to explain. What mattered was that I was enjoying being teetotal.

I still attended CID lunches, and still joined colleagues down the pub – though not as frequently as before, and when I did my tipple was now ginger beer. I would wake the next morning clear and fresh and feel gratitude that I was handling my life without alcohol in the mix.

My new posting was Fulham, part of F Division. It was a smaller police station with fewer officers than the divisional HQ at Hammersmith. Its proximity to Stamford Bridge, the Chelsea Football Club ground, kept everyone busy. A notorious crew by the name of the Chelsea Headhunters, which perversely called itself a 'firm', would gather to commit violence in pubs before and after the matches. This outfit, which was populated with skinheads and had links to the far right, took up a lot of resources from uniform colleagues. Police officers known as 'spotters' used intelligence to identify suspects or known troublemakers in the match-day crowds and were familiar with the core members of the gang. I persuaded my bosses that it might be useful to bring in the CID to work with spotters from the uniform section to boost intelligence gathering.

Many uniform officers were experts on football hooligans and attended all matches, whether at home or away or even abroad. The network of hooligans was difficult to break. Our focus was to find out planned spots for violence and to identify and arrest gang members outside and within the stadium – ideally before they had a chance to commit carnage.

In 1995, Fulham benefited from the new central computer system being rolled out across the Met: the Crime Reporting Information System (CRIS) was where crime reports would now be logged. It was far more efficient than the manual system and enabled much quicker and readier access to crime reports and officers' case updates. We were sent on in-house training courses to learn how to use the software. Luckily, I took to it like a duck to water.

It wasn't the first piece of technology used by the Met. Computerization to date included, for example, computer-aided despatch (CAD), which since the early 1980s had identified the location of a 999 call once logged by the call handler in the central information room. The Home Office Large Major Enquiry System (HOLMES), introduced in 1985, provided an indexing system for all information received regarding a particular murder. As for mobile phones, they were not issued to police officers during my career. Instead, we used pagers, which would bleep us a number to call when we were out and about or on call.

Around this time senior officers were also given individual computers. I recall a senior and older officer vowing that he wouldn't be switching his on. But I could see that technology was the way forward and I resolved to engage with it.

One of my duties as head of CID was responsibility for the Crime Squad. Shortly after my arrival at Fulham, I shook things up a bit after realizing that most of the squad's officers had already accrued enough experience, passed their selection board and were just waiting for a date to go to detective training school. For them, the Crime Squad had served its purpose. I decided to return them to uniform, to give other police officers a chance to garner detective experience in the squad. Unfortunately, those I sent back to uniform were up in arms at my decision.

Although no official complaint was made, a notice was slipped under my office door. It read: 'Are you being bullied at work?' – which I guessed was aimed at me and had been sent by someone disgruntled about the decision I'd taken.

One of the applicants to be considered for the Crime Squad vacancies was an officer called Mark. Apparently, he had previously been accepted onto the squad and then sent back to uniform because he was deemed to have taken too long to complete a particular job he'd been given and was not seen as a team player. Mark was a good thief taker and a very capable officer. A mild-mannered guy, always smartly dressed, Mark was also Black in a predominantly white outfit – as indeed every section of the Met invariably was. After I'd interviewed him, I reselected him for the Crime Squad. I was approached by another detective who disagreed with my decision, but it was my call to make – and yet it would be undermined when I suddenly found myself off sick.

My absence was caused by tripping up the steep stairs at work one morning; I must have been distracted at the time, but the pain as I landed concentrated my mind. My knee swelled instantly as a sharp stabbing sensation seared through my joint.

Barely able to walk, I hoped that a few days would suffice to bring it back down to size and for the pain to subside. Alas no. Swollen and extremely painful, my knee forced me to take time off sick for the first time in my working life. I did not enjoy the enforced downtime, or the thought of my work piling up back at the office. My heart sank when a consultant diagnosed severe arthritis and warned me that I would need a knee replacement down the line. My sights were still firmly on the next rung of the career ladder, and for that fitness was definitely required, so this was news I didn't wish to hear. I returned to work, but the excruciating pain periodically surfaced and would blight the rest of my policing life.

When I came back to work after three weeks off, I found that in my absence Mark had been taken off the team again. I was told the decision was due to an alleged minor infraction related to his return from holiday. A flight delay meant that he was back a day later than expected. I found it unbelievable that this was the basis for kicking him off the squad. A delayed flight was out of his control. I wondered whether his ejection was a blind spot or something more sinister.

All the evidence suggested that Mark was a good officer who produced results, so the decision to deny him the chance to prove himself made no sense. Would a white officer have been kicked off the squad for the same incident? I spoke to my boss, who had decided to remove Mark after a detective sergeant spoke to him. My boss, who was a fair man, was sympathetic to what I was saying, but the decision had already been made. I had to wonder exactly what information he had been given. I cursed the fact that I had been off sick when this happened, since I would have fought Mark's corner and I'm sure common sense would have prevailed. All I was left with was the distinct suspicion that Mark had been removed because he was seen as different, but I couldn't prove it, as is so often the case.

I felt desperately sorry that a good cop with potential had missed out on the opportunity to become, I have no doubt, a fine detective. Despite his evident disappointment, he found the time to pop into my office when I was out to leave a book on my desk with a note inside that read 'Enjoy'. The book, by Susan Taylor, was called *The Spirit* and was about taking a positive attitude to life changes.

The good news is that Mark eventually did become a detective, after getting back into the Crime Squad on his third attempt some 18 months later. He was later promoted to detective sergeant and worked on the Counter Terrorism Command until his retirement.

When we recently spoke about his experiences as a Black police officer, Mark told me that the negative comments about his sharp dress sense never went away. He didn't know if he was being oversensitive or not, but what he felt was being conveyed was 'Who do you think you are?' He told me: 'I always felt targeted – because I didn't see others getting the same treatment. I've had some unfortunate treatment in my career but to be fair the good times far outweighed the bad. Sometimes colleagues just don't think about the impact their words and actions have on others. But even with all the negative experiences, I knew I would never give up on my career as a cop.'

Inclusivity and understanding of difference undeniably still had a long way to go in the Metropolitan Police service. In 1989, concern about the number of Black and Asian recruits quitting early led to Black and Asian officers from across the Met being ordered to take part in a two-day seminar in 1990 at Bristol Polytechnic so that the Met could understand the reasons behind the premature departures. Around 350 Black and Asian officers attended. Among the issues to emerge was that many felt isolated and without support; inappropriate humour and behaviour from colleagues were not addressed by supervisors, and people felt that their career opportunities were restricted – particularly in CID, according to a paper by Paul Wilson, a former Met superintendent who is himself Black. In his memoir, *Rocking the Boat*, Wilson recalls delegates at the seminar reporting racist abuse, personal lockers being broken into and the tyres of their cars being slashed. The upshot of the Bristol seminar was that it brought many Black officers together for the first time, and it sowed the seeds of the Black Police Association. Launched at New Scotland Yard in September 1994, the BPA's key objective was to 'improve the working environment for Black personnel within the Metropolitan Police Service, with a view to enhancing the quality of service to the public'.

When the BPA was launched, the then chair of the Metropolitan Police Federation, Mike Bennett, was reported in the *Guardian* newspaper as saying: 'There would be a huge outcry if white police officers decided to set up their own staff association. There is a growing feeling in the police force that white heterosexual officers are an endangered species.' The obvious response to this ridiculous claim was that the Metropolitan Police had been white, male and heterosexual since 1829 and remained overwhelmingly so.

In a parliamentary debate on policing in London held on 5 February 1996, the then shadow home secretary Jack Straw told MPs that 1,277 ethnic minority officers (2.6 per cent of the force) were recruited to the Met in 1994 – a slight increase – but 1,384 had quit the service: '100 more, and a higher number than the total of all officers who retired at the end of their service. That is plainly unsatisfactory, and suggests . . . that, although from the outside the service is attractive to ethnic minority recruits, something is going wrong when they get into the service.'

*

It was a boost for me as crime manager when the then home secretary Michael Howard congratulated Fulham police 'on their excellent performance in fighting crime' in light of its 'substantial increase' in solved cases. Our clear-up rate for crime in 1996 was 25 per cent.

It felt particularly rewarding given the staffing challenges in CID. I had inherited two uniform inspectors to fill vacant detective inspector roles as a result of a decision by Commissioner Sir Paul Condon that supervisory ranks could be interchanged between uniform and CID. This meant that someone who had worked in uniform for the entirety of their career to date.

could be switched over to performing the same role in CID and vice versa. The trouble was that people with rank but no prior experience of CID would require more supervision until they learned the ropes, however talented and skilled they were. I had to develop these two individuals as well as manage a CID office that was also operating under strength in DS and DC rank because the commissioner had imposed a moratorium on detectives attending the detective school.

In the meantime, life on duty continued as usual. One day in June of 1996, I attended the scene when a man was found dead in an expensive block of apartments. The victim was a Syrian-born occupant called Habib Saliba. As I entered the flat, I saw Habib lying on his back in a pool of blood. This appeared to be murder. In a suspected murder case, the area major investigation team would be brought in to investigate and a senior investigating officer would be appointed. Crime-scene preservation is essential at any murder or major crime scene, so the number of people in attendance is kept to a minimum.

I handed the case over to the homicide team and left them to it, although I was obviously very interested to discover who had committed the crime. Outside the flat I talked with Mr Saliba's close friend, who seemed inconsolable at Saliba's death. Habib, he said, had on a few occasions paid a woman for sex at his home and was concerned that a diamond ring valued at £8,000 that belonged to his deceased mother had been stolen.

Habib had told his friend he had called the woman to his flat to confront her about the missing jewellery. He hid a tape recorder in a bookshelf to try to get proof that she was the culprit.

I learned later from colleagues that a forensic examination of the tape machine revealed Habib's own dying screams as he was being attacked with a huge carving knife in the hallway of his home.

The woman was quickly identified as Samantha Enoch. Just 20 years of age, Enoch was arrested with her boyfriend and both were subsequently charged with the murder. The trial was held the following year; Enoch tried to pin the murder on her boyfriend, but was found guilty and sentenced to life.

According to a report of the case in the *Independent* on 16 April 1997, Judge Henry Pownall QC said, 'In this court, there have been some calculated, calculating and callous defendants, but few to touch you . . . You are dangerous, devious and wicked.' The boyfriend was acquitted.

*

It's fair to say that 1996 was not a good year for me. I applied to do the superintendents' assessment for a second time. Yet again, I failed the maths. My weakness in this area put the next rung of the ladder out of reach. I felt utterly defeated. But this was nothing compared to the pain I was to experience a few months later when my best pal Sue Weston was diagnosed with cancer of the colon.

Within weeks of her diagnosis in October, Sue was admitted to the wonderful Royal Marsden Hospital in Sutton, where she was given a room on the breast-cancer wing. Between her myriad friends, including her very close pal Faith Lelyveld, we always made sure that one of us kept Sue company in her final weeks.

I can still remember vividly the moment we were told Sue's cancer was terminal. I was called to a meeting in her room. The consultant pulled up a chair, took hold of Sue's hand and told her the cancer had spread to the liver. He was on the verge of tears when he told her there was nothing more that he could do. The cancer in the liver had spread like shotgun pellets.

'Is it going to be quick?' Sue asked. The doctor nodded. She turned to me as I stood at the end of her bed and pointed her finger directly at me.

'Don't you drink on this,' she said.

'Don't flatter yourself,' I quipped, mustering all my strength not to cry at the devastating news.

Sue was well aware of the dangers of turning to drink at such a stressful time since she too had been in recovery for about two years by then.

In the job, I'd seen death many times, but hearing my trusted and formidable friend's awful diagnosis was something else. It was the run-up to Christmas, when we should have been looking forward to parties filling our social calendar. Instead, we were clinging to the final days of a long friendship. I didn't touch a drop of alcohol, but I did pick up a cigarette again after quitting some months before – though this lapse only lasted a couple of weeks.

Prior to her diagnosis, Sue had bought us tickets to a Tina Turner concert just before Christmas. Since we could no longer go, she'd passed on the tickets to another friend called Ann. I left large notices on a board in Sue's room for Ann, mischievously claiming that the Tina Turner concert was cancelled. It made Sue laugh.

So many people wanted to see or speak with Sue in her final days that in many ways it seemed like a never-ending party. A few of us helped decorate the ward with Christmas decorations. I spent long days at the hospital, alternating my visits with other friends of Sue's to be by her bedside. She was never alone.

On the night we should have been watching Tina on stage, I watched Sue in her hospital bed as her breathing became laboured, so much so that I would periodically rush to get a nurse. Holding my friend's hand and watching her slowly slip away proved to be a very lonely experience. I was grateful to see Ann pop in on her way home from the gig. We sat together as Sue took her last breath shortly before 3am. She was 40 years of age.

Driving straight from the hospital to work early the next morning, I felt on mute as I watched the commuters walking over Putney Bridge. Sue had been such an important part of my life. I wanted the world to stand still while I digested my grief, but no such luck.

Sue's friend Faith slipped Sue's warrant card to the funeral director to put in the coffin to honour Sue's wish. Sue's cortege received a police escort to the crematorium in Watford. Police motorcyclists with blue lights flashing stopped traffic at roundabouts and junctions to make way for the coffin and funeral cars. There is nothing quite like a police escort and the respectful silence as people watch. Sue would have loved the fuss.

Nothing would ever be quite the same again for me now that Sue had gone. Things had changed in other ways too, both in my own life and on the job. I'd been in recovery for five years now, and my outlook had shifted to such an extent I didn't feel that life would end if the job did. Added to that, I was unhappy with the way some officers in the Met responded to a new government target to increase arrests. For example, in the past, if an officer came across four people and one was smoking a cannabis joint, that individual would have been arrested for possession. Now some colleagues chose to arrest everyone: the person with the spliff for possession with intent to supply, and the other three for possession if they admitted to having even one puff of it. This potentially meant four arrests rather than one, though usually all four would only end up with a caution. I objected to what seemed to me like fiddling of the figures. Moreover, the new emphasis on arrests disadvantaged the work done by CID. For example, a detective could spend weeks investigating a rape case, but if a uniform officer happened to be the one to arrest the suspect, it would be notched up to uniform. The fact that the arrested suspect would be taken straight back to CID, and the detectives would then be the ones expected to solve the case, didn't register in this new system.

This constellation of factors made me wonder where I was heading in life. In early 1997, I found myself entering the Roman Catholic cathedral in Westminster after arriving early for an appointment with the Met's chief medical officer to talk about my knee, which continued to cause me considerable grief. This was one of my favourite churches. Sitting in the tranquil space, I prayed for my much-missed friend Sue and then found myself pondering on the course of my own life. I vowed that I would surrender to whatever the CMO said. An hour later, I knew the answer.

The CMO looked at me over the rim of his glasses as he said: 'I think that we should let you go.'

'OK,' I said, my throat tightening at the thought.

As I left his office, my head swam: I loved being a police officer, and I believed that the superintendent rank was within my grasp, if only I could get on top of the pesky maths segment of the assessment. The higher the rank, the more power I would have to change things for the better. But the consultant was right.

After 28 years in the police, I decided to pay heed to the CMO's advice. It was a decision I made with a pretty heavy heart, but with my head held high.

On my last day of service, I was called as a prosecution witness at Southwark Crown Court to give evidence in the case of a prison officer who had taken an antique gun to work to show a colleague. As the on-call duty DCI who had interviewed the prison officer, I gave evidence regarding my dealings with him on that day. It seemed to be a fitting way to end my service, and I wore my gold Flying Squad brooch on my jacket lapel in a nod to a professional life spent predominantly as an operational detective.

'What do you know about guns, DCI Malton?' asked the defence counsel.

'Not a lot, sir.'

My brooch caught his eye.

'I see you're wearing a Flying Squad brooch, so hence my question: did you serve on the Flying Squad?'

'I did indeed, sir.'

'As I understand it, officers on the Flying Squad are routinely armed during their operations, is that not right?'

'Some officers choose to be armed, sir. I chose not to be. I was one of the nicer officers on the Flying Squad.'

My light-hearted comment seemed to go down well as the jury and even the judge chuckled.

'I understand it's your last day of service, detective.'

'Yes. Indeed it is.'

'Well, I have no further questions for you save to say I wish you all the best in your retirement and enjoy your pension.'

And that was that. My last job. As I left the court building, I punched the air and whispered 'Yes!' to myself as I headed back to Fulham Police Station for the last time. It says a lot that I didn't even enquire about the outcome of the case and the fate of the prison officer. All I could think was that I was free!

The moment of elation gave way to sadness later. Despite its dysfunctions, the police had been a family to me, one to which I had devoted myself fully, and I had absolutely loved all the jobs I had done during my service. Unlike some who prefer to slip out quietly by the back door to little fanfare, I opted for a big leaving do for colleagues and friends.

I was prepared for the sense of bereavement that ensued after leaving the police in April 1997. It felt like a divorce – without the acrimony. I had watched many colleagues leave the force and settle into a quiet life, but aged 47, I felt far too young to be mooching around or pottering in my garden all week. I needed to figure out what I would do next. I played golf and caught up with friends, but the void I felt was pretty constant.

The brutal reality of being out of the job was rammed home to me when I met up with a friend still serving in the Met.

'So what are you working on?' I asked.

'Oh, I can't tell you that. You're ex-job now,' she said. Ouch.

I felt in complete limbo. I missed the buzz of the station, the unpredictable nature of the job and, crucially, the crime detection, which I had always found so compelling. I did my best to transition into post-police life, even attending a yoga class to help manage the pain in my knee that so often left me feeling demoralized.

Is this it? I asked myself with a mild sense of despair as I adopted the downward-dog pose, head down and bum in the air, and reckoned with my new civilian status and a future without any direction. Is this all my life is going to be now? Hobbies and classes to pad out the week? All I could see was a slow fade to oblivion, boredom and emptiness.

My fears proved short-lived when, two months after retirement, I received a call from someone who worked on *The Bill*. They told me that the show's executive producer, Michael Chapman, wanted to know whether I'd be interested in working as a story consultant.

'Hello, sir,' I said when we met a week later.

'My name's Michael,' he smiled.

'Sorry, force of habit from the job,' I laughed.

I was offered a contract by Thames Television to work on the show three days a week. I grabbed it with both hands. A job that allowed me to do what I knew best, understood most, in the relaxed setting of the TV world. I would be applying my knowledge and experience to the dramatized portrayal of policing and crime. I had not left policing and crime behind, after all.

CHAPTER 17

A NEW BEGINNING

I woke up each morning before going to work counting my luck in landing the perfect gig.

I had watched *The Bill* on ITV since the series launched in 1984, when I was working at West End Central. *The Bill* seemed to have a 'Marmite' effect on colleagues: some loved it, some didn't watch the show because it felt like a busman's holiday to them. It's true that if you wanted to switch off from the job you might want to give it a swerve. *The Bill* focused on station life and policing on the streets in London. It offered a socially realistic and up-to-date portrayal of the daily life of police officers working at the fictional Sun Hill Police Station: from the friction between detectives and their uniform colleagues, to junior officers being ticked off for not properly following procedure.

Among the characters I most enjoyed in the early series was no-nonsense Detective Inspector Burnside, played by Christopher Ellison, who knew most of the villains around because he'd 'nicked' most of them. I also loved the character Ted Roach, played by the late Tony Scannell. He was an old-fashioned copper with a short fuse who enjoyed a glass of Scotch. Roach forms an unlikely partnership with a transvestite sex worker called Roxanne, played by Paul O'Grady, who becomes his informant.

I came with a fair bit of prior experience, which began when I helped *The Bill* production team with a rape storyline in the mid-1980s. I had sought permission from Scotland Yard to supply the show with storylines, which first had to be cleared as suitable by our press office. I had continued to drum up the odd idea for episodes in my spare time over the ensuing years.

One idea came after a visit to a clinic outside London that treated sex offenders in the 1980s. Curious about a type of criminal that I could never understand and found very difficult to deal with, I called up a clinic led by a former probation officer, Ray Wyre, who had worked in prisons. He became a pioneer in the treatment of sex offenders. I'd read an article about him and wanted to know more, so I asked if I could go and see him. I went in my own time and sat in a group therapy session as perpetrators were encouraged to talk through the 'offender cycle wheel': the thoughts and emotions that arise prior to them committing an offence, and the steps taken to turn their warped fantasy into reality. The therapeutic context invited honesty, free from the judgement of others.

One of the men in the group had used his status in the community as a successful businessman as a shield for his abuse. Charming and handsome, he was believed when he branded his daughter a liar when she claimed that he was sexually abusing her, but his conscience eventually got the better of him.

'I am the type of man who is very, very plausible and could get away with it,' he said, 'but there came a time when I couldn't face myself anymore, so here I am.'

I stopped sending storylines to the team at *The Bill* after I became involved in *Prime Suspect* in the early 1990s, but that show's success in turn triggered a flurry of calls from the TV world. I was approached by a script editor at Granada called Patrick Spence to work on the first couple of episodes of *Cracker*, a drama based on a psychological profiler played by the late Robbie Coltrane. I also advised on the first episode of *A Touch of Frost*, the successful show with David Jason as lead, and the late Kay Mellor's *Band of Gold*, about a group of sex workers. Then there were the drama series created and written by Lynda La Plante: *She's Out* and *Killer Net*. This back-catalogue meant that I didn't feel too nervous when I arrived at Thames Television to start my new job.

The studio and offices were situated in an unattractive building on an industrial estate in South Wimbledon, but as is so often the case, appearances are deceptive. The people who worked there created an atmosphere that was relaxed, friendly and upbeat.

Everybody was on first-name terms. There was no 'sir' or 'ma'am' to be heard, and conversations were on a footing of equals, not rank. My tendency to think outside the box, which had often seemed a problem in my policing career, was positively encouraged in my new job. It seemed more of a natural fit for my personality.

It was good to work with more women, many of them in senior roles – something that I wasn't used to. Working on fictional storytelling was of course far easier than dealing with the high stakes of policing crime. It took me a while to let my guard down a little and acclimatize to the more relaxed culture after so many years in the Met. A few weeks after arriving at Thames Television, I bumped into one of *The Bill*'s set designers in the corridor.

'Hi, Jackie,' he smiled. 'That colour you're wearing really suits you.'

I looked at him distrustfully, my eyes narrowing.

'Are you taking the piss?'

'Er, no. I was just struck by the red jacket.'

My face turned a matching shade. Thankfully, he saw the funny side. I had grown used to the fact that being a woman worked against me in the police force; here was someone complimenting my femininity. Clearly,

I needed to adjust to taking compliments at face value rather than assuming that someone was pulling my leg.

The show aimed to reflect modern policing in the Met. My role was to suggest storylines for *The Bill* on a weekly basis and to inject an episode with as much authenticity as possible. I developed the plot with writers, while two police advisers checked scripts and worked on set to ensure that the police-procedural aspects were properly implemented. We also checked that a balanced view of policing was portrayed. The commitment to social realism meant showing the mundane as well as the exciting, the mistakes as well as the successes.

We tried to be as broad as possible in terms of the spectrum of crimes that uniform officers and detectives were expected to deal with: sexual offences, stalking, domestic violence, street robberies, thefts, assaults, drug dealing, petty shoplifting and the escalation of minor squabbles between neighbours. Foot chases and the odd car chase were part of the mix. The message in each episode was that crime never pays. To make Sun Hill as authentic as possible, the production crew sourced the same cups and saucers used in the Met canteens, and used the same furniture suppliers.

I always made sure I arrived with some ideas in the bag, drawn from a range of sources: the large reserve of cases I had been involved in or was aware of from my policing time, or new cases I had read about in the press or heard about from my contacts. My contacts for the most part were police officers – current and former – but I also had prison officers, probation officers, criminal lawyers, barristers, forensic pathologists and scientists in my address book. Stories based on real cases were always the best, subject to key changes being made to give them an original feel and to protect the identity of those involved.

My hostage-negotiator training proved useful for one plot line. I drew on a training scenario from my course whereby a female patient took a GP hostage. The fictional version involved a father in a custody battle who takes a teacher and Sun Hill's Sergeant Cryer hostage on school premises. A trained police negotiator tries to end the siege peacefully with firearm officers on standby, but Sergeant Cryer is injured and retires from the job.

Part of my role was to keep writers and the story team abreast of latest developments through briefings and meetings with individuals working in the criminal justice system. We invited a forensic profiler to come in to talk to us to spark ideas; a police officer from the Met Arts and Antiques Squad also came in to outline his work and the kind of cases that came across his team's desk; and a senior investigating officer came to talk to us about investigating a serial killer.

*

About a year after I joined the show, we began thinking about adding a Black detective to CID. This was 1998, 14 years into the series. My former colleague Paul Wilson agreed to come in to talk to the scriptwriters. Paul was by then a uniform inspector, and spent an hour talking about the experiences of many Black police officers in the Met. Given that Paul was chair of the Black Police Association, which he had been instrumental in setting up, he was able to give a very informed picture. The Met, he said, struggled to face up to the racism that blighted many Black officers' lives. He highlighted the casual and routine discrimination and the racist language that he and colleagues had to put up with.

When the actor Karl Collins was cast to play DC Danny Glaze, Paul invited him to Scotland Yard and the pair discussed how a Black detective would be received within CID. One of the questions Collins asked Paul was how his large Afro hairstyle was likely to go down in a CID setting. In his memoir *Rocking the Boat*, Paul recounts how he took Karl along to see a DCI in CID to ask his opinion. Would he have

Collins working for him if he went to work sporting the Afro? 'Absolutely,' came the reply. And so he kept his hair just as he liked it. Collins made a huge success of the role and was popular with viewers. Warm and funny, Danny Glaze was an attractive character who kept his head down in a white-dominated office and got on with the job. An able detective, his ability to reach victims and perpetrators alike during police interviews got him noticed by colleagues.

Part of my job was to create biographies for new regulars on the show, based on the guidelines set by the executive producer. I would often draw on the characteristics of former colleagues, then mix them up a bit. I particularly enjoyed working with the actor Roberta Taylor on her character Gina Gold.

Inspector Gold was the first female uniform inspector at Sun Hill. She loved boxing matches, smoked cigarettes, had the occasional drink in her office after work and didn't always play by the rules. She was diligent in the job and looked after her team. The character was so popular among policewomen that one year Roberta Taylor was invited to speak at a policewomen's conference in Hampshire.

I often felt that when some of the actors and production team started on the show, they held preconceived ideas about policing and officers. After being in the role for a while and talking to me about what it was like to be a police officer, some of them would say words to the effect of: 'I'd never appreciated what a police officer has to put up with.'

As for the police view of *The Bill*, serving officers told me that they watched the show to find out what was happening in the Met, because it was usually spot on about new policing initiatives that were coming down the track. Many were willing to help us with storylines, which fuelled my sense that it was quite respected as a show among those in the policing community who chose to watch it. Over the years, at least two police commissioners visited the studios where *The Bill* was filmed. Positive comments from my former peers always made me feel extremely proud to be part of the show.

After a few years, I was invited to join the development team at the show's production company, TalkBack Thames. We would work up ideas for potential new shows. Projects included *Murder Investigation Team*, which ran from 2003 to 2005, and a two-episode crossover with Germany's equivalent of *The Bill*, called *Soko Leipzig*, which involved me making regular trips to Berlin and working with writers and production teams in both countries. It was times like this that I'd pinch myself and realize how fortunate I was in the way my life had panned out since leaving the police. Using real-life policing to tell compelling stories for entertainment was proving to be a lot of fun.

Not long after becoming a story consultant, I acquired an agent, who advised me to set up a company for script consultancy and TV police advisory work. It paved the way to more projects: I spoke to the writers developing *Life on Mars* about my experiences as a woman police officer in the early 1970s and worked with the writer Barbara Machin when she was creating *Waking the Dead*. Both series were broadcast on the BBC. I also worked on nine series of *Trial and Retribution* for ITV, written and created by Lynda La Plante.

Working in the creative environment yielded some unexpected benefits. Thanks to a supportive nudge from a young script editor called Kara Manley, I finally went to university.

'I never went to university because I was always too scared of failing,' I'd confided in Kara. 'It's far too late now anyway.'

'It's never too late, Jackie,' she countered. 'I know that you'd love it. Try a course in creative writing: it's the field you've been working in for the past few years, so it's the obvious choice for study.'

Kara's words registered with me. It made sense to study something that I had shown flair for; a familiar subject might take some of the anxiety out of confronting a long-held fear of academic failure. So, at the age of 57, I finally found the courage to apply to university. I was accepted on an MA in creative writing at the University of Sussex, which I attended at weekends.

It was there that I discovered the work of the American short-story writer Raymond Carver. I loved his characters' clipped dialogue and his observations about the worst and the best of the human condition. I later learned that Carver had also been a recovering alcoholic. His work influenced my own narrative style in the play I produced for my MA dissertation, entitled *Be Mine*, about two alcoholics who first meet while in prison. Taking the form of a series of monologues by various characters, the work was inspired by the AA volunteering that I had started to do one evening a week in a men's prison. A writer on *The Bill* offered to read it, and after doing so she showed it to a radio producer. To my amazement it was commissioned by BBC Radio 4 and broadcast in 2012.

*

Thirteen years after I joined *The Bill*, the show's falling ratings brought it to an end.

To mark the final episode in August 2010, the journalist Denise Winterman wrote a piece for *BBC News Magazine* about the 'fictional south London cop shop', for which she interviewed serving police officers. One told her that the detail and accuracy in the drama 'brought policing into the public domain' and 'helped people understand the job and the pressures that come with it'.

Another commented that it had shown the 'leg work we do that is a necessary part of the job. It showed we weren't always doing raids or having cups of tea but are out in the community or at our desks doing reports. It got all of that right.'

The day that the final credits scrolled on the screen was a sad one for me. While being with the Met had felt like loving a dysfunctional family, working for the good of Sun Hill had been a more straightforward and relaxed experience, with many laughs along the way. It was the first place where I felt that I really belonged and was seen and respected for my contribution. All in, I worked on more than 400 episodes.

The final episode of the UK's longest-running police-procedural drama was dedicated 'to the men and women of the Metropolitan Police, past and present'.

The years rolled by, and I kept busy with various projects as a story consultant, and as a contributor to the odd crime-related documentary, including writing an episode of the Channel 5 series *Suspect*, produced by Paul Marquess.

Opportunity knocked again in 2018, when a TV director called David Howard sounded me out about fronting up a new television series. The programme he had in mind would focus on what it took to track down the prime suspect in a real murder case.

'Tell me more,' I said. 'This sounds really interesting.'

'It's going to be called *The Real Prime Suspect*. We want you to revisit some of the major murder investigations in this country and talk to the detectives and other professionals about how they caught the culprit.'

My own show. I was speechless, which is a rare thing for me.

Commissioned by CBS Reality, the series would comprise ten one-hour documentaries about notorious murder cases that had taken place in the UK or the US. In each show, interviews would be interspersed with reconstruction scenes.

Its unique selling point was that it would be the first crime documentary presented by a former detective, whose experience would enable illuminating interviews with those involved in past murder investigations: ex-detectives, forensic experts, pathologists, solicitors and so on. The thinking was that people who had worked as police officers might speak more freely to someone who understood the job and the pressures that they were under during the investigation.

The pitch grabbed me instantly: the theme of the show was tracking police work from the murder right through to the conclusion of the case. *The Real Prime Suspect* would take viewers on a journey through different eras of policing and attitudes and the investigative techniques and tools of detection available at a given point in time. More importantly, we would hear directly from some of the detectives who had worked on the cases.

The offer was, as they say, a no-brainer. And so, at 67 years of age, I signed up to present a crime series. I teamed up with Monster Films, run by David and producer Rik Hall, who led a small and dedicated production team based in Cardiff. I knew that I could put my policing experience to good use by ensuring that the questions to the retired officers were pertinent and searching.

As I would say at the start of each episode: 'Once a detective, always a detective; it never leaves.'

As a police officer, I had investigated plenty of crimes, and many deaths, but I had been involved in only a few murder cases. When I was involved in a murder case, I wasn't always there for very long. I had been moved to the Flying Squad just months into the investigation into the disappearance of young Vishal Mehrotra in the summer of 1981 – a case that remains unsolved 40 years on. And therein lies the sobering truth of crime detection in real life. Unlike what we see on TV dramas, not every case is solved.

Revisiting old cases for the show highlighted just how limited the police toolkit for gathering, analysing and storing evidence had been. Some of the murders that we looked at hailed back to a time when fingerprinting was the very best possible evidence you could get (short of a confession); a time when blood-type matches could only narrow the odds, rather than prove beyond doubt that the person in custody was the culprit. Incident rooms had to manually sift through huge amounts of information. Databases that could easily be cross-referenced by police forces did not appear until the Home Office's new computerized system, HOLMES, was introduced in 1985.

All the cases we covered occurred before CCTV; before mobile phones were smart enough to track locations; before social media was around to offer clues; and crucially before DNA fingerprinting could conclusively match perpetrators to the crime through the evidence left behind at the crime scene.

The limitations of forensics meant that culprits sometimes got away in the immediate aftermath, only to have their crimes exposed years later as new scientific methods widened the scope for matching the evidence to a name, coupled with good detective work on cold cases.

Many of the officers who appeared on the programme had never previously spoken publicly about the details of their investigations, or how they had affected them. I researched each case as thoroughly as possible to be fully abreast of the details. Some of the former officers I approached were keen to meet up first to check that they were not participating in some gratuitous show that would in any way denigrate the dignity of the victims or their memories. Once reassured, they agreed to appear. For me, one of the most important features of the show was retired police officers talking about the lasting impact the cases had on them. Some of the interviewees later said that talking to me, a retired police officer who could understand their experiences, had made the interview easier for them and given them the confidence to be more expansive in their accounts.

I vividly remember speaking with Philip Maskery, the detective who in 1975 found the body of 17-year-old Lesley Whittle in a drainage shaft leading down to a tunnel under Bathpool Park, Staffordshire. She had been kidnapped and murdered by the serial killer Donald Neilson. We had arranged to speak on the phone to discuss the preliminaries.

Phil said to me: 'Do you realize, Jackie, that you're calling me at 28 minutes past 3 on the 7th of March, which is exactly the time and date that I discovered Lesley's body.'

I obviously knew the date was the same, but I had absolutely no idea about the time that Lesley had been found.

'Oh my god,' I said. 'How surreal is that?'

When we filmed the programme, we played the recording Neilson had made of Lesley telling her mother that she was all right. He played the tape to her parents over the phone, as part of a ransom demand. On the recording, Lesley's voice is calm and composed and you got the feeling that she thought that she would eventually come home. Given what we knew happened next, it was utterly chilling to hear her voice, and so incredibly sad. It was clearly still upsetting to Philip. Lesley had stayed in his thoughts for more than four decades. 'It goes through my mind frequently that she would have been in her early sixties now, probably married, with children; she was denied all that.'

The professionalism and determination of those who had worked to identify perpetrators of the most high-profile murders in British crime history, and then secured their convictions, were humbling. Their achievements were laudable. The compassion the officers felt for the victims and their families was evident; without exception, it was clear that their work on the cases had been affecting. I could feel their emotion still.

Listening to retired officers talk about their experiences resurfaced the regret I felt about some of the cases I'd worked on that we didn't crack – in particular the New Cross fire and the murder of Vishal.

There are some cases you just never forget. This was echoed by Jeff Norman when he was interviewed about the police enquiry into the murder of a vulnerable 15-year-old girl called Karen Price, whose skeletal remains were found wrapped in a carpet in a back garden in December 1989. 'As you well know, that kind of investigation never leaves you. For quite a long period of time, we didn't even know who this person was. Not only did we identify her, we got the results that we always strive to get for victims of these kinds of crimes.'

Monster Films was commissioned to do another six episodes of *The Real Prime Suspect* in a second series the following year. Each time I worked on an episode, I was taken back to my time as a detective, even though it had been more than 20 years since I left the job. Working on the show helped me to reconnect to all the reasons that I had loved being a police officer. Despite the disappointments of some of my unresolved cases, I gained a feeling that I had done some good in finding justice for victims.

CHAPTER 18

BEHIND BARS

'Who would have believed it?' chuckled Frank as we walked down a corridor. ''Ere's me, an armed robber, and you being former Flying Squad, in prison together.'

'Yeah,' I replied. 'Never in my wildest dreams did I imagine that happening.'

Frank was a veteran of the crime world serving a double-digit stretch for armed robbery. He was the kind of career criminal I had once sat opposite in police investigation rooms, listening to them insist their innocence with a solicitor by their side. The type of suspect that as a former Flying Squad officer, I would have been intent on sending to jail.

Now, we were side by side. I was trying to help him, and people like him: men whose addictions fuelled their crimes and landed them in jail.

Prison wasn't where I started doing AA service, but it is where I have ended up. Like numerous other alcoholics, I have committed to repaying my debt for the life-changing support AA gave me by providing my services to others. Before prison, I helped out with the AA fellowship in a number of ways. I started by making the tea at meetings and later worked on committees at regional and national level in campaign-related work. We organized a billboard campaign in south London with the message: 'Is alcohol costing you more than money? Call Alcoholics Anonymous on 0345 697555.' For three years I served on a committee that ran an annual event at the House of Commons to help form policy around the treatment of addiction. We also tried to get the message out to police, probation, health and social workers about A A as a solution to addiction – a free service that was available 24/7.

Then, in 2006, I received a call from a man called Sam inviting me to be the chair at an A A meeting in a prison where he worked as a volunteer. In A A speak, being a chair means being a guest speaker at a meeting to talk about your personal recovery experience at some length. I can't deny that I felt a little bit daunted about revealing to inmates that I used to be a police officer, but I agreed to come along.

My destination was a Category C prison – essentially a resettlement prison, which provides inmates with opportunities to learn workplace-related skills and also houses long-term prisoners (lifers) in the last third of their sentence, in preparation for their transfer to a D category prison with open conditions. Built in the 1960s, the modern building didn't look like a prison, but the barbed wire on a perimeter wall gave it away.

Sam was waiting for me in reception. As I entered the building, the unmistakable smell of cabbage hit me. I left my valuables in one of the visitor lockers, then an officer checked me for contraband. I followed Sam as he clanged open and shut a slew of doors to take us to the meeting; the sound always reminds me of the opening credits of the 1970s popular comedy drama *Porridge*.

We arrived in a room next to the prison chapel. Chairs had already been set up in a semicircle by one of the inmates. Another member of the group offered me a coffee, and I chatted with him as the men began to arrive for the meeting after being released from their respective wings of the prison. Some nodded to me, others said, 'Evening,' while others didn't look at me or speak.

I had weighed up beforehand whether to mention my former career as a police officer when sharing my life of drink and recovery with prisoners. I worried that it would alienate the men, but then again recovery is all about honesty and authenticity, so telling the truth was the only option. I talked about my spiral into alcoholism, the shame that I had sought to disguise through drink, how drinking only made things worse, and the moment of enlightenment when I realized what I needed to do to break the cycle: quit the drink and change the way that I thought and behaved.

'So you see,' I concluded, 'you may see me as your worst nightmare, given my former job, but we have more in common than you might think.' I smiled. Some grinned back at me, a few acknowledged my point, and that was enough.

Other members of the group then shared their own addiction stories. For many of them, their rock bottom was ending up in prison. Some had been inside before but now they had reached a point in their lives where they had just had enough. It was sobering stuff. My interest in the men was sufficiently piqued to attend another meeting.

News that a former Met Police officer had attended an AA meeting had already done the rounds by the time I arrived at the prison for the next one.

Walking along a corridor, I heard a voice from the communal area call out: 'Excuse me, miss. You were in the Flying Squad, weren't you?'

'Yeah,' I said, with all the nonchalance I could muster, while privately thinking, *Here we go* . . .

The guy grinned. 'I was nicked by the Sweeney. That's why I'm here!'

He made being nicked by the illustrious Flying Squad sound like a badge of honour.

My second meeting was chaired by a former prisoner called Chris who had served a long sentence for murder.

'Not for the first time, I woke up in a police cell,' he told the group. 'I was being permanently arrested for drinking offences, so I wasn't shocked to be there. But this time, when a detective walked in to take me for an interview, his face looked serious.

'"What have I done this time?" I asked.

'"It's as serious as it gets," the detective said. "You killed your girlfriend."

'I couldn't believe it, and I certainly couldn't remember it. It was a total blackout.' Chris sounded remorseful as he talked about how he had beaten his partner to death after losing control of his emotions while drunk.

When a devastated Chris was sent to prison on remand, they put him in a cell with a man who was in recovery.

'I was in pieces over the fact that I had killed my girlfriend. My cell mate said: "You never have to drink again, mate. Come on. You're coming with me to an AA meeting." I told him to get lost. Then I calmed down. I thought about it. Eventually I decided to go to a meeting with him.'

Chris has now been sober for decades and since his release gives regular AA service in prisons around the country to instil hope in others. Listening to his honesty that day made me realize that I wanted to support men who were destined to remain perpetrators of crime unless they learned to manage their addiction. It was at that moment that I realized prison was the ideal place for me to do AA service.

When Sam asked me if I would be interested in being a co-volunteer with him, it was an automatic yes from me. After all, I had seen first-hand how addiction caused countless victims, be it of theft or violence or, in the tragic case of Chris's girlfriend, murder. Addiction serves as a distraction and temporary relief from sometimes unimaginable and unmanageable pain, but it can fuel violent behaviour and deception as desperate addicts find any means to get their hands on their drug of choice. If I could support people like Chris in their recovery, I thought, maybe I could help them get away from the revolving door of prison life, and prevent them inflicting further pain on others and on themselves. I agreed to volunteer at the prison group on a weekly basis.

Not everyone gave me a warm welcome at first. My former career made some bristle, since many hated 'the old Bill'; for others it sowed doubt about whether I could be trusted. A couple of members said they couldn't share their stories with me in the room, but they were encouraged to stay after being assured that I was not there to catch them out.

Whenever the matter was raised, my stock answer would be: 'I'm not a cop any more – and in any case, the police didn't put you in prison: you did.' I didn't usually get a comeback when I said that.

Within the confines of prison, the group was open to anyone with an addiction. The deal was that prison staff would not be present. It was just me, a new fellow AA volunteer after Sam stepped down, and around 20 men. The meeting place was the same room adjacent to the chapel, where a religious service often took place at the same time. I had a whistle on a chain to call for help and a radio in case all hell broke loose, but in truth I never felt scared by my situation as a woman surrounded by men. I was used to it.

In 2009, about three years into my weekly volunteering, I applied for an MSc in addiction psychology and counselling at London Southbank University. Completing my MA in creative writing put paid to self-doubts about my capacity for academic work. As part of the course, I was required to do a one-day weekly placement to practise the counselling theory that I was learning in class. The obvious thing to do was to put myself forward for the prison's six-month programme for inmates whose offending was driven by addiction, run by the Rehabilitation for Addicted Prisoners Trust (RAPt), now known as the Forward Trust.

A trainee counsellor is expected to maintain firm boundaries and focus on the client, whereas AA is a peer-support scheme wherein everyone shares their experiences. Doing both at the same time in the same venue would be a conflict, so I relinquished my voluntary role in the AA group during my year of training. Now, instead of devoting an hour each week at the prison, I would spend an entire day as a trainee counsellor.

For the first time, I was given my own set of keys to allow me free access around the prison. To get the keys, I had to do some training to avoid the perils of being tricked by desperate men who might mistake me for a soft touch. For example, the prisoner who might innocently hand me a letter saying: 'I've missed the post, miss. Do you mind posting this on your way home?'

The letter might be intended for someone they were stalking, or contain threats, or instructions. Similarly, a prisoner might ask you to bring in the most innocuous thing, such as a tiny screw that fixes the arms of the glasses to the bit of the frame that holds the lenses in. It would seem like an act of kindness when you realized how frustrating it would be for someone to be unable to see or read properly for want of that screw. But prison officers warned us that if you obliged, you crossed an important boundary. Before you knew it, you could find yourself manipulated into bringing other things in that could have greater ramifications.

*

The RAPt programme was designed to encourage the men to reflect on their addiction by exploring all aspects of it: the underlying reasons that led them to become addicts; the physical and emotional toll; the damage it caused in terms of relationships and the other opportunities lost.

The first stage involved assessing participants' readiness for change. After four weeks, those deemed suitable were moved on to a four-month intensive phase that involved one-to-one counselling and group sessions. The men would be expected to do a lot of written work, which would be shared in group therapy. The final stage was the relapse-prevention strategy, where the men would work out how to avoid falling down the usual rabbit holes of addiction on leaving prison.

I facilitated a group alongside a qualified counsellor. The initial phase often saw people in defence mode: men with their arms crossed, brows furrowed or heads down. Some looked anxious; others carried hostile expressions on their faces to mask their fear of being exposed, not least among men with whom they co-existed 24/7 in a community that thrived on gossip. The men were asked to identify the myriad ways their life had become unmanageable as a consequence of their addiction. Many of them were paying for their addiction with years of incarceration, repeated time and again.

For some, my presence as a former police officer on the therapeutic programme underlined their fear that if they described a past crime for which they had never been caught, it might be reported now. In truth, the fact that I was an ex-detective was neither here nor there, since any counsellor on the team who heard talk of an offence described in identifiable detail was duty-bound to report it.

Slowly, people began to open up. The arms would unfold, the brow would relax, the voice would soften – and more than once, tears would fall. The men's ages varied widely, as did the offences they were imprisoned for: murder, serious wounding, robbery and burglary. One had been a drug addict for almost 30 years and his life had revolved around a succession of prison stints for robbery. He knew all too well that unless he managed to kick his addiction before being released, he would return to the same miserable life and his time out of jail would be short-lived.

Several of the men assessed as having drink or drug addictions turned out to have a stronger addiction to crime. Some spoke of an intense experience in the preparation phase: the fear, the excitement, the buzz. The thought of instant money would create a huge adrenaline rush; pulling the job off made them feel superhuman and would be fleetingly satisfying before the void returned.

These men were displaying the hallmark characteristics of addiction that you would hear from a drinker, a gambler or a drug addict. The stories stayed with me. Simon, for example, was taught to be a thief from a very young age by his crooked father.

'My dad would say, "Don't buy anything, son, just take it and walk away." So anything I needed, anything that I wanted, I just nicked it. Even a sandwich for lunch, I'd nick it.'

Despite his upbringing he knew that his compulsion to steal was wrong, so he buried the conflict by using drugs. And dealing in drugs is how he ended up in prison.

'I just don't know anything else,' he said. 'I don't know how to be normal like other people.'

Any repeated behaviour becomes a habit after a while, and altering it required Simon to understand the underlying thoughts and feelings that were bound up with his automatic tendency to steal whatever he wanted or needed. It was a case of making the unconscious processes conscious ones, and it was going to take a lot of hard work.

Daniel was roped into illegality by his mother at an early age. He was a drug addict from birth, courtesy of his mother's inability to stop using when pregnant. Abandoned by his father, Daniel was left to fend for himself.

'My mum was always stoned and gave me nothing unless I sold weed for her first,' he said. 'If I needed new shoes, she'd say, "Yes fine, but you need to earn it."'

Substance misuse often started early in those seeking to escape their miserable young lives. Barry, for example, was brought up by a single mother who was addicted to tranquilizers. He was also badly bullied at school. When he told his mother, her dysfunctional advice was that he needed to sort it out himself – with his fists. It put him on a rocky path. He became addicted to drugs and when we met, he was serving time for robbery.

Readily available substances like glue and gas canisters were often the gateway to cannabis, which in turn led to more powerful substances such as coke, crack or heroin. As the drug dependency escalated, so did the offending. Chaos reigned and blighted not only other people's lives but their own, culminating in the deprivation of their freedom and a criminal label.

A common feeling that emerged in the group was shame. The shame they felt about themselves, their lives and their crimes. It was a sentiment that I could relate to fully too. They suffered from low self-worth mixed in with a dose of grandiosity – the classic symptoms of an addict.

The next phase of the programme required a frank and rigorous look at all aspects of their childhood and their journeys into addiction and into offending. Dysfunctional parents and emotional neglect were key themes, and it made for painful listening. What you heard above all else as the men talked was the pain that they had carried since childhood, which they buried by shutting down their emotions. The void this left was then filled by turning to booze, drugs or gambling.

The accounts I heard of casual and systematic cruelty by parents took my breath away: youngsters left to go hungry; beatings; sexual abuse; neglect; abandonment. A dearth of love and an absence of security. You don't have to have a terrible start in life to become an addict, but those who found themselves in prison seemed to have experienced more than their fair share of adversity at the beginning of their lives, and their addiction served as a crucial emotional prop. The use of violent or aggressive behaviour among some of the men was often a maladaptive way to feel powerful and to mask vulnerability, neediness and a sense of inadequacy. It took courage to resurrect the painful early experiences that shaped them.

The missing sense of belonging was what led many of these men into hot water. 'Joining a gang made me feel like I had a family that cared about me, and that's what I wanted,' said John, who had been convicted for a string of robberies. 'I finally felt part of something,' he told me. 'I loved my crew. We were doing robberies, but we were in it together and I enjoyed the feeling. The money helped me feel good about myself as well.'

The stories I heard reminded me of my years spent patrolling the streets of Highfields in Leicester as a PC in the 1970s, where the blight of poverty and deprivation too often disfigured the lives of parents and children alike. Difficult childhood circumstances present obstacles that everyone could do without as they grow up.

What struck me was that dogs were often a lifeline. Being separated from their beloved pets while in prison caused some of the men significant distress. The pets were seen as loyal, true friends, who never hurt them, disappointed them or rejected them.

'My dog's been with me through everything that I've been through,' Steve told me. 'He's been into crack houses with me, he's woken me up in the local park after blackouts, and he's been in every pub in north London. He's my best pal when I'm sober as well. He's my best pal – end of.'

Joe wasn't the only one crying as he talked about the wonderful time his father bought him a puppy for Christmas as a small boy, and the devastation he felt when his dad later killed the dog in front of his eyes to punish him for some misdemeanour or other.

While the pain some of these men had experienced at the hands of others was often truly shocking, blaming those who had treated them so badly wouldn't fix anything. They needed to take responsibility for the damage they had in turn caused to innocent victims. This was their only chance of recovery. It required dropping the tough and fearless personas that many had adopted as an armour, which for a lot of these men was a daunting and sometimes terrifying prospect.

'I'm not bad-looking, I look tough and I walk down the corridor with a swagger – that's my mask,' said Jay, who was in jail for robbery. 'What happens if I don't like what I see when I remove it?' The bigger question was what would happen if he didn't: a future defined by addiction and no doubt more crime and invariably more prison time. I knew from first-hand experience what a difficult ask it is to strip back the layers and be more authentic about who we are, but it was necessary nonetheless.

Some men were a pleasure to deal with while others were more challenging. Lee was a bright and articulate man serving a lengthy stretch of time for a series of particularly nasty robberies. His paranoia was well and truly triggered when I was assigned to be his individual counsellor. Convinced that I was working as an undercover police officer to catch him out, he made his feelings about me clear. He was not an easy customer. We got there, though. At the end of the programme, he conceded that his worries about me had been wide of the mark.

It's all about building trust: I listen to what the people I'm working with have to say and mirror back that I've heard their concerns. Then I challenge their irrational patterns of thinking and cognitive distortions: in Lee's case, I told him his assumption about me was untrue.

Darren, convicted for grievous bodily harm, had never felt that he fitted in with kids from more stable backgrounds. His father was mostly absent in his childhood due to a long prison sentence meted out for murder. When he was a teenager, Darren discovered that alcohol gave him confidence: 'I felt like I could fit in anywhere.'

With drink came drugs. His family mingled in circles dominated by a macho culture, where being weak was frowned upon and a gangster image was lauded. He cultivated the persona of a violent thug that instilled fear, but deep down lay someone else: 'I didn't want people to see the real me or to look down their nose at me as a nobody. It also got me everything I wanted, because people were too afraid of me to ever say no.'

Tellingly, Darren described hurting men 'like my dad, so the story would get back to him'. But he knew he was a fraud, and increasingly got high to cope with the guilt about his violent behaviour. It all came to a halt when he was sentenced to prison after killing someone while using drugs. His decision to do the RAPt programme was his lifeline to stop the cycle of crime. This was his chance to avoid adding to his tally of victims.

The process of going into recovery could be seen as an act of weakness within the prison setting, and out of a vast prison population only a few took part. To avoid falling prey to drug dealers and peddlers of booze made by wily prisoners on the sly, the men on the programme were placed on a designated wing. But not mixing at all was impossible, and during particularly vulnerable times some of them could be susceptible to an approach in the communal areas of the jail. If the addict succumbed to the lure of drugs, initially offered for free to tempt them back to their old costly ways, the RAPt programme's weekly drug testing would tell us that they were using again. They would be discharged from the programme and given a period of time to reflect on their lapse before being considered for re-entry. This may seem a tough course of action, but recovery can only come from addicts themselves – nobody can do it for them, so being discharged from the programme gives them some time to think, to see if they're ready to embrace recovery.

My work at the prison ended up taking more of my week than originally planned. Within a matter of a month or two, I was asked whether I would consider extending my one-day placement to two days, and then three. By then *The Bill* had been axed, so I agreed.

The day I qualified as an addiction counsellor in 2012 was a very proud one for me. I had learned so many new skills, so much from the men that I worked with, and so much more about myself. Coupling my first-hand experience of recovery with academic teaching and therapeutic practice was a fruitful endeavour, but I decided that I was more comfortable returning to my unpaid role running the AA group and focusing on the 12-step programme using my newly acquired therapeutic skills. I saw my own identification as an addict as a useful point of connection with the men, and I didn't want to get paid to help others to recover when I had been given my own sobriety for free.

Listening to the men reinforced the power of being honest about our lives, however difficult this may be when so many wrong turns have been taken. It is the only way through. The hardest part of recovery is facing up to the choices you made that led you to the unpleasant place you find yourself in now, and resisting the temptation to blame others for what has happened to you.

Recovery allows the possibility of a new way of living. Is redemption possible? I believe it is. Some former addicts have been able to find the things that they had craved in their life: a loving family, a home and a dog. Of the many men I've kept in touch with since they left prison, all bar one managed to steer clear of their addictions, to stay out of prison and to lead respectable lives. No mean feat.

Over the years of helping men recover from addiction, I have encountered thieves, robbers and wife beaters. I have met around 30 murderers – far more than I ever did as a police officer – all of whom had killed while under the influence of drink or drugs. No excuses can be made for any of these crimes, but I often wonder whether so much carnage would be wrought if more support was offered early on to those who are struggling: mental-health support; decent housing; more rehab services made available to addicts; and more youth services for teenagers to give them something to do and somewhere to go, like a boxing club, for example, led by skilled youth workers offering them additional guidance.

A failure to support those living troubled or dysfunctional lives often spells disaster further down the line; it means that everyone loses out. One day, these men will leave prison. Isn't it worth ensuring that we are safe among them and that they are safe within themselves?

Working in a prison has shifted the 'cops and robbers' mindset that I once had about criminals. Yes, they do bad things, but they are also people with vulnerabilities. Most do feel shame, more than people may imagine.

Policing nowadays is much more focused on crime-diversion schemes than it used to be. Jason Kew, for example, is a recently retired police chief inspector who led the Thames Valley violence-reduction unit, where people found with controlled drugs (as defined by the misuse of drugs legislation) are assessed and directed to health-based drug-intervention programmes, rather than arrested or interviewed by the police. Crime-diversion schemes are not a silver bullet, but they are most definitely part of the solution to the complex issue of addiction, which is a leading cause of crime.

My work is with those already in the criminal justice system. I am one of an army of volunteers supporting people whom many want to forget once they are behind lock and key. For me, it is a grounding experience, and a constant reminder that the comfort of addiction is a poisoned chalice that leaves us incapable of living our best possible lives. Helping the inmates also helps me. And I am grateful to them for that.

EPILOGUE

At about nine o'clock one evening, I arrived home after a convivial supper at a neighbour's house to hear my trusted Jackapoo barking hysterically. As I entered the hallway, a strong smell of bleach immediately hit me. The odour trailed upstairs to the front bedroom and I realized what my dog was trying to tell me. We had been burgled. Copious amounts of bleach had been sprayed over my furniture. Two masked men in black, seen prowling the village earlier that evening by a neighbour, had invaded my home and used the bleach to prevent their DNA from being detected. The thought of strangers rifling through my belongings and cherry-picking their loot was chilling. I experienced that sense of vulnerability I had so often seen in burglary victims when I was a serving police officer. These strangers had invaded the peace of my home. They had taken treasured family heirlooms whose value was more sentimental than financial. It took me a while to get my head straight, and much longer to sort out the mess the burglars had made.

Two young police officers came round the next morning to make a report. It was autumn 2021. The officers sitting in my front room were part of Police Now, a two-year national graduate leadership programme to encourage leaders in local policing. Supervised by a police tutor, they asked all the right questions in exactly the right manner. Looking at the woman in uniform sitting alongside her male colleague made me reminisce about my own policing years.

I have always felt thankful for the way my parents supported my decision to join the police, seen then as a masculine profession. It opened the door to an interesting professional life full of variety.

Equally, I am glad that I voiced some of the challenges of being a woman in the Met to Lynda La Plante. The tinge of guilt that I later experienced about sharing my experiences was due partly to conflicting loyalties to myself and to the Met. But it was mostly because I had internalized unacceptable behaviour in the workplace and thought it normal, as so many of us do. What reassured me that I had done the right thing was hearing from younger women that they'd seen Jane Tennison as a positive role model to aspire to in their own careers. I remember one officer telling me: 'I watched the show and I think most female detective inspectors will say to you that they want to base themselves on DCI Tennison.' By the time I left the Met in 1997, any residual niggling doubts were long gone. Women police officers needed a voice, and they still do.

I sincerely hope that the young female police officer who came round to my house that autumn day in 2021 will have every opportunity to thrive in her career without needing to make unacceptable sacrifices, and without feeling the loneliness that I did as I climbed up the ranks.

Thankfully, there are now more channels for women to address work issues that impact on their daily lives and wellbeing. Twitter discussions such as ones led by #WeCops, run by a City of London officer called Caroline Hay, foster an online community that allows men and women to discuss sexism and sexual misconduct and to share information and ideas on how to improve policing.

Flexible working patterns to aid childcare and improve the work–life balance are now commonplace. There is a national working group focusing on a spectrum of issues affecting family life. The fact that there are now more women in the Met, and – crucially – more women in senior ranks, has surely played a part in this changed landscape. By March 2021, women made up 32.4 per cent of police officers across 43 forces in England and Wales and 15 female chief officers headed up police forces.

To my delight, Dame Cressida Dick smashed the ultimate glass ceiling in 2017 by becoming the Met's first female commissioner. I first met Cressida when I arrived at West End Central in 1984, and I liked her instantly. She was cool under pressure, honourable, with huge integrity and an absolute passion for policing – a promising blend of traits that destined her to rise up the career ladder. None of us at the time could have envisaged a female commissioner, but if I'd had a bet as to who this candidate might be, I would have put my money on Cressida.

In the last two years of her tenure, though, the Met was hit by a number of scandals that shook public confidence in the police. The kidnap, rape and murder of Sarah Everard at the hands of a serving police officer in March 2021 shocked the nation to the core. Wayne Couzens was an officer in the Met's Parliamentary and Diplomatic Protection Command who abused the use of his warrant card to stop this young woman as she was on her way home after a night out with a friend. He received a whole-life tariff for his crimes, meaning that he will never leave prison. An investigation into Couzens's phone seized after his arrest revealed that he was part of a WhatsApp group with other police officers which revelled in misogynistic and racist messages.

In December 2021, two Met Police officers pleaded guilty to misconduct in public office and were each jailed for two years and nine months after taking selfies alongside two murder victims while guarding the crime scene. PC Deniz Jaffer took pictures of the bodies of Nicole Smallman and

Bibaa Henry – two sisters tragically found stabbed to death in June 2020 in a northwest London park. Jaffer sent some of these pictures to PC Jamie Lewis, as well as to a WhatsApp group that included members of the general public. Lewis, meanwhile, edited some of the photos and posted them, along with a couple of photographs he had taken himself at the crime scene, to a WhatsApp group of officers who called themselves the 'A-team'. The *Guardian* reported that he had texted, 'Unfortunately, I'm sat next to two dead birds full of stab wounds.' This is of course simply obscene.

More terrible news for the Met followed in early 2022 when the Independent Office for Police Conduct published a report that highlighted the sharing, between 2016 and 2018, of misogynistic, racist and homophobic messages by police officers, mostly of constable rank, and mostly based at Charing Cross Police Station. Social media gave officers a covert channel via which to share their indefensible bigoted views without being rebuked or reported by colleagues.

Unfortunately, bigoted attitudes still lurk in some corners of the organization, just as they do in wider society. Those who vented their ignorant attitudes underground via WhatsApp showed themselves to be pretty lousy police officers as well as despicable people, since they left digital evidence in their trail. Covert behaviour is difficult to police, and no doubt many remain elusive. The officers involved have disgraced the uniform and let down their colleagues and the public as well as themselves.

Cressida resigned after she lost the support of the London Mayor Sadiq Khan, but it's not as if the fault lines weren't known before her tenure. Lynda La Plante shone a spotlight on the misogyny, racism and homophobia that had been going on in the Met for decades. More than 30 years after the show was first transmitted, and (at the time of writing) seven Met commissioners later, the problems still appear to be rife, but only the first female – and gay – Met commissioner was forced out over it.

The damage done to public trust in the Met must be restored, but like most good things, there are no quick fixes – certainly not in a vast organization like the Met.

Those who harbour vile views about fellow human beings based on their race, their gender or their sexuality need to have their warrant card removed. Having a more diverse workforce would clearly help.

Within the Met, I very much doubt that any commissioner, however able, can create the perfect police service, but it seems to me that a more transparent and more open culture would be for the good. The vast majority of police officers are upstanding and professional; but officers who come across poor conduct need to feel confident and safe about speaking up without fear of a backlash.

I would not wish on anyone the personal toll that reporting Inspector Smith back at West End Central caused me. It was me and not Smith who was seen as letting the side down, despite his decision to fit up innocent people and consign them to a criminal conviction to boost his arrest rates. His actions not only damaged the reputation of us all, but also led to significant pay-outs to people wrongly accused of possessing drugs.

Years after Smith was convicted, a number of claims were made against the Met by victims who sought damages in relation to fabricated drug charges, with costs awarded. Some of the claims took years to resolve, and several of them involved out-of-court settlements. One man was awarded £21,000 in damages at the High Court, ten years after his arrest on a fabricated drugs and assault charge arising from the activities of some of the D-relief officers under Smith's spell.

As for me, I had my say on national television 36 years later. It was on a BBC2 series called *Bent Coppers: Crossing the Line of Duty*, broadcast in April 2021. The title of the documentary drew on the popularity of *Line of Duty*, the BBC drama created by Jed Mercurio about a fictional unit called AC12 whose officers investigate police corruption and wrongdoing. The documentary looked at real-life corruption in policing over the years and the unit tasked to root it out. On camera, I talked openly about the negative impact of reporting police wrongdoing and of being treated like a traitor by some. It had been 'life defining', I said. 'It was this sense of belonging in an institution that was so powerful,' I explained. 'If you're on the outside of all of that and you challenge it, it's crushing. . . You were seen as the baddie. You were seen as having done the wrong thing. That feeling of isolation; there was just nowhere to go.'

As I spoke, I began to cry. My reaction after so many years surprised me, but I didn't ask for filming to be stopped or to do a retake. I was no longer ashamed of how I felt, no longer prepared to pretend. 'It's madness,' I said, 'because I've dealt with it. It's being vilified for doing something that was right. I wanted them to say, "You did the right thing, Jackie. Well done." They said the opposite to that. But that feeling of wanting to belong to this huge organization and wanting them to like me for it, was the pain that it caused, because they didn't. They didn't respect me for it, they didn't like me for it. And that's what hurt.'

Recognition can come when you least expect it. In a TV review in *The Times* the next day, entitled 'Bent Coppers: Crossing the Line of Duty – the woman who stood up to the Old Bill bullies', Carol Midgley wrote:

> Until last night I had never considered what it must be like to
> be a straight copper testifying against a bent one. The answer is:
> traumatizing. The former detective Jackie Malton, who was the
> inspiration for DCI Jane Tennison, played by Helen Mirren,
> in *Prime Suspect*, became visibly distressed at the memory nearly
> four decades on in the final instalment of *Bent Coppers: Crossing
> the Line of Duty*.

She walked into the police canteen and everyone just stood up and walked out. 'You get crushed,' she said. 'It was the toughest thing. There was just nowhere to go.' I hope she comforted herself by imagining how jealous they all later became on watching the brilliant *Prime Suspect*.

The feedback over the next couple of days was heart-warming. Messages of support for me doing my job fearlessly flashed up on Twitter. One said: 'Jackie – I joined a little while after you. All I can say is that you were known as a legend among the best detectives.' Another wrote: 'I know many who worked with and for you – you have their personal and professional respect as a person and police officer. One of our very best.'

An old colleague from my time in Leicester wrote: 'I remember you at Charles Street, Jackie. You would stand no nonsense from anyone and stood your ground. But even so it must have been tough for you. Well done you. Also you deserve all your subsequent success.' For me, it was wonderful and very moving. Two old and very close friends got in touch to say that they had no idea how tough things had been then – because at the time, I had kept my cards so close to my chest.

In the past, when a police officer was struggling, the advice was often something along the lines of 'If you can't take the heat, get out of the kitchen' followed by a visit to the pub to drink and forget. Today there is a more compassionate approach, and more understanding. In her book *The Policing Mind,* Dr Jessica K Miller explains that an individual needs three things to be resilient: 'safety, satisfaction and connection. If these needs are met in any context at an individual or organizational level, there will be resilience.' I felt slightly disconnected within myself and the pressures at West End Central made things worse because I didn't feel safe there. I certainly didn't feel any satisfaction at being punished by colleagues for doing my job, and I felt isolated. It was a recipe for disaster.

The police service has come a long way when it comes to mental health. The horrific case of David Fuller and the support provided to officers who worked on the case comes to mind. In 2021, Fuller was found guilty of two murders committed in 1987 after being linked in a review more than three decades later of the DNA found at the scenes. On arrest, police uncovered video recordings at Fuller's flat that he had taken of himself committing sexual offences on the bodies of dead women in mortuaries at two hospitals where he worked in electrical maintenance. Many officers from Kent Police were involved in the huge task of identifying the bodies and then informing the victims' families about what had occurred. Highly trained counsellors at Kent Police provided support and counselling to the officers involved in the case, from family liaison officers to the detectives collecting and viewing the digital evidence.

There are now systems in place to support officers' mental health – a welcome development. Oscar Kilo (OK) is the home of the National Police Wellbeing Service, launched in 2019 to provide evidence-based support and guidance to police forces so that they can develop wellbeing services for their staff.

Police Care UK is a charity for serving officers and staff, including retired officers, who have suffered physical and psychological harm as a consequence of doing their job. Research funded by the charity and conducted by a team from the University of Cambridge found that one in five serving officers is living with post-traumatic stress disorder (PTSD) or complex PTSD because of the cumulative effects of exposure to multiple traumas.

This kind of provision is crucial to support officers, who face far more traumatic situations in their career than most people do in a lifetime. The job they do is hard, exhausting and often thankless. Like most public-sector organizations, it is only when mistakes are made that the spotlight is shone in their faces. Rare are the reports about acts of bravery and compassion displayed by the police but that's not because bravery and compassion don't exist; doing the job to the best of one's ability is simply taken for granted.

Despite some misgivings about the institution that I once worked in, I would join again today. Being a police officer is a job like no other. We deal with the human condition and all of its complexities. It was a privilege to have an insight into the behaviours of mankind, both good and bad.

Police officers never know what their day will bring, hour by hour, minute by minute. They confront danger without a second thought. The nature of the work can be exciting, stimulating and sometimes make you despair. Police officers make split-second difficult decisions in high-risk situations that are later pored over.

Things have changed beyond recognition since I retired from the Met. What is very clear is that the police service needs to be more diverse to reflect the population it serves. Just 7.6 per cent of police officers in England and Wales identified as being from an ethnic-minority group, according to Home Office figures (March 2021). That 7.6 per cent further divided into Black officers (1.3 per cent), Asian officers (3.4 per cent) and those who identified as a mixed ethnic group or another group (2.9 per cent). Of this group, there was under-representation in senior rank, with just 5 per cent of officers at the rank of chief inspector or above. Clearly there is a long way to go in recruiting more Black and Asian officers and in retaining them once they have joined. There are also more openly gay police officers, but not everyone chooses to disclose their sexuality, so it is difficult to establish the true number of gay police officers in the country.

What is undoubtedly true is that police officers nowadays are doing a far more demanding, complex and sophisticated job than we were doing at the end of the last century.

Forensic searches of a suspect's digital technology (such as phones and computers) were not available in my day. Technological advancements and the digital era may have seen an exponential rise in cyber-crime, but they also provide great potential as crime-detection aids, which I do envy. Automatic number-plate recognition (ANPR), for example, widespread CCTV, mobile-phone data and online financial records are all useful investigative tools. However, it still requires police officers to follow up leads, ask the right questions and listen to what people are telling them.

By the same token, technology has made police officers more accountable than ever before, with the use of body-worn cameras, custody suite CCTV and filmed interviews. On top of that, everyone seems to have a camera to record what they see and can upload the footage for the viewing millions on social media. Transparency must always be welcome. Colleagues tell me that the introduction of body-worn cameras has led to a significant reduction in complaints from the public about their treatment.

As the world has changed, so has the law and so have crime patterns. Officers now respond more proactively to public-protection offences such as those involving child exploitation, modern slavery, grooming, and in dealing with people with alcohol and drug addiction or mental-health issues. Although police officers have always dealt with the vulnerable in society, it is fair to say it was not always seen as a priority compared with crimes of theft, burglary and robbery where targets were measured.

One positive development is that whatever the crime, the presumption of believing an allegation and following it up sees a welcome shift away from the culture of disbelief that seemed to be the prevailing attitude towards certain kinds of crime in the past. To avoid innocent people being sent to jail, the focus should always be on discovering the truth, remembering the caveat of 'credible evidence'. As Andy Higgins so aptly put it in an article for the Police Foundation in 2015, it isn't the case that 'to eradicate disbelief, one must believe . . . surely it is not beyond the capacity of the police officer to suspend belief and disbelief while dealing with someone presenting as the victim of crime.'

My message to anyone in the police force today – or indeed in other walks of life – is plough your own furrow, even if the ground that you are tilling seems unyielding at first. I believed in collaboration with people from different walks of life with unique areas of expertise before it was fashionable to do so, but now it is widely accepted as a force for good. As late as 2022, Her Majesty's Inspectorate underlined in its annual report the importance of the police working in partnership with other agencies to prevent crime. Similarly, the report highlighted the link between adverse childhood experiences, drug and alcohol addiction and mental health which I had observed first-hand during my years as a police officer and do now as a prison volunteer. Moreover, the report noted that 'Although the police's primary purpose is the prevention of crime, in cases where mental ill health is an appreciable factor, it would be unrealistic to expect the police to make significant progress as long as the public provision of treatment for mental ill health continues to be chronically insufficient.'

People are responsible for the crimes that they commit, but it's undeniable that emotional neglect and deprivation play their part in the choices affected individuals make, and that crime reduction should not just be down to the police.

Listening to prisoners talk about often deeply disturbing childhoods has reinforced what I grew to realize in my years on the job: that policing is often used as a sticking plaster for deeper ills that society as a whole needs to tackle. Law and order cannot be put in isolation. In over 50 years since I joined the police, I have watched successive governments opt for short-term fixes for long-term problems, none of which have been successful in addressing social deprivation. Safeguarding issues such as domestic abuse, sexual abuse and the protection of children and vulnerable adults have now become a priority for the police. For example, the Care Act 2014 requires local authorities to set up Safeguarding Adult Boards so that all local partners, including the police, can work together to safeguard adults at risk. Governments need to be willing to invest in a strong network of well-resourced public services and a robust safety net to limit the problems arising in the first place. Instead, the reality is that more demands are being placed on the police service due to the dwindling provision of prevention and support services elsewhere because of austerity measures, particularly in the areas of social care, mental health and early-years support. More provision of services such as education and skills training for troubled families and easier access to mental-health assessments are needed.

The police service has itself been hit hard by austerity cuts imposed in the last decade. There are now far fewer dedicated police stations with front counters for the public, as hundreds of police stations have been sold off to the highest bidders in order to get some cash to ease the cuts. Even the prestigious building called West End Central in Savile Row, Mayfair, has gone. The disappearance of police stations is unlikely to do much to improve relations with the local communities.

Cuts have also impeded contact between police officers, since some of the police stations that remain have lost their canteens, where a lot of officers once used to informally exchange information and local intelligence during breaks. Canteen culture wasn't all bad, it has to be said.

*

Life is a mixture of luck, accepting that life events are not in our control, and personal agency to make the best of any situation. However, I wouldn't be human if I didn't admit to some regrets, the biggest of which relate to the cases that I worked on that were never solved.

Time has not healed the frustration and sadness of not knowing what caused the fire in New Cross in 1981 that led to the deaths of 14 young people, nor who was responsible for murdering Vishal Mehrotra not long after. These two cases have stuck with me the most. The families deserve answers.

The case of Vishal's murder was picked up a few years ago by a tenacious BBC journalist called Colin Campbell, who is dedicated in his efforts to find justice for Vishal. Colin has been trying to highlight the lines of investigation that could potentially bring closure to Vishal's family, and I have been happy to help him in any way I can.

When I left the police, I moved further out into the countryside, not too far from Rogate and Petersfield. Sometimes, I drive off the A272 and park close to Alder Copse, where Vishal's partial remains were discovered. I find it sad to think of him in the boggy soil, alone and cold.

Vishal would be 50 now, had he lived, but I still see the smiling face of an eight-year-old boy wearing a navy-and-white striped T-shirt and black cord trousers. I feel a responsibility to never forget him.

The Mehrotras welcomed me as part of their family in 1981 and still do so today. Vishambar remarried and after retirement became a magistrate for several years. Now he is getting older and, like all parents of a murdered child, he and Aruna need to know as much as they ever did who killed their child, and why and how. I hope that one day they will get the answers. I believe that even now there may still be clues lurking in the ground that could help the police with the investigation, given the advances in DNA.

As for my own family, if I had one wish it would be to have both my parents back in my life, even for one day. On the day that my mother died in 2010, I was about to catch an early train to London to meet the writer

Peter Morgan for breakfast in a Pimlico café to discuss his television series *The Jury*. My sister Sue contacted me to say that she had been called to the hospital where my mother was being cared for after suffering a stroke. 'Carry on with your meeting,' she said. 'I will update you.'

The train was heaving when I got on, so I followed the woman in front of me as if she would magically know where free seats were to be found. She sidled into the middle of a three-seater, opposite which there was another vacant space.

As the journey ensued in the usual commuter silence, my phone rang. It was Sue. Mum had died. The news hit me like a ton of bricks. Tears ran down my face. When the train reached Waterloo, the woman sitting opposite, whom I had meekly followed along the train, looked at me and said: 'I heard the conversation – you're coming with me.'

Like a child, I once again followed her along the corridor and off the train. She took me to a station café on the concourse, bought me a coffee and sat with me a while. It turned out that she was a teacher on her way to a conference. I'll never forget that moment. The kindness of strangers.

The loss of my mother was devastating and losing my father a couple of years later just as painful. Dad fell and broke his hip just before his ninety-third birthday and died shortly before being discharged from hospital.

The third blow was losing my brother Trevor in 2015. He had settled in a remote town called Henley on Klip outside Johannesburg and was found dead by his cleaner one January day. Thankfully, I still have the love and support of my sister Sue and my brother-in law Peter.

One of my regrets in life is not facing some of my fears a lot sooner. My fear of academic failure kept me captive for far too long. People told me that I was bright, but four O levels led me to believe otherwise. Completing an MA, followed by an MSc, confirmed that I had harboured a false idea of myself – as did so many of us who felt branded due to failing the eleven-plus.

This formative experience in education so early in my life was in many ways defining, and the injury sustained to my confidence lasted decades. In 2019, I received an honorary doctorate from London South Bank University for my lifetime achievements. Not bad for an eleven-plus failure.

The biggest achievement in my life was putting down my last alcoholic drink. My commitment to the AA fellowship remains unwavering. No one chooses to become an alcoholic when they grow up, but in many ways alcoholism was the very best thing that happened to me. My job as a detective didn't make me an alcoholic, but some of my experiences in the Met served to amplify something that I been wrestling with long before I joined. I was plagued by two conflicting sides: the go-getting, ballsy and fearless Jackie, and the chronic self-doubter too easily unsettled by rejection or disapproval.

Admitting to my addiction allowed me to learn two important things: that I am enough, and that what other people think of me doesn't really matter, because recovery is an inside job. Had it not been for my experiences at West End Central, perhaps I would never have joined AA, so in one way I can feel grateful to those who made me feel like a pariah at work. Out of darkness, as it were, can come some unexpected goodness. Sobriety has enabled me to be clear-headed, more aware of who I am and where I begin and end.

I am so glad to have met Lynda. The most successful stories are the ones that ensure that nothing is ever the same again, and so it was with Lynda's influence in my life. It opened so many doors for me.

Jane Tennison did not have a follow-up series about life after leaving the police, but I can testify to the fact that, however much we love our jobs, however rewarding they are, there is a life beyond for the taking. I've been lucky that mine has been such a fulfilling one so far. There are still chapters to be created, one day at a time.

BIBLIOGRAPHY

Cavender, Gray and Jurik, Nancy C, *Justice Provocateur,* Champaign, IL: University of Illinois Press, 2012

Halford, Alison, *No Way Up the Greasy Pole*, London: Constable and Company Ltd, 1993

Home Office Judges' Rules and Administrative Directions to the Police, London: Her Majesty's Stationery Office, 1964

Jermyn, Deborah, *BFI TV Classics: Prime Suspect*, London: Palgrave Macmillan, 2010

Kinnock, Glenys and Millar, Fiona, *By Faith and Daring: Interviews with Remarkable Women*, London: Virago, 1993

Lamb, Ben, *You're Nicked*, Manchester: Manchester University Press, 2020

Lock, Joan, *The British Policewoman*, London: Robert Hale Ltd, 2014

Mark, Sir Robert, *In The Office of Constable*, London: William Collins Sons & Co Ltd, 1978

Mason, Gary, *The Official History of the Metropolitan Police – 175 years of Policing*, London: Carlton Books Ltd, 2004

Miller, Jessica K, *The Policing Mind*, Bristol: Policy Press, 2022

Moss, Alan; Swinden, David and Kennison, Peter, *Behind the Blue Lamp: Scotland Yard's Police Stations* 1829–2020, London: Blue Lamp Books, 2021

Newman, Sir Kenneth, *The Policing Principles of the Metropolitan Police*, London: Metropolitan Police, 1985

Paddick, Brian, *Line of Fire*, London: Simon and Schuster UK Ltd, 2008

Reed, Jennifer and Strange, Robert J., *Voices from the Blue*, London: Robinson, 2019

Satchwell, Graham, *An Inspector Recalls*, Cheltenham: The History Press, 2016

Sandhu, Parm, with Prebble, Stuart, *Black and Blue*, London: Atlantic Books, 2021

Sutherland, John, *Blue*, London: Weidenfield & Nicolson, 2017

Sutherland, John, *Crossing the Line*, London: Weidenfield & Nicolson, 2020

Wilson, Paul, *Rocking the Boat*, London: SRL Publishing Ltd 2021

Young, Malcolm, *An Inside Job*, Oxford: Clarendon Press, 1991

With particular thanks to the British Library.

AUTHOR'S ACKNOWLEDGEMENTS

I have been asked many times since *Prime Suspect* first aired in 1991 to write a memoir, and not once did I feel the time was right. It was only when I met my co-author, Hélène Mulholland, by chance, that the idea came to fruition. One cannot overestimate the skill and persistence a writer needs in extracting the complexities, minutiae, nuances and emotions of another person's life. Hélène, you have been magnificent and tenacious in drawing out every thought, behaviour and emotion of the last six decades of my life, even when sometimes they were painful to revisit. Thank you very much for capturing my voice so eloquently. I hope you are as proud of the book as I am.

And my thanks to a very special man Hélène allowed me to share with her, Professor Alan Simpson. Your calmness, presence, objectivity and wisdom have been gratefully received. My Jackapoo Frank will miss his London walks with you and your love.

The power of Twitter can be amazing: it's how I first 'met' my agent, Kate Barker. I cannot thank you enough, Kate, for keeping the ship steady and on a straight course. Your serenity, coolness and placidity were very much appreciated throughout. I am eternally grateful to you.

A book cannot be on the bookshelves without a publisher. Hélène and I were fortunate this book was acquired by the most brilliant editor,

Claudia Connal, from Octopus Publishing, who championed the idea from the off and guided us both with her experience. Your expertise and knowledge are hugely appreciated. Thank you so much, Claudia.

Thanks also to Hélène's agent, Laura Williams, an integral participant in the process.

I want to thank my Mum and Dad, Olive and Jeffrey Malton, for so many good things they instilled in me while I was growing up, especially a sense of what's right and wrong, a strong work ethic and being of service to others. I miss you both very much, as I do my older brother Trevor, who died a few years ago at a relatively young age.

My very best friend is my sister Sue, who quite frankly I'd be lost without. You know me inside out and have been by my side for all of my life. Thank you for your support, love and kindness, especially when my life felt dark at times. My love for you is immeasurable.

Sue is lucky enough to be married to one of the kindest and most popular men I know, Peter Keller. We have shared many fun times together, including the ups and downs of your football team, Stoke City, and your golf handicap, where your 'bandit' reputation still lingers on. You're such a lovely man.

I wish my nieces and nephews lived nearer, but they don't. The distance between us all doesn't detract from the love I feel for you: Sarah in Singapore, Richard in Australia and Nicholas in South Africa, not forgetting your respective spouses: Chris, Manuela and Bianca. I would love so much for us all to be together under one roof for a while.

And to my great-nieces and -nephew, Georgia, Kayla and Kian, the only advice I can give you is to always stay true to who you are.

My oldest friends are Gareth Miller and Trevor Nunn. Thank you for idyllic childhood times in Leicester and all the decades since. I very much value our friendship.

To my ex-colleagues in Leicestershire Constabulary: you were my apprenticeship and grounding in policing, for which I will always be grateful – thank you.

Special thanks go to Neil Bell, the 'Force Historical Archivist', for his knowledge and research in helping me remember some of the details of my early days as a young and naïve police constable in Leicestershire.

Huge respect and admiration go to retired Commander Graham Stockwell, Metropolitan Police. You were an outstanding leader and detective, way ahead of your time. Thank you also to Commander Stockwell's family – Reidun, Ellen Peyton and Clive Stockwell QC – for your help.

Thanks also to two Flying Squad colleagues for help in remembering some of the details: Chris Buckle and Roy Daisley. We did have many fun times, too.

Retired police officer Philip Rule and the Police Memorial Trust remember each year the lives lost outside Harrods in 1983. Phil kindly checked through my recollection of this awful tragedy. It is officers like Phil who never forget their colleagues and the civilians who died. Thank you.

Although it was and sometimes still is a painful memory, I wish to reinforce my admiration for 'Stella', who had the courage to speak out about her misgivings regarding the actions of some officers at West End Central. I know how difficult that must have been for you. We have had many chats since as to the effects of that time. You will always have my huge respect and friendship.

Thanks to PC Tony Bruce and to PC John Murray for their heroic battle in getting justice for the murder of WPC Yvonne Fletcher in St James's Square in 1984.

To ex-detective Dr Bob Sherwood and retired Detective Chief

Superintendent Sue Hill, thank you for your continued friendship from our days at Hammersmith and being my 'critical' readers of the book.

To Stephanie Knight, thank you for your passion and commitment in helping me set up the domestic-violence unit at Hammersmith Police Station. I couldn't have done it without you and its success was all down to you.

Thanks to Neil Blacklock from Respect, and the founder of the Domestic Violence Intervention Project, for his memory of those early days in Hammersmith.

When you leave the police, you never know quite where the journey will take you. To four ex-police officers, now writers, thank you for your generosity of spirit in sharing your knowledge, advice and wisdom: Dick Kirby, Graham Satchwell, John Sutherland and Paul Wilson. I admire you all.

To Caroline Hay from #WeCops, for informing me of the latest issues and developments affecting women police officers .

Thanks to 'Mark' for revisiting your experiences.

Special thanks to retired Detective Chief Superintendent Kate Halpin QPM, vice chair of the Police History Society, for checking my memory regarding details and dates.

To my academic friends Dr Clifford Williams, Professor Jennifer Brown and Gavin Hales, Senior Research Fellow, London Metropolitan University, my grateful thanks.

I'm a proud member of the Metropolitan Women Police Association and my thanks go to the members and to the archivist Siobhan Clark, who all answered many questions, since a collective memory is better than one!

To Joan Lock, an extremely valuable police historian, who was very generous with her time.

To the wise and extremely experienced Duncan Campbell, who helped with feedback on the book proposal and manuscript. I wish all journalists were as thorough as you! Thank you.

Kate Fletcher from the Gay and Lesbian Police Association, who was generous in her time briefing myself and Hélène on this front.

Lynda La Plante helped change the course of my life and I am forever grateful to her for listening to my story and creating the iconic character DCI Jane Tennison.

Thanks to David Howard and Rik Hall from Monster Films for believing I could be the presenter of *The Real Prime Suspect*. And to Sam Rowden from CBS Reality who commissioned the series and gave permission to use the title for this book. It was a privilege to work with you all.

For years my photograph has been taken in cells, tunnels and other dark places to reflect the darkness of a detective's job. Thank you to Roger Turner for allowing me to smile in our photo shoot.

It is 41 years since the murder of Vishal Mehrotra and, along with Shaun Keep and Colin Campbell, a hugely committed journalist from the BBC, we continue to 'make enquiries' regarding the crime. To Vishambar Mehrotra and his wife Lovina, who I remain in contact with, I admire your dignity and determination in finding the killer of your son. Colin Campbell, my respect for you is enormous.

A special thank you to the Metropolitan Police and to all the serving members of police forces throughout the country. I know you go to work each day, wanting to do your very best for the public you serve. You rarely get applauded for the heroic acts you perform. We do have the best police forces in the world. Thank you for your service.

To my friend Dame Cressida Dick DBE QPM, thank you for breaking the ultimate glass ceiling for women in policing by becoming the first female Metropolitan Police Commissioner. Your achievement showed women from all walks of life that we should not hold ourselves back from reaching for what we want in life, whatever that may be.

To my girl 'gang' of friends – thank you for your friendship, which I continue to treasure.

To Lizzie and John, thank you so much for your love, and sharing with me your family when mine live so far away.

To the men in prison who have trusted the process of sharing with me their deepest fears about themselves. It's a privilege to listen.

To a very special friend, Carmel, who I first met in the rooms of Alcoholics Anonymous nearly 30 years ago. Your continued friendship and unconditional love have been an integral part of my recovery. Thank you.

And lastly, to the fellowship of Alcoholics Anonymous, who helped me to find my way back. I am forever indebted to the 12-step programme and the founders of AA, Dr Bob and Bill Wilson.

Thank you.

Jackie

ABOUT THE AUTHOR

JACKIE MALTON was a police officer for twenty-eight years. During her career she worked in the drugs squad, CID, the Flying Squad (famously called the Sweeney), fraud squad and as a hostage negotiator. She rose to become one of only three female detective chief inspectors in the Metropolitan Police. Jackie acted as an adviser on *Prime Suspect* and has consulted on many popular police dramas, including *Cracker*, *The Bill* and *Life on Mars*. Most recently, she presented the TV series *The Real Prime Suspect*, in which she revisited notorious murder cases. Jackie regularly gives talks on policing and currently volunteers in a male prison supporting offenders recovering from addiction. @thursley.

HÉLÈNE MULHOLLAND has been a journalist for over twenty years and previously worked at the *Guardian* as a political reporter. Hélène now works on a freelance basis.